Short-term Psychotherapy
and Structured
Behavior Change

Short-term Psychotherapy and Structured Behavior Change

E. Lakin Phillips, Ph.D.
Psychological Clinic
George Washington University

Daniel N. Wiener, Ph.D.
Veterans Administration, St. Paul
and University of Minnesota

McGraw-Hill Book Company
New York, St. Louis, San Francisco, Toronto, London, Sydney

Short-term Psychotherapy and Structured Behavior Change

Library of Congress Catalog Card Number 66-18212

49784

1234567890 MP 7321069876

To F. W. and J. B. W.

and

To the Memory of M. L. P. and C. B. P.

Preface

Psychotherapy can be an exciting venture in problem solving, taxing both the therapist's and the patient's ingenuity and intelligence to their limits. It is seldom so stimulating and challenging, however. Why?

We believe therapy as conventionally practiced is usually loaded down with a superstructure of theory—somewhat unified in such cases as psychoanalytic and nondirective therapies, a potpourri of theoretical fragments in eclectic and other approaches—which diverts therapists and patients from the problems and solutions at hand. Instead, it burdens them with speculations which may be intended for use in carrying out grand concepts and advancing scientific study—but not primarily in helping individuals as directly and effectively as possible. Parsimony is ignored. It is as if therapists had been trained to look at patient problems through glasses which distort, suppress, elongate, and fore-shorten, so that the view of therapy may be delightful, creative, or fantastic, but never entirely realistic.

Because the therapist's (or the patient's) views so modify direct observation of behavior, problems are constantly being stated and progress measured indirectly. The sense of unreality about conversations, rewards, and activities in most therapy today puts a chill on the warm, fermenting experience of solving life's real problems. Therapeutic theorists have written the recipe, and therapist and patient often are simply following directions blindly.

Not that we would abjure theory. This book is about a theory of psychotherapy, but one which is closely tied to direct, observable behavior. We would write the therapeutic program for each patient (or group of patients) according to his own particular problems—and according to other problems as they arise—and their efficient, pragmatic resolution, until the major problems are solved and the techniques of problem solving are learned. If the primary problem—and most efficient solution—lies with the family, the school, or the community, we would program similarly for it, to the extent that we are permitted, structuring the situation to define concrete goals, specific methods of accomplishing these goals, and objective ways of judging results and modifying methods of solution accordingly.

Human-behavior problems, in our view, are not to be treated as individual diseases, nor are they most efficiently solved through individual treatment. While much of the book is written within the context of individual psychotherapy, the model presented does not depend upon the personal patient-therapist session. We subscribe to Dubos's (1959, p. 21) view:

> The modern American is encouraged to believe that money can create drugs for the cure of heart disease, cancer, and mental disease, but he makes no worthwhile effort to recognize, let alone correct, the mismanagements of his everyday life that contribute to the high incidence of these conditions. . . . Is it not a delusion to proclaim the present state of health as the best in the history of the world at a time when increasing numbers of persons in our society depend on drugs and on doctors for meeting the ordinary problems of every day life?

So, while we would create a technology of human-behavior problem solving—for individuals as well as for groups—we stress our belief that the *giant* steps toward the solution of human problems in living will come through the structuring and control of large social units, just as sanitation control contributed far more to life expectancy than the most sophisticated use of drugs and surgery.

We hope that our views may contribute to the development of a proving ground for all theories of psychotherapy. Surely the production of significant behavior change as efficiently as possible would be the goal of all therapists. Too often, however, the goodness of fit between practice and theory—leaving out concrete behavior change—has been the way of judging the success of the therapy or the competence of the therapist. If the criterion were effectiveness of the patient's behavior in his life, all therapeutic practices could be similarly measured. "Effective behavior" would still have to be defined. Even this, however, would not seem to be a difficult task, provided that the patient's views, the significant persons he chooses to live with, and his societal functioning were considered without interposing other theoretical views.

Whatever our deficiencies in accomplishing this purpose, we would plead for agreement upon ways to judge methods and results. It may be good for the therapist's ego to believe that he can establish his own criterion for success, but this contributes only to anarchy, not to scientific progress.

When problems and criteria for judging outcome are concretely defined, the importance of theoretical questions about superficiality or depth of problem and treatment diminishes. Why should problems of living that are attacked in therapy be considered serious, wide-ranging, and inaccessible to direct solution? Why should such problems require permanent solutions, so that if therapy does not provide them, it is viewed as a failure? Why, if direct methods are considered superficial, or unavailing with serious problems, are therapists unable successfully to treat with "depth" therapy the most serious problems in living—those of the psychotic and the sociopath?

Another question that concerns us about the emerging science of human behavior and about its vital contributions to our views and practice is pointed up by Dubos (1959, p. 20): "Clearly, modern medical science has helped to clean up the mess created by urban and industrial civilization. However, by the time laboratory medicine came effectively into the picture, the job had been carried far toward completion by the humanitarians and social reformers of the nineteenth century."

It seems quite possible that vast humanitarian movements can change our current living problems and solve them far more efficiently than the tiny increments from laboratory science can. An example might be a sweeping fervor for viable quasi-religious self-help groups. But we hope that solutions, for individuals or groups, can be more efficiently discovered, directed, and accomplished so that progress will not depend upon unpredictable and uncontrollable concatenations of historical events.

Efficient behavior-change methods may well have to come from more viable sources than the traditional training in psychotherapy, be they clinical psychology, psychiatry, social work, religion, sociology, or informed public movements. If changes do not come from within the professions, they will have to come from external forces, from social configurations that come to grips with the problems of man most forcefully. Our hope remains, however, that changes in practice and in theory can come from the professions purporting to devise ways man can best solve his problems.

We are engaged, then, in the search for better methods that can be used efficiently. This search is in the tradition of the Promethean reach for creative control, the human reach for mastery of self and environment, and the breaking of chains forged by concepts of chance, mystery, and overwhelming complexity.

To list contributors adequately would require analysis of our personal histories. We limit ourselves instead to the most immediate influencers. Dr. Salak El-Batrawi stimulated useful conceptual notions, and Dr. Saleem Shah suggested several useful directions for the early manuscript. The George Washington University Psychological Clinic staff and students were an appreciated sounding board for ideas. Jonathan Wiener made valuable suggestions, from the viewpoint of sociology, for Chapter 10, "From Microcosm to Macrocosm: Structure in Society," although the responsibility for its final form is ours alone. Dr. Leona Tyler and Miss Marian Norby provided valuable criticism. Finally, our wives gave to our lives the stability needed for productive effort and the sense of proportion necessary to get us unstuck when we were mired in difficulties.

E. Lakin Phillips
Daniel N. Wiener

Contents

1 The Therapeutic Process: New Goals for Today and Tomorrow

Introduction

Since the mid-1940s, interest in psychotherapy has grown at a rapid rate. At the same time, concern about mental health generally has become widespread. Perhaps symbiosis is occurring: as the need for psychotherapy becomes more evident, research, theory, writing, thinking, and study grow more active, and in turn wider interest fosters the recognition of the needs of the mental health movement. The generic study of behavior change is gradually emerging as an important part of this broad interest. Psychotherapy is not only a specific professional pursuit but also, broadly, the effort to change behavior. It is discussed here in both contexts.

There have been many trends in the research and practice of psychotherapy over the last 20 years. Rogers's views spread, some additional neoanalytic schools sprouted and grew, and eclectic therapies began to be formalized. Psychologists vigorously applied learning-theory principles to psychotherapy. Operant conditioning and renewed interest in classical Pavlovian conditioning have also been applied to clinical and psychotherapeutic problems. To describe the whole range of these developments in psychotherapy, however, is outside the scope of this book.

It is not easy to distill these changes and generalize on their meaning or to say how they can be most cogently conceptualized. Each of today's leading psychotherapists would no doubt offer a different conceptualization of these events if he tried to trace the ebb and flow in thinking, research, and practice in therapy.

This volume attempts to relate psychotherapeutic research to a single consideration: *how to make psychotherapy more efficient*. This question should not be regarded as an attempt to make today's therapy shorter or cheaper, that is, not just efficiency for its own sake. The therapist or client cannot remain neutral on the subject of whether long- or short-term therapy is better under optimum conditions.

Many believe that good short-term therapy is only a poor substitute for good long-term therapy. To them, short-term therapy is for the poor, the lower classes, the naïve, the "unmotivated," and the nonfluent of speech, and is equated with superficial insight and temporary effects. Long-term therapy, on the other hand, is likely to be regarded as "deep," "intensive," "long-lasting," and more "insightful."

Our view, which is not neutral, is that long-term therapy is not, in fact, the most desirable, not even for those who can afford it or who prefer it. It is not the matter of efficiency alone that makes us favor short- over long-term therapy. Instead, our belief is that structured therapy (which tends to be short-term) is better than long-term, conventional therapy for this reason: structured therapy is *purposely* as short-term as possible. By "purposely," we mean *structured to solve specific problems*—regardless of whether they are chronic and serious or only mildly disabling.

In short-term structured therapy, it is necessary to define problems differently. Such therapy also leads to measuring change differently—hour by hour. This approach is not needed by the long-term therapist, who is not pressed for time and who is committed primarily to uncovering and interpreting past behavior and then applying these insights to current behavior—or who, if he is limited by time, tries to tailor the long-term approach to meet undesired limits. The long-term therapist often longs for the ideal case, while marking time with ordinary cases that "clutter" his practice.

Long-term therapy can, of course, be structured in the sense of reviewing historical material systematically, or it can be structured in a general way, such as when it centers around the elimination of alcoholism, frigidity, or job dissatisfaction. But without the pressure of time, this therapy moves obliquely toward its goal, as though self-understanding were the central problem and would be the total or crucial part of the solution. Even when short-term therapy is relatively unstructured, it is more likely to progress toward problem solving because it attempts to define specific problems *first* and deal directly with them.

The reader will find that the term "structure" is used here chiefly to express the concept of the framework man can impose upon his life and world (that is, structuring, in the sense of shaping and of giving a concrete description of, and meaning to, life). More specifically, structuring refers to the *purposeful selection,* by the therapist and the client, of *variables* basic to behavior change. It implies not only the willingness of the therapist to intervene in various constructive ways but also his ability to select variables for control, manipulation, and study, as part of his interest in a mutual goal—the efficient behavior and personality change of his client.

When structure is lacking in the person or in his environment, the goal may be to construct or firm up structure in both. It is such structuring which gets man (the client) where he wants to go. Structuring will help reveal whether his goals are unrealistic and should therefore be changed. This, as we shall show later, is a "response-centered" theory (Phillips & Batrawi, 1964). In it the patient is first the *manipuland* and later the *manipulator.*

In the long run, effective structuring of the social environment may prove to be the major solution for man's pervasive problems today. For the individual whose environment is amenable to some (therapist) control—for example, the criminal, the student, or the child—the most efficient solution may be the therapeutic structuring of his environment by others. But the individual who can master his environment or who can be induced to act and think independently about major problems can often do this structuring largely by himself, with the intervention of his therapist. The environment itself must necessarily be used as the most accessible and useful tool in promoting behavior change on a large scale.

Determining the Pivotal Consideration

"How to shorten psychotherapy" is an old but worthwhile question. It has been asked—and answered—by many therapists since the days of Freud. A glance through the list of topics in the *Annual Reviews of Psychology* will show that there has been a repeated interest in short-term therapy but that very few therapists have ever dealt extensively with methods of shortening therapy. Even fewer have attempted to develop a concept of short-term therapy within current psychological theory. Part of our task here is to glean the best ideas from the work of others and to use them in shaping our own conclusions. In this way we hope to arrive at some practical considerations and theoretical leads that will serve others now beginning to practice or conduct research in psychotherapy. Perhaps this effort will encourage the systematic pursuit of new empirical and theoretical leads that will lift psychotherapy to a new level of rationality.

Relating therapy to a single variable such as time (and its structuring effect) offers great promise. Although other variables may be relevant, we know of none so stimulating and basic.

Yet time is not a true variable here (and perhaps is not in any science). Rather, it is a concept that *carries,* or ushers in, other variables; that is, time may serve as a backdrop against which other variables are revealed more clearly.

However, the use of time as the pivotal concept in therapy requires us to think in larger conceptual terms, since from Rank on, it has forced to the forefront the notion of structure. When time-limited therapy is practiced, *all other variables and considerations are brought into bolder relief;* that is, they are in a new context. Without the limitations of time, therapy may have form, but the relationships among variables are usually less clear.

As in any matrix, when one variable is singled out as pivotal, the relationships among other variables change, and as Ashby (1958) has shown, the great search in science has been for single-valued concepts. No single, exclusive conceptual organization for psychotherapy is presumed here. However, the emphasis on time and, as a consequence, the stress on the need for structure are moves in that direction.

When the pivotal consideration is time, changes in goals result, as has been noted by many investigators (Rank, 1947; Shlien, Mosak, & Dreikurs, 1962; Taft, 1933). Once one becomes accustomed to thinking in terms of the importance of time, other ways to begin the structuring process naturally follow. But there are also additional approaches to shaping a situation or a problem.

A commitment to *action,* for example, can lead to a restructuring of variables. The patient is encouraged to attempt a concrete behavioral solution to a given problem sooner. "Take effective action" may be an oversimplification of the key to behavior change and to psychotherapy, taken out of context, but it is a central notion. Action taking forces structuring, for it tests out a given problem and tells us whether it is stated aptly, whether a given proposal solves a problem, and whether the person taking the action is benefited.

Many therapists are reluctant to suggest action for their patients to take. Arbitrary advice would seldom be wise, such as to get a divorce, to quit school and get a job, or to leave town, even though such a decision might later evolve from the therapy. Well-considered counsel to act, however, refers to a cogent suggestion for an alternative way to handle a problem that cannot be tested until action is taken—even though the decision as to the alternative and its consequences rests with the client. In therapy, action resembles the empiricist's behavior in science—it is the final way to define a problem and validate a solution. Action as a means of testing therapeutic technique has its counterpart in the testing of a scientific hypothesis.

There are many opportunities for structuring in psychotherapy, for example, teaching the patient to take responsibility for his conduct; helping him to realize that a solution to a problem, while it may be arrived at theoretically during a therapy session, can and must be tested by him alone in his life outside the session; and helping him discover that while his background strongly influences his outlook and behavior, the only behavior he can ever change is his current (and future) behavior.

However, the structuring process can be promoted by selecting specific variables for manipulation. Setting up specific tasks or time schedules, ordering or arranging behaviors to achieve a specific goal, and challenging the client's assumptions basic to a previous action and asking how the outcome would be affected by a different assumption, might be selected as examples. There have been some interesting variations of this type of guidance. Wolpe, for example, bases his therapy on teaching the patient to do the opposite of what he would previously have done (termed "reciprocal inhibition" therapy).

Another approach to the selection of variables is inherent in Rotter's "social learning theory" and Kelly's "personal construct." Two other methods are operant conditioning and Pavlovian classical conditioning.

Our culture sometimes seems to make a fetish of efficiency. If efficiency and "getting things done" become the goal instead of the means, they may become meaningless. Efficiency or shortening of therapy should not be emphasized to the extent that meaning is sacrificed. Limits must be set to efficiency, to restructuring, to time setting, to action, to responsibility taking, and to all the other steps that are so desirable and necessary in effective psychotherapy—but only in relation to clear goals. There is no way to arrive at any final answers to this problem of how far efficiency can be carried to facilitate goal achievement except through patient research.

Time is emphasized here because it is immediately cogent, assessable, and clear. It lends an immediacy and sharpness, and it brings an urgency to planning that makes structuring inevitable, so that there is less drifting and improvisation in therapy. Then one can move on to the generalization and abstraction that raise time considerations to a more complex level.

Each step in structuring the elements in the client's life is a step toward the solution of his problems. The client needs to develop structure and purpose and to gain a knowledge of what leads to what. He must become more aware of how events and forces may be shaped to lead to a predictable outcome—this is part of the structuring process. Psychotherapy can help to harmonize these elements in a more orderly manner.

Change outside Psychotherapy

Another preliminary consideration of great importance in understanding psychotherapy and behavior change has to do with the traditional practice of psychotherapy in the consulting room. Although it has been defined in many ways, the term "psychotherapy" usually suggests two people in a social exchange. One is the "helper," the other the seeker of help. Some of the other characteristics, according to Stieper and Wiener (1965, p. 11), are:

1. There is a prolonged interpersonal relationship between two or more people.
2. One (or more) of the participants has had special experience or training in changing human behavior.
3. One (or more) of the participants has entered the relationship because of his dissatisfaction with his life.
4. The methods used in this exchange are psychological.
5. The relationship is designed to lessen the difficulties of the person(s) seeking help.

But such a definition does not account for the persons who change for the better without ever seeking formal help. How is this fact explained, a fact that few therapists discuss but that none deny? How is therapeutic change related to teaching or persuasion, and what is its significance in relation to propaganda, indoctrination, and coercion? The therapist must be aware of more than the traditional consulting-room therapy. Consulting-room verbal exchange is only one kind of psychological therapy, but by "psychotherapy" the profession has usually meant this limited "talking" therapy.

Obviously, psychotherapy needs a much wider interpretation. It is regarded here as the attempt by professionally trained persons to help others change behavior through psychological means. For example, a teacher in the classroom may ask a psychologist, a psychiatrist, or a social worker how to handle given behavior problems of children, or she may devise methods herself. She may put certain suggestions into effect and be pleasantly surprised both at the simplicity of the suggestions and at the effectiveness of the outcome (that is, the change in behavior). How is this explained? Is this psychotherapy? Perhaps not in the usual sense of technique, but in the larger sense of outcome, it is an instance of accomplishing behavior change. Under specific conditions, it may even produce a personality change, with or without the professional intervention of mental health specialists.

But there are other, broader forces that may also change behavior of a whole society. For example, the United States Supreme Court issues an edict aimed at integrating schools and many public places. Dramatically, and in relatively short order, wheels are set in motion which, in a decade, advance the nation further toward a stated goal than it has moved in a century. Although social behavior has changed, it has not been subjected to conventional psychotherapeutic methods. Prejudiced politicians have not been taken into the consulting room to acknowledge the harmfulness of their ways. There has been no change in their "motivational structure," no unburdening of repressed conflicts. Instead, a new structure has been precipitated by the Supreme Court action, which produces widespread changes in behavior with far-reaching effects upon individual personalities and ways of living.

The person who moves to a new home and therefore must travel a different route to and from work will undergo a change in behavior. So will the child who learns a different way to solve an arithmetic problem, the adult who learns a new skill, or the elderly person who moves from his isolated room to share an apartment.

It is sometimes surprising how easily behavior can be changed. Moreover, the changes are sometimes sweeping and permanent. Many professionals in the mental health field who have become committed in their practice to severely limited methods overlook this vital fact.

Often, of course, behavior does not change even in the clinic devoted to that goal. This may be true even after years of painstaking search for the origins, causes, and conditions of problems and their solutions. Therapists are still largely ignorant about the conditions under which behavior changes—and about why it will not—and this ignorance has made many psychotherapists cynical about even the study of behavior change. Many of them regard it as impractical, scientifically impossible, or trivial.

But the scientific approach holds that it is not through caprice but through *a set of conditions different from those being utilized* that behavior changes. This is the lesson taught by discoveries in many other scientific fields. Chemists, physicists, biologists, and many other scientists search continually for different sets of conditions to account for the phenomena they study. What must not be overlooked is that this different set of conditions means a different structure, a different set of elements, or a different set of relationships, in whatever environment is under study.

Behavior can change under a variety of conditions. The scientist's task is to understand, predict, control, and manipulate these elements and their relationships. If he can specify his manipulations to achieve some predictable ends, he presumably has the elements of an effective science, and of understanding in the grand sense of the term.

Not every person who needs help can be treated in the consulting room. Of the schoolchildren who need help, not every one can be sent to a hospital or clinic. With many, behavior change cannot be achieved through extensive personal therapy in the private office. Some will not talk; others cannot. Some will not come for help; some will not stay long enough if they do come. Anyway, the total cost in time and personnel of such treatment is much too great to meet the social need.

To meet the problem, it must first be acknowledged that behavior change can occur anywhere under a vast range of conditions. Then the questions must be asked: "Which elements can actually be changed and which ones cannot?" and "How does behavior change, that is, by and through what conditions and means?"

"Behavior change" can be a more useful term than "psychotherapy." In special cases, of course, individual psychotherapy may be desperately needed, and probably has been for a long time. But behavior change, which is a broader approach, is the paramount need in society.

In speaking of behavior change, rather than psychotherapy, the clinic and the laboratory can also be drawn closer together. Later, construction of a clinical practice on a harder core of knowledge—knowledge available from experimental learning areas of psychology and from cybernetics—will be emphasized. A behavior-change model is a useful alternative to the medical disease model.

Conditions for Behavior Change

It is easy to believe that only intensive psychotherapy can change damaging, self-defeating behavior of long standing. It is usually accepted on faith that such behavior has long been inaccessible to strong rational efforts to change it and that nothing short of radical indirect methods can modify or affect it now.

This belief is now being challenged (Jahoda, 1958). There is already evidence that psychotics have often *not* been exposed to strong rational efforts to change their distortions and misdirected behavior. There is also extensive evidence in the behavior of clients whose efforts to reach their goals, without benefit of systematic assistance, have been misdirected. These clients often are willing to try new ways that are pointed out, clearly and directly, as structured steps toward their goals. In fact, the readiness and ease with which such a patient can make changes strongly supports the hypothesis that he has not been previously exposed to appropriate structuring—even when he was more pliant.

Some things cannot be learned through talking, for example, driving a car or playing the piano. They must be *done*. This may be true of behavior change in many instances. How does a husband stop fighting with his wife, his boss, or his children? Talk may be a preliminary step. In many cases, however, it need not be preliminary and does not even relate to the objective of not fighting. The outcome is changed behavior, that is, not fighting. Of course, the preliminaries will vary with the activity. In this case, if fighting is thwarted or redirected through direct manipulation of the situation and if a solution to the problem is forced upon the participants long enough (by an authoritarian relative, a minister, a counselor, or the mere presence of a stranger), the new behavior may be permanent, even though the intervention is nonprofessional.

Methods of behavior change should include practically any set of conditions that will change behavior. The list is long. There is no preeminently effective method, such as talking, although it has a place. There are many methods.

Our precepts are (1) develop structure, (2) change behavior as directly and efficiently as possible, and (3) realign variables. Set tasks and do follow-up. Use any reasonable and ethical means effectively to change behavior. Try many devices, recognizing that changing behavior can take many directions. Above all, judge results critically, and change accordingly.

Time was our first consideration; then the notion of structure followed quickly. Structure is important because it subsumes time and measures many other variables as well. Structure is an abstraction; time is concrete, easily identified, and readily measured. Action and responsibility are more vague, although they can be related to specific acts, instruments, and conditions.

To sum up, the psychotherapist is only one of many behavior changers, and psychotherapy is only one of many methods for behavior change. Hopefully, since he is especially trained and skilled, the psychotherapist is capable of directing the work of others who will help in accomplishing change and is not limited to the practice of psychotherapy in the consulting room. Krasner (1962) writes of the psychotherapist as a "reinforcement machine." Granted, this is one role, but priority should be given to the choice and control of change media and goals. Otherwise, what is reinforced may be a matter of chance or drift. The highest priority should be given to what is chosen to be regulated, controlled, directed, and shaped. The reinforcement should come naturally from the (new) behavior outside therapy, after it has been generated in some behavior-change situation. This natural reinforcement is vital in our concept of behavior change.

The therapist is to be an "architect of change." He may act as a reinforcer himself; he may teach others, such as parents and teachers, to take this role; he may act to manipulate variables as well as people (who may be considered "variables") in order to bring structure to a given person or situation; and he may work in the consulting room with a single human being. But, as an architect of change, he should be able to work in a school, in a clinic, in the laboratory, or in larger units of society. He should be able to work on emotional problems in individual behavior or on the social problems of individuals or groups.

More needs to be known about the structure of variables in the therapeutic situation, and especially about the use of time as the pivotal concern. More needs to be understood about the importance of concrete, complex variables, such as responsibility, action, and the therapeutic outcomes. This book is a plea to the psychotherapist to operate broadly and effectively as an architect of change, and it presents a framework for such action.

This approach is derived from, and supported by, research (including original research), learning theory, and cybernetics. It is intended to contribute a useful set of principles about behavior change for use by the tyro therapist, the laboratory-minded experimental clinician, the classroom teacher of psychotherapy, those responsible for the direction of others (such as parents and teachers), and all others who attempt, systematically and professionally, to change behavior to benefit the developing or troubled human being.

2 Considerations Underlying Short-term Therapy

There is an urgent need for new and more powerful action directed toward overcoming man's vast behavior problems. There is a variety of vantage points from which these problems may be approached. However, in choosing any particular one, it must be recognized that other views and tools may also be relevant.

When the extent to which these problems erode daily lives and social functions is observed, one must be impressed with the acute need for more efficient methods that will reach more people. The fact is that current methods of treatment are seldom very effective or efficient in solving behavioral problems. However, the continuous appeals for ever more money and personnel to expand the application of established conventional methods ignore the grave weaknesses of these methods and tend to perpetuate them—at the expense of large-scale innovation.

Inevitably the problem of diagnosis appears when there is an effort to develop more effective or short-term treatment. Traditional diagnostic practice is intimately related to the concept of "mental illness." In our purview, behavior change is regarded as a different problem from psychotherapy for emotional "sickness."

There are many ways to view short-term therapy. Primarily it should deal with current problems in living. It has little concern with an exploration of the past or the inner life of the client or with a broad philosophical search for hidden meaning. The emphasis and focus upon current problems are vital in making psychotherapy more effective and more efficient.

How does one live a life "effectively"? How does one operate from day to day in a fairly reasonable way? Most planning for life appears to be short-term, even though it is generally supported by long-term goals. One may commit himself to a house mortgage that involves large obligations for a period of 20 or 30 years. A man may marry and have children with the intention of remaining with both enterprises for the rest of his life, as the majority of people do. But along with all long-range planning there are numerous short-range goals that sustain continuous efforts en route, so that the effectiveness and the validity of long-range plans depend on many short-range goals and achievements which can be measured and dealt with on a daily basis. In short, the accomplishment of long-range goals depends upon many short-term goals.

In medicine, as in social work, law, and other service professions, limited help (first aid or a small boost) is an accepted technique of treatment or of solving problems. Minor aids, judiciously applied, can be crucial in avoiding defeat or damage and in turning the organism toward success—as seen in the development of children. The Hutterite society, described at the end of this chapter, offers another kind of example of how the small steps in structured group living can deflect human behavior in important ways.

The Mental Health Problem

Today, "mental illness" is considered a massive problem of growing proportion (Leighton, 1959; Plunkett & Gordon, 1960). It is estimated that nearly eighteen million people now need some kind of formal treatment. This "silent" need is seldom verbalized, even though it is often dimly sensed by the sufferer as well as by the public. Moreover, it is estimated that only about 10 per cent of this number, or approximately 1.8 million, are identified each year as in need of help or are being treated at clinics or hospitals or by private practitioners.

Lang (1958) points out that 1.75 million serious crimes are committed each year, that society has nearly four million problem drinkers, that one out of every four marriages ends in divorce, and that each year more than 250,000 children between ages 7 and 17 are brought before juvenile courts.

It is estimated also (National Association for Mental Health, 1963) that at least 50 per cent of all the medical and surgical cases treated by private physicians and hospitals have an emotional complication that is often a central contributor to the illness.

Moreover, only a small percentage of emotionally disturbed children receive any formal help even though more than eighteen thousand children and young people are admitted yearly to public mental hospitals (National Association for Mental Health, 1963), often for sporadic, inefficient, and impersonal treatment.

There are too few clinical resources, outpatient mental health units, and hospitals and private resources available—or even feasible—to cope with such vast needs. If the present number of public and private clinics (about fifteen hundred) was multiplied $2\frac{1}{2}$ times, it is unlikely that there would be more than 1 clinical resource available to every 50,000 people. Since nearly 10 per cent of the present population is expected to need help at some time in life, even this number of clinics would, according to conventional conceptions, eventually be trying to treat far more people than is considered reasonable.

In New York State alone, in 1940, according to studies by Goldhamer and Marshall (1953), 1 person in every 15 had spent some time during his life in a mental hospital. Moreover, Landis and Page (1939) found that incapacitating mental illness affects 1 person in 10 at some time during his life.

The use of modern drugs, which make early discharges possible, has reduced the number of patients in mental hospitals and the length of treatment. However, the total number of recidivists and of persons needing some kind of formal help with mental or emotional problems seems to be increasing. Perhaps a need for better identification of problems is involved also.

Any measure that can prevent or alleviate the development of serious personal or social problems should be welcomed. And while the number of seriously disturbed persons is great, the number of people who suffer a milder or more moderate degree of emotional disturbance is much greater still.

Inefficiency in Treatment

If behavior-change efforts can be concentrated on those most likely to profit from ameliorative help, before they are forced to resort to more costly and stigmatizing treatment in a hospital, the advantages of short-term treatment may be more clearly seen.

Unfortunately, clinicians tend to adjudge many patients as "too sick" to profit from modest outpatient efforts. There is a great range of individual judgments about who should be hospitalized and who can be treated outside; at least some practitioners believe and practice as if judicious outpatient help, rather than hospitalization, were adequate for a much higher percentage of persons than receive it. Such wide variation may well stem from the methods that the practitioners use.

It is difficult to judge and get agreement upon the extent of a disturbance. It is even harder to say which treatment is most likely to succeed. Too often the rule of thumb appears to be: "When in doubt, hospitalize." This is a convenient decision, since it leaves most of the care to hospital staff. It is also socially safe to confine the patient, since the public will criticize occasional assaultive, suicidal, or bizarre behavior more severely than ineffective therapy (Hollingshead & Redlich, 1958).

But short-term structured treatment can prevent both social disruption and hospitalization. It can also be valid treatment in hospitals as well as out, with whatever the degree of disturbance. As a method, such treatment should always be weighed against the use of drugs, shock, and custodial care or against the superficial conversation and social activity that too often characterize the treatment of seriously disrupted persons. Its effectiveness should be measured against that of "intensive," or "depth," treatment. It would practically always seem useful at the very least to try it first before turning to longer-term and less direct methods.

Even such confirmed psychoanalysts as Alexander and French (1946) have presented a strong case for short-term help—not as a stopgap, but as a first-rate therapeutic effort. They disagree with conventional views in this way:

> It is argued by some psychoanalysts that quick therapeutic results cannot indicate deep, thoroughgoing changes in the dynamic structure of the personality, that years are required to bring about such fundamental changes. Others excuse the lack of therapeutic results in prolonged analysis by the patient's "resistance." They have comforted themselves by saying that the patient is not yet "fully analyzed" and they are convinced that further treatment will eventually bring the desired results. Then, when results still do not come, they often take refuge in deciding that the patient is a "latent schizophrenic."

In an effort to clarify the analytic position, Fairbairn (1952) writes that, in its long-term effort, psychoanalysis is not so much set on exploring the past as it is on determining the unconscious motivations for present behavior. Significantly, the premise here is that, as in short-term therapy, therapy should focus on current behavior. But the path is to trace the origins and meanings of problems that often have their locus in infantile or childhood experiences. It is precisely this decision to explore the past that points up a major difference between short-term and long-term treatment (Knight, 1941).

When a patient does not progress readily, the degree or tenacity of the problem may, of course, be profound. But it may be that the therapeutic effort is being mishandled or that the circumstances of treatment are inappropriate for this client at the current time. Short-term therapy can provide alternatives for testing in relatively short order, and it may capture the best and most constructive resources of the disturbed person. Prolonged treatment, on the other hand, which is generally based on untested hypotheses for long periods of time, may aggravate or miss the behavior problems, nor is it likely to facilitate the development of treatment alternatives when therapy is ineffectual.

Outcome studies are subject to much criticism. Yet there is a gathering core of evidence about therapeutic effort and outcome that is generally accepted. Summaries of the percentage of patients who improve under various therapeutic regimens are published continually, although the bases for comparisons are weak. In one good summary, Appel, Lhamon, Meyers, and Harvey (1953) reported on studies published from 1936 to 1951, covering research on outcomes from therapy in a diversity of settings from 1910 to 1947. If we accept Eysenck's review (1952) as a reference point, there is little evidence that the improvement rates have materially changed since then.

Appel et al. (1953, pp. 24–27) write that ". . . there is in these various reports a general agreement as to the rate of improvement from therapy of the psychoneuroses which falls within the range of 55 to 76 per cent. . . ." These figures include follow-up résumés of the patient's standings. They generalize further: "A review of . . . statistical reports shows that improvement takes place in roughly 67 per cent of psychoneurotic and 39 per cent of schizophrenic patients."

There are gross and numerous deficiencies in the reported studies, particularly concerning such factors as selectivity of clients, dropout rates, quality of therapists, length and nature of follow-up, and control groups. But the burden obviously lies heavily with the therapist to justify the length and costliness of his procedures when he claims that unusual length or intensiveness is necessary or desirable, since these outcome figures tend to be similar for all approaches. Some more precise recent research, to be discussed, even favors the short-term structured approach.

The Semantic Problem in Traditional Diagnosis

Habits of classifying often lead clinicians to regard patients as more disturbed than they may be for treatment purposes. The use of an apparently specific diagnostic term, such as "pseudoneurotic schizophrenia," "paranoid state," or "manic-depressive psychosis," for example, implies the need for hospitalization, and a kind of treatment which may be unnecessarily restricted.

Moreover, such terms as "Oedipus complex" and "castration" may convey notions that are not central for personality change. In fact, the use of such terms may divert the therapist from useful practices for therapeutic help. In commenting on the social aspects of emotional problems, Whitehorn (1953) points out some of the confusions that may arise from use of certain diagnostic terms.

If preoccupation with classifying pathology were replaced by a specific description of patients' weaknesses *and* strengths and of their problems in handling their environments, methods of treatment could become more constructive and concrete. As Ruesch and Bateson (1951, pp. 234–255) have written:

> For the present we observe that psychiatry is predominantly concerned with the perception and description of the abnormal and undesirable and that the technical vocabulary is almost entirely focused upon the pathological aspects. . . . It is a science rather inarticulate about its operations with its theoretical focus concentrated upon the diagnosis of abnormality and the analysis of normal dynamics in abnormal circumstances. The dynamics of normal circumstances and the methods of implementing the therapeutic process are comparatively little studied.

It is generally agreed that present diagnostic categories are not very valid. In fact, Szasz (1960; 1961; 1964) has argued that the entire concept of "mental illness" is invalid. And Szasz is not the first seriously to challenge prevailing descriptions. In spite of this trend, most clinicians at one time or another rely on these commonly employed categories and, as a result, think of their patients as "sick." As a result, their trial of different forms of behavior-change efforts is hampered. Moreover, the use of formidable psychiatric terms tends to reinforce anxieties of the therapist about his clients.

In most of the published works of therapists who rely on or commend short-term therapy, patients are described in terms of directly observable behavior, not in diagnostic categories. Leaving behind the formality of psychiatric diagnoses seems to facilitate more flexible thinking about disturbed people and their problems and about the instruments and methods of solutions (Szasz, 1960).

Although derived from a general criticism of the application of the medical disease model to psychotherapy and behavior change (Eysenck, 1960, pp. 1–10), this criticism must not be equated with a desire for anarchy in the diagnostic field. It has its greatest value in pointing out the limitations of the disease model in the study and application of behavior-change methods. It should also hasten the development of models better suited for psychotherapy.

Short-term Therapy Based upon Current Problems

Although everyone has problems, most people seem to solve or control or reduce most of their problems most of the time. Even if 1 out of 10 persons does go to a mental hospital at one time in his life, 9 out of 10 do not. It is vital to discover why these 9 are apparently successful in handling their problems.

Although Wolberg (1954) considers that the value of short-term therapy can be overemphasized, he agrees that its gains can be considerable. He tends to view it as "second best," however. He believes that it is most effective with those who have limited goals in treatment, with those who have already worked out their difficulties on a nonverbal level, and with special therapists competent with the technique. In Wolberg's opinion, persistent, long-term problems do not yield to short-term therapy; however, he agrees that brief therapy does not preclude extensive personality change (1954, pp. 103–105).

Because of his tendency to look for shortcomings, symptoms, and dynamics, the clinician might rate many a successfully functioning person as "sick." Of course, the clinician does not manufacture problems, but he does find them to fit his theoretical or diagnostic notions. The clinician, if he is influenced by the field of general medicine, usually thinks in terms of diagnostic categories and mental *illness*. In general, he has not adopted the physician's practical attitudes toward normalcy and his concept of a wide range of "healthiness." Minor mental symptoms tend to be viewed more seriously than minor physical symptoms, even by those trained to act therapeutically toward both. The therapist might well give greater stress to what people can do and to their special competencies—not just to their inadequacies.

Since nearly 7 out of 10 patients admitted to a mental hospital return to life outside the hospital, and since mental hospitals, in general, are not noted for the quality of their treatment, a practical set of criteria is needed to evaluate the cause and nature of such change. While a 70 per cent improvement rate is not necessarily good—and may represent only naturally occurring improvement—it does suggest a degree of progress from incapacity worthy of analysis.

The recent emphasis on rehabilitation also attests to a kind of "total push," environmental assistance, or manipulation in the interest of helping the patient arrive at a modicum of satisfaction. In the formal field of rehabilitation, the criteria are centered chiefly on job performance as the measure of improvement (Rusk, 1949; Rusk, 1958; Rusk & Taylor, 1953). The rehabilitation team does not ask whether a patient is symptom-free or has reached some insightful state reconciling his conscious and unconscious thoughts. Rather, it asks whether the patient is able to function in a fairly adequate manner sufficient to sustain himself and those for whom he is responsible, to an extent reasonably commensurate with his measurable potentialities. In short, both rehabilitation medicine and rehabilitation psychology are based upon objective, behavioral criteria of performance and improvement.

Some depth-oriented therapists also emphasize practical criteria. For example, Miller (1950) suggests the use of more flexible mechanisms in adjusting to life as a goal. And in his writing on homosexuality and its treatment, Bieber (1962) bases his data on overt behavioral criteria; his conclusions are founded upon behavioristic criteria from everyday life (although many of his concepts have an "internal" reference).

In her discussion of the motivations and purposes of psychoanalysis, Fromm-Reichmann (1950) asserts that she intends to "make the unconscious conscious" when facing the practical problem of weighing outcomes. However, the only specific criteria she discusses are related to overt behavioral manifestations, that is, job satisfaction, social activity, marital adjustment, and ability to keep out of trouble.

In short-term, structured psychotherapy, the goals are direct and concrete from the beginning. Its therapeutic procedures are set with specific outcome criteria in mind. If bed-wetting is part of the presenting complaint, a large share of the therapeutic effort is directed to this problem (Lovibond, 1963; Mowrer & Mowrer, 1938; Phillips, 1961). The outcome is then evaluated in terms of progress toward changing this behavior.

In learning how to do psychotherapy, the budding clinician is often taught to reject or mistrust his direct observations. He is trained to substitute unobservable concepts derived from theory. He is taught that what is initially observed in the patient is not the "real" problem, but only a symptom, usually several degrees removed from the basic issue. He may even be taught to look *past* what he observes is directly at hand and is manipulable; he may be taught that he is seeing only the top of the iceberg, which indicates a large, deep, unseen presence. What "makes" a person do that which is "superficially" observable is some profound and obscure condition which should not be dealt with on the surface.

But when the scene of the therapeutic effort is removed to some obscure referents of an earlier time and place, psychotherapy does not treat with the available problems or the potentially available resources of the patient. Therapy that deals chiefly with the recovery of lost memories or obscure causes cannot succeed quickly even when that otherwise might be possible.

Any problem that troubles the individual or any behavior that creates a problem for others and is not being solved is worth treating. The patient may have only vague symptoms such as tenseness, ulcers, or a sense of panic because he does not or cannot define the more concrete problems in his daily life. Even these symptoms can be dealt with directly or used immediately in measuring the problem and a solution. That a given item of psychopathology is not "the" problem in a psychodynamic sense is of little moment. What constitutes the central problem is a conceptual matter, even if based on factual observations. The therapist who refuses to work with direct observations and solutions is more likely to go wrong, for while scientific sophistication must often incorporate the unseen, it must also be able to test parsimonious solutions rigorously.

To sum up, then, whatever is the problem in daily life can be used as the therapeutic problem as well and is also the most tangible basis for evaluating outcome. This is not to say that the observed problem(s) constitutes the *whole* problem. Other problems may exist, to be sure, problems that are important as well as problems that may be harmlessly passed over. Certainly, few therapists would contend that they deal with *every* problem of their clients.

Short-term Steps (toward Long-term Goals)

Most people seem to focus their planning upon immediately upcoming events in their lives. The parent wants to help his child improve in reading—by the end of the school year. A man looks for ways to make good—on a new job. A woman looks for ways to attract a proposal of marriage—from a certain man or by a certain time. While long-term planning is desirable and should be encouraged, therapy in this regard can seldom do more than help develop or envision the master framework: each specific step in implementing the broad plan must usually be short, setting up the model and developing the habits likely to achieve these long-term goals. Therapy seldom lasts long enough actually to see these plans through.

In a recent volume, Stieper and Wiener (1965, p. 43), in reviewing length of time associated with beneficial therapeutic outcomes, suggest that the patient usually has in mind a period of time or a particular phase in his life which guides his participation in therapy and determines his readiness to continue or drop it.

In a university psychological clinic, the length of the school term sets an arbitrary time limit on therapy. Although this is an outside limit, it often sets the goal of professional help: the student who seeks help, as well as the university staff, must see evidence of improvement by the end of the term, or by some specific point in time, to know what to do next.

In nearly every aspect of one's life, phasing or structuring must fit a time limit of some sort. Nearly every patient asks the practitioner some time during the first hours of therapy: "How much will this cost?" or "How long will it last?" Nearly everyone must budget time, money, and energy.

Often, the therapist views these limitations as too restrictive. "If we only had more time," he remarks, or "If the patient could only afford more." Sometimes the wish correctly implies unrealistic restrictions upon psychotherapy. But therapy must fit the normal life space and time projections that shape and limit all human activities. Therapy is just another human enterprise subject to most of the common basic rules and boundaries.

Curtailing Long-term Therapy

For the moment, we shall set aside the question of when, if ever, long-term treatment is a justified goal from the very onset of therapy. In an eclectic or institutional setting, such a goal is not generally intentional, nor is a long-term treatment likely to be predicted at the beginning. Instead, the therapist feels his way along; he seldom has specific goals unless the patient imposes limitations on treatment because of such factors as finances, the need to move, or an acute disruption in his life requiring immediate change. The therapist may limit treatment because his services are needed by others, although this is not the usual occurrence, since therapists apparently prefer (and are usually permitted) to continue working with an old patient rather than take on a new one.

Under these conditions, the therapy may continue indefinitely, without planning on the part of client or therapist, unless a decisive environmental force intervenes or one of the participants becomes restive or disenchanted with the treatment. One of the authors has observed clients who have been coming to a clinic for treatment for nearly two decades whose cases show no signs of terminating or being terminated.

Usually two reasons, intertwined, are advanced for continuing such patients for such long periods of time: (1) The patient would get worse if he were not "supported" or "maintained" at the *status quo* by the therapist's friendship; (2) the patient appears to need supervision or drugs permanently, to supply a kind of basic "irreversible deficit" in his personality—such as the diabetic's lifelong need for insulin.

Although the relevant physiological, neurological, or psychological information is lacking to support this analogy to diabetes, the therapist obviously assumes a rather egocentric mantle if he considers no more sanguine goals, in the belief that he himself can make no further improvement and that neither could anyone or anything else available. Certainly this drifting, long-term therapy should be tested continuously for its presumed effect in warding off greater trouble.

The problem of interminability in outpatient psychotherapy has been examined in at least four related studies on the same population. In their study, Stieper and Wiener (1959) divided patients into two long-term and two short-term groups, among whom there were no differences in education, intelligence, or diagnosis. They found no correlation between length of time in therapy and the extent of the patient's improvement. Moreover, they observed that ". . . . the great majority of long-term patients were being seen by a small minority of the therapists. A likely reason appears to be failure on the part of 'long-term' therapists adequately to formulate therapy goals, and to impersonalize the therapeutic relationship." Another study also suggests this relationship. Assigning clinical patients specifically by clinical judgment, rather than randomly, appears to make no difference in the outcome of the treatment (Garetz, Kogl, & Wiener, 1959).

Two other studies have been directly concerned with the effects of arbitrary termination of long-term or "interminable" therapy. In the first (Wiener, 1959), two psychiatrists were leaving the clinic. This fact presented an opportunity to terminate the treatment of all their patients, most of whom would ordinarily have been transferred to other therapists. No dire consequences were observed during the 6-month follow-up period, and although they were told that they could come back at any time (they even *had* to return if they wanted a refill of medication), about one out of four did not try to return. Those who had been in treatment the longest were most likely to return, but there was no correlation between age, education, or type of diagnosis.

In the other study, which dealt with the effect of removing medications from long-term users (Wiener, Feinberg, Nagobads, Westendorf, & Warren, 1963), there appeared to be no untoward effect on long-term users, in comparison with the control group (who were continued on the drug regimen). In fact, there were certain improvements. The evidence was strong, however, that when the study was over, even the most successfully withdrawn (improved) patients were returned to drugs. Although their therapists could seldom offer any reason for this return, the authors concluded that they returned because the therapist had not formulated an alternative way of treatment—or termination.

What should be concluded, then, from these and similar studies? Certainly, they offer powerful evidence that long-termness in psychotherapy—other than the occasional cases of psychoanalytic therapy, where it is a goal at the beginning—is often determined by factors unrelated to diagnosis, intelligence, the initial intent of the patient (or therapist), and other aspects of the patient's determinable needs or attributes. Even in psychoanalysis, the question of length of therapy takes on similar properties because vastly different therapy regimens occur, ranging from one to five interviews per week, from 2 to 10 years or longer, and from a minimum of 100 to 200 hours up to over one thousand hours. Long-termness or interminability of treatment seems most likely to be determined by the dependency and conceptual needs of the patient and by the personality and theory of the therapist, and it apparently has little direct relationship to improvement in treatment.

Effects of Limited Help

In pursuing the idea of "phases," as discussed above in connection with the work of Stieper and Wiener (1965), the amount of judicious help most people need, to get moving satisfactorily, may turn out to be surprisingly modest—often more modest than the therapist is ready to believe. While some patients may continue in therapy indefinitely, a large majority of outpatients seem likely enough to respond sufficiently to well-directed limited help to make it worthwhile to develop such help. The theoretical aspect of why this is the case will be discussed in a later chapter.

In one study (unpublished), one of the authors found that in a group of 110 students offered psychotherapeutic help at a psychological center, about one-third refused to accept it, saying that they preferred to handle their problems by themselves. The entire group had been given a battery of psychological tests to discover and describe any personal, social, and academic difficulties, and therapeutic help was immediately available. Those who were offered professional help were selected on the basis of their expressed desire to understand their problems better and on the basis of two or more substantial elevations on the Minnesota Multiphasic Personality Inventory.

A follow-up study of all 110 of these students approximately 6 to 8 months later indicated that three-fourths of those who declined help were still functioning well and, in their own evaluation, still had no need for help.

Although the clinicians, basing their opinions on objective criteria, thought these individuals needed help—and they indeed might have profited from help—it is significant that over three-fourths of them continued to solve their problems adequately or at least to live with a modicum of satisfaction. Perhaps the potential clients were wiser than the clinicians in predicting a capacity to get along on their own. Of course, the therapist may say that this reaction reflects pathology, such as masochism, fear, or resistance, but the burden of proving pathology when denied still must rest on the therapist.

The point here is that therapists may be so attuned to psychopathology and to believing that people need help that they fail to see, or may underestimate, strength and problem-solving resources in many who may seem to need—or even ask for—*some* help. In either case, the problem and resources may need only a small amount of definition to permit the client to master or control the situation.

Conversely, the thought may occur to the research-oriented practitioner that to engage these very persons in long-term depth therapy might, in time, be of unusual value (and in any case not harmful) even though the focus of therapy would necessarily be more nebulous than the usual attempt to solve currently disruptive problems efficiently.

Perhaps this very vagueness of purpose may be the reason why so many come for therapy only to decide that they have not found what they want (or have found what they did not want) and elect not to continue. Whether or not the patients' own evaluations are correct, the clinicians have much to learn from them, for many can fend for themselves after a modest effort to overcome what disrupts or disturbs their lives. It may be that the sheer fact of reporting a problem to another person, of exposing oneself to objective scrutiny about highly personal matters (Mowrer, 1963), makes some constructive difference and thereby permits one to move along on his own.

Alexander (1953, pp. 18–19) believes that short-term therapy fulfills dependency needs, provides some guidance and catharsis to support defenses, and permits some effective manipulation of life situations. (He defines such therapy in very short terms—as few as one or two interviews—while our own description is more elaborate, theory-based, and wide-ranging.) He appears here to regard short-term therapy as ameliorative and supportive, rather than as producing substantial and persisting behavior change, and since the more profound research questions implied by this difference of opinion are essentially empirical, they can be answered only through further research.

The Importance of Structure in a Society

Data from another culture can sometimes lend valuable perspective on the culture in which today's therapist functions. The Hutterite society, which is a compact subculture within the United States, is vastly different from the society of the country as a whole in most aspects which affect behavior problems. We are not competent to generalize from other societies, nor is it valid to single out a society which functions in a specified way as proof of one's point without evaluating an entire population of societies. There seems always to be a society—or case—to illustrate any view. This brief example is cited only to illustrate how clarity and firmness in structure seemingly can produce certain social results—not as proof of a theory.

In their study of the Hutterite society, Eaton and Weil (1955) found it relatively free from crime and mental illness. Their study is significant to this discussion because it underlines the importance attached here to the concept of structure in human relations. The rearing of Hutterite children differs sharply from that suggested by currently popular mental hygiene strictures (Lang, 1958):

> The Hutterite Brethren's child-rearing methods are consistently in opposition to the advice of the Children's Bureau bulletins of 1914 and 1942, as well as 1951. Still the children thrive. Though not everything in their lives is fun and though they may not grow into what we consider "happy" adults, still, both as children and adults they are contented and successful enough, and they are nearly free from emotional turmoil.

The Hutterite society is noted for the simplicity and clarity of its relationships. While it is not the typical complex urban society so prevalent in the United States, it does reveal some of the advantages of a firm structuring of human relations. Few who are used to the "American way of life" would probably choose to live under the relatively primitive conditions of the Hutterites. But there may be a useful lesson in their way of living, for it emphasizes a simplicity and structure that might well be central to mental health—not only in the whole society but in its treatment of the emotionally disturbed.

Hutterite children are disciplined more strongly than most American children. The social group also gives the disturbed person more social support than is the case in present-day American society. While emotional problems are usually taken to indicate some kind of inferiority, the Hutterites, in spite of their more severe attitude toward human conduct, generally support the disturbed person readily, in nonjudgmental and nonaccusative ways. Moreover, although it is a highly structured society, there are many individual differences in behavior (Eaton & Weil, 1955, p. 181): "Hutterite individuals differed widely. They were not cases in the same mold, but if viewed as a group they provided an extreme example of the relative importance of ideology and belief among the many personality dimensions which help to shape infants into adult human beings." And again: ". . . our study of Hutterite individuals disclosed no simple standardization of personality structure, despite a high degree of communality in social and cultural patterns (Eaton & Weil, 1955, p. 181).

The Therapeutic Meaning of Structure

It is often said that individual welfare and mental health are injured by structure in any aspect of human relations (except, perhaps, for obviously necessary requirements such as paying one's check at a restaurant or driving on the right side of the road in traffic). In the same sense, structured, short-term therapy is often criticized on the grounds that it violates the uniqueness of the individual. Its critics say that the structuring of responses in situations involving choice deprives the patient of his individual initiative, interest, creative potentiality, or other virtues.

Our thesis is just the opposite. Our conclusion is that structure is what makes human relations satisfying and provides the basis for problem solving. This is particularly evident when the person is suffering from relatively serious emotional disturbance. The example of the Hutterite society is not offered in support of any type of therapy, but as evidence that a highly structured set of living conditions need not injure mental health and that such structuring can be of substantial benefit.

The emphasis on the technique of structuring, the specifics of therapy, and the need for self-discipline as presented in subsequent chapters is based on a growing body of research which appears to be logical and valid in given contexts. The problem becomes largely that of applying reason, predictability, and control in therapy, as in many other human relations areas.

There are many interpretations of "structure." Here the emphasis is on the therapist's use of external controls and manipulations that will lead to self-control and direction where needed. More specifically, structure in therapy means observing the relationship between given antecedent and resultant elements; interfering in pathology to realign variables so as to produce a different outcome or effect; using environmental manipulations (encompassing persons outside of therapy) to bring about desired effects; introducing and assuring as much certainty and dependability and control in heretofore uncontrolled and uncertain situations as possible; and, above all, making these changes in ways consonant with the integrity and values of the individual (or social unit).

What structure specifically does not mean here is permissiveness with nebulous purpose; reliance on creative, sporadic, or unpredictable bursts to solve problems that have been chronically unsolved; the belief that nonenvironmental or internal conditions and motivations will solve problems through unfocused or indirect measures; and an indiscriminate rejection of control and order as somehow injurious to mental health.

Structure can be studied in a simple, obvious situation such as asking a child to close his comic book and get to work on his spelling lesson, or even in the most pervasive situation, such as ordering the environment of the psychotic patient to screen out pathological behavior and induce more normal behavior. In its broadest context, structure operates as a generic condition, ranging from simple verbal-persuasive techniques to the nonverbal environmental manipulation of large segments of behavior in a design for a whole society.

To sum up, this view of structure subsumes verbal therapy measures that are engineered to change behavior, as well as many types of laboratory methods (related chiefly to conditioning, either of a classical or operant variety). And, finally, it embraces a wide range of social measures that seek to control variables entirely outside the classroom, laboratory, or consulting room.

3 Relevant Reports: Methods, Implications, and Concepts

Attempts to shorten psychotherapy have followed two broad trends. One trend has been to develop shortened approaches to therapy, without regard to a specific therapeutic orientation. These attempts have been largely in response to the urgent demands that arose during and immediately after World War II. In studies on such shortened therapy, which somewhat resembles first aid, there is little interest evidenced in posing theoretical questions or in placing short-term therapy in the perspective of a distinctive method.

The other trend, which is more recent, has arisen chiefly from a behavioral emphasis and, as discussed later, stems mainly from laboratory (or laboratory-inspired) studies of learning and behavior change. In this approach, learning principles are applied to psychotherapy, but with the behavioral emphasis discussed in the preceding chapter. This trend, which has had the benefit of much more theoretical guidance, has sought to bring together the work of the laboratory and the clinic.

Although these studies raise methodological, philosophical, and theoretical issues, this chapter is concerned more with the problem of transition, from shortening therapy in the clinic as a practical measure, to the behavioral restatement of clinical problems, psychosomatic complaints, and psychotic conditions.

The growing number of important studies on the implications of short-term therapy and behavioral change raise many questions about traditional clinical approaches. In examining these questions, the details of some laboratory-based behavior-change and short-term methods should be considered. There are several avenues open to the therapist intent upon shortening treatment. There are important theoretical issues in short-term therapy and behavior-change efforts which can carry the theory-minded therapist far beyond the scope of conventional clinical work. The application of laboratory-derived methods to clinical problems promises even further insights into how to make therapy shorter and more effective.

Early Reports

Illustrating the heightened interest in shortened treatment during and after World War II, Gutheil (1944), who favored shorter psychoanalytic therapy, indicated 18 kinds of disorders where good results might be expected from brief therapy. In their study of the responses of patients to brief psychotherapy, Harris and Christiansen (1946) found that among 53 patients who were slowly recovering from physical disease or injury, those who responded best to short-term therapy had greater rated ego strength and greater stability and modifiability of personality structure.

In their study of brief therapy of patients in a military convalescent hospital, Prugh and Brody (1946) reported that brief therapy was effective where the problems were "situational war neuroses." Anxiety reactions, mild conversions, and hypochondriacal or psychosomatic problems all responded well to short-term therapy.

Among cases discussed at the Third Psychotherapy Council (Chicago Institute for Psychoanalysis, Third Psychotherapy Council, 1946), held at the Chicago Institute of Psychoanalysis, were two cases conducted according to principles of "brief" or "flexible" therapy—short at least by psychoanalytic standards. One patient, who had a peptic ulcer, was treated in 36 interviews over 10 months by Alexander; another patient, who was suffering from migraine headaches, was treated by Johnson in 75 interviews over 19 months. The authors state that ". . . the same type of unconscious material [was obtained]," and they report comparable therapeutic results, although their brief therapy was not based on daily interviews, as in concentrated psychoanalytic therapy.

The observations of Grinker (1947), also writing from the military setting, are based on brief psychotherapy, which was brief because there were not enough therapists to carry on prolonged therapy. Although he gives no statistics, he cites an exemplary case and recommends procedures that are suitable for brief therapy.

Baker (1947), who recommended psychotherapy as a "first-aid" technique when long-term therapy is impractical, cites six steps as essential to the practice of brief therapy: intellectual clarification of the problem; advice; catharsis; interpretation of transference and resistance; the use of prolonged supportive therapy devoid of personality-change efforts; and favorable attitude of the therapist. He believes that situational difficulties respond best to brief therapy and that if the source of the problems lies far back in the patient's life, short-term therapy is contraindicated.

Even though some therapists, such as Baker, Grinker, and Prugh and Brody, seem to practice short-term therapy only out of necessity rather than as a preferred choice, they have helped to prepare the way for consideration of shortened therapy on its own merits; they have opened the door to the study of their shortened methods compared with both their preferred ones and those of learning theorists.

In pointing out the importance of short-term therapy in the medical setting, Malamud (1948) wrote about its goals and methods, but cited no unique approaches. A community setting in which short-term therapy methods were explored has been described by Koye (1949). The goal was not to restore the patient to maximum functioning but to help him develop a modicum of a working relationship with his environment.

In doing treatment with limited goals (or "sector therapy") which was psychoanalytically oriented, Deutsch (1949) described his methods in a recorded series of 14 interviews. This work represents one of the early attempts by an analyst to come to grips with briefer therapy in theory as well as in practice.

In his evaluation of brief psychotherapy, based on Rotter's social learning theory, Morton (1949) used a matched control group. He found psychometric gains for his experimental (psychotherapy) group over the controls. This was one of the first studies explicitly to use both a brief-therapy and a control (no-therapy) group. It served as a heuristic lead for many others to follow (Morton, 1955).

A book by Cameron (1950) anticipated some of our concepts and attitudes in discussing behavior change and psychotherapy. In the first *Annual Review of Psychology,* Snyder (1950, p. 228) noted a steady trend in psychotherapy toward briefer efforts.

Salter (1949; 1961), who was an early and forceful exponent of conditioned-reflex therapy, systematically challenged many assumptions in psychoanalytic theory. He tried to develop a thoroughly objective basis for psychotherapy and behavior change, and his concept of "behavioral prescriptions" resembled the subsequent approach of Wolpe (1952), as well as some of the earlier practices of the psychoanalyst Herzberg (1941; 1945). The growing movement today to make the therapist more resourceful and efficient was anticipated by Salter, Herzberg, and Wolpe, even though their early efforts were often ignored and frequently criticized.

Wolpe (1952) seemed to have found relatively effective ways to state his theoretical position on the use of learning theory, in which he stressed a "response-centered" type of therapy (see Chapters 4 and 5). In his method of "reciprocal inhibition," the patient is taught behavior that is inimical to his neurotic or anxious behavior. There is a deliberate effort to interfere with, or counteract, maladaptive behavior through inhibitory methods. In his first report, Wolpe cited statistics from 70 cases, seen for from 4 to 125 interviews and classified into four outcome groups: apparently cured (49 per cent), much improved (37 per cent), slightly to moderately improved (10 per cent), and unimproved (4 per cent). While these are his own unsubstantiated judgments of outcome—and thus are not scientifically acceptable—his findings have been remarkably stimulating and have inspired more highly controlled, laboratory types of study (for example, Lang & Lazovik, 1963; Lazovik & Lang, 1960) than would ordinarily occur solely on the basis of clinical psychotherapy reports.

In a later study (1954), Wolpe collected evidence of improvement on test scores as well as on clinical signs for 122 patients. The general rate of improvement, about 90 per cent (showing mild to great improvement), was approximately the same as he reported earlier. Wolpe's recent book (1958) and other work (1961a; 1961b; 1961c) are further evidence of the stimulating nature of his ideas, which are now attracting wide interest.

Although the number of psychoanalysts who are showing an interest in short-term therapy is growing, few of them have accepted it on theoretical grounds. For example, Pumpian-Mindlin (1953) is a psychoanalyst who has been attracted to short-term therapy apparently more from necessity than from any theoretical conviction. Yet he writes that severe or gross psychopathology is, itself, no contraindication for short-term therapy. He stresses the power to "grasp and use the material" of therapeutic discussion, and other characteristics of the patient, as being related mainly to the reality situation. He is fairly explicit about short-term goals, the techniques to be used, and how to choose cases according to given criteria.

Principles for the practice of brief psychotherapy have also been noted by Bonime (1953). Another psychoanalytically inclined therapist, Rothenburg (1955), reports on patients whose neurotic symptoms were reduced by short treatment. Faries (1955) found that students counseled on a short-term basis in a college setting were more likely to graduate than noncounseled students.

In their study of short-term, parent-child psychotherapy in child guidance, Phillips and Johnston (1954) compared the results for cases treated by conventional methods—mainly modified psychoanalytic therapy—with those for cases treated by a prearranged short-term method. This comparison revealed that in the short-term cases there were fewer dropouts before completing therapy and that fewer interviews were needed to reach a completion or termination level. On a questionnaire, the parents expressed greater satisfaction with the short-term therapy.

Later Reports: Methods of Greater Precision

In his summary of newer approaches to psychotherapy, Ellis (1955a) found that psychoanalytic orthodoxy was waning by 1955, as compared with a decade or two earlier. Also, he found a more collaborative and active patient-therapist role in evidence. Based on a review of more than four hundred articles, he found that, in the decade following World War II, there had been mounting interest not only in new methods and concepts of therapy but also in briefer therapy.

Although these later studies examined by Ellis arose mainly to provide practical solutions to clinical problems, they have begun to assume theoretical importance. Later studies tend to differ from earlier ones in that they broaden the assessment of therapy beyond the mere reporting of overall clinical impressions of change. Generally, they use various psychometric techniques and compare types of cases or therapy regimens, relative to attempts to shorten therapy. There also are efforts to relate the conduct, and success or failure, of the therapy to various characteristics of the patient, the therapist, and their interaction. In brief, there are important refinements of design and concept in these later studies.

In shortening his therapy, Shlien (1956) used a time-limited arrangement, somewhat similar to that discussed earlier in connection with the Phillips and Johnston study, by which he set the number of interviews in advance with the client's consent. The results of this time limiting were so encouraging that he later made a more complete study (Shlien, Mosak, & Dreikurs, 1960; Shlien, Mosak, & Dreikurs, 1962), in which clients were given either client-centered or Adlerian therapy, under both time-limited and unlimited conditions. A control group was held in abeyance for 3 months after the termination of therapy. The time set for limited therapy was 20 interviews; under unlimited time conditions the client-centered patients averaged 37 interviews. The criterion of change was the Butler-Haigh 80-Item Q-Sort. The client-centered, time-limited cases showed movement from the beginning of therapy to the end of follow-up, represented by a correlation between self and ideal Q Sorts of $+.05$ and $+.54$, respectively. The control cases yielded a self-ideal correlation of $+.55$ during the time the clinical cases were in therapy.

Shlien's study was valuable not only because it introduced an explicit approach to brief therapy but also because it compared the entire movement of the therapy cases on the Q Sort with controls. Although no detailed criticism of research studies can be attempted here, it is worth noting that *overt* behavioral changes were not studied by Shlien et al., nor can they be inferred from the Q Sort findings.

Any attempt to introduce controls and independent measurements in such research makes the study more vulnerable to specific criticism and controversy than a straightforward report of clinical impressions and judgments does. Regardless of the merit of such criticism, Shlien's work is of the type to be welcomed by science, for it points a way to further research on the shortening of therapy. Used with more reliable and objective criteria of change—especially behavioral evidence—such research will undoubtedly have increasing usefulness and will stimulate other new work.

In their study of cases terminated by consent of both therapist and patient, Pascal and Zax (1956) found that treatment could be described in three categories: Type I, environmental manipulation, taking 5 or more hours; Type II, brief therapy, of 30 or more hours; and Type III, long-term cases, of 100 hours or more. The total number of cases studied was 30, selected from 350 cases (320 cases did not qualify for their study on the basis of too few interviews); these were, in turn, a random sample from 1,022 cases in their files. The average number of hours of therapy was as follows: Type I, 10 hours; Type II, 60 hours; and Type III, 184 hours. The first two can be considered short-term therapy. Of the 30 cases studied, all but two (from Type II) showed improvement.

It is not easy to evaluate these results, especially since they are based only on a highly selective sample of a much larger number, which, in turn, was about one-third of the total cases in file (1,022). However, they show that there was little difference in outcome between short-term therapy and therapy that lasted from 3 to 18 times as long.

The possibility that outcome is correlated with the number of interviews has been suggested by Taylor (1956) in an article examining the relationship between success and length of therapy. He found there was a "failure zone" between the twelfth and twenty-first interviews. Whether this generalization applies in different therapeutic approaches or when there is a systematic effort to shorten therapy is a moot question; that is, what might be a failure zone in long-term (or unlimited) therapy might not exist, as the Shlien et al. report suggests, when there are intentional preplanned time limits to the therapy.

During and shortly after World War II, the "placebo effect" began to attract considerable attention as the enhancement of therapeutic results through the patient's suggestibility. In addition, as pressure increased to offer service to more people, drugs came into wider use to supplement psychotherapy or to ready the patient for help. In reviewing the research on the relationship between psychotherapy and the placebo effect, Rosenthal and Frank (1958) concluded that there are many nonspecific factors which influence psychotherapy. Perhaps these nonspecific factors are more closely related to the individual potential for behavior change than such standard variables as insight and catharsis are.

In another report on similar research, Gliedman, Nash, Imber, Stone, and Frank (1958) equated the use of drugs and short-term psychotherapy in the sense that each is a method used to "reduce symptoms." In this context they found that both help the patient to mobilize the healthful aspects of his personality and diminish his secondary reactions to illness. Any therapeutic maneuver that helps the patient to start moving may place him in a position to experience much-needed success in living. Their report suggests that it is of secondary importance which method is used to encourage the patient's resourcefulness.

In his review of psychotherapy in the 1957 issue of the *Annual Review of Psychology*, Winder (1957, p. 318) summarized a number of studies involving a wide range of approaches to change in psychotherapy. Treatment goals included reduction of neurotic symptoms, strengthening of defenses, reduction of psychotic symptoms, improvement in interpersonal relations, changes in self-concept, and insight. Although a wide range of therapeutic persuasions was represented, all had one feature in common: changes in behavior were often accomplished by very simple methods. Changes were not sweeping or dramatic in any type of psychotherapy, but were generally palliative and practical.

In a study that shed light on evaluative techniques, Cartwright and Rath (1957) made a factor analysis of the outcome of 31 cases of client-centered treatment. The change matrix yielded two factors that were not related: the client's views and the therapist's views. Wiener, Feinberg, Nagobads, Westendorf, and Warren (1963) report a similar finding in drug therapy with psychiatric patients. It may be too much to expect that client and therapist views of therapeutic outcome would match completely; yet to find little or no relationship suggests that these two essential participants regard the therapeutic process very differently and points up a pressing need for concepts and measures to resolve this difference.

The context in which therapy is conducted also has an appreciable effect on the type of outcome. Starting with the (incorrect) premise that the longer therapy lasts, the better the results, the therapist may miss a salutary outcome from a very few interviews. In this case, the patient's view is easily overlooked. If there is a concerted effort to shorten therapy and focus upon the patient's views, combined with more conventional criteria of outcome, the therapist is more likely to make a practical and heuristic evaluation that he can discuss with the patient. A therapist-imposed view of the essential depth and long-term nature of effective therapy may by itself cause a difference of opinion between therapist and client as to what the therapy was worth and what it produced. This lack of communication is critical and should be cause for grave concern.

On this subject, Winder writes that it is a mistake in psychothera-peutic practice to overlook amelioration as a basic goal of treatment. Perhaps the fact that often the therapist does not accept ameliorative goals or consider short-term therapy a creditable process helps to explain why the views of the therapist and patient differ. As Winder says: "In general, it would seem that in many instances effective therapy must deal directly or indirectly with a situation rather than with the individual alone. The problem posed would seem to be: what interpersonal and intrapersonal fields are susceptible to restructuring, in what ways, and by what procedures?" (1957, p. 309).

In another study, by Whitehorn and Betz (1957), of short-term ther-apy by both experienced and inexperienced therapists, comparing ther-apy with insulin and without it, the results suggest that insulin acts more as a motivator toward change when the therapist is inexperienced. Per-haps the experienced therapist is better able to stimulate enough change in the patient otherwise, so that the drug is unnecessary.

In their study on the relationship between therapy length and out-come, Stendal and van der Veen (1957) found a correlation of +.58 between length of treatment and movement toward personal integration (an average of 31 interviews for 73 clients). Although short-term therapy was the mode of operation, it was not intended to be. Any generaliza-tions about the relationship between length of treatment and outcome should always allow for the originally selected method of therapy. For example, client-centered therapy does not ordinarily seek historical ori-gins at length, as depth-oriented therapy does. It is likely that the cor-relation obtained would have been lower if the mean number of inter-views had been in the hundreds.

Kirtner and Cartwright (1958a) studied success and failure in short- and long-term therapy in relation to interview behavior in 47 cases of client-centered therapy. In addition to failure and success groups in long- and short-term treatment, they studied a fifth group of intermediate fail-ures (13 to 21 interviews). The patient is encouraged to focus *internally* (on his subjective psychological processes) in client-centered therapy; the patient who focuses on behavior outside himself is less likely to be con-sidered an apt patient. While none of the cases was extremely long-term, that is, extending over hundreds of interview hours, and while all were treated with the client-centered approach, there is some evidence that somewhat longer treatment in this context was slightly more beneficial.

In another study, Kirtner and Cartwright (1958b) found, on the Thematic Apperception Test (but with only 26 subjects and unstable results), that the length of therapy has much to do with the personality structure of the patient at the beginning of therapy.

Child-guidance cases were studied by Phillips (1960), comparing results for parent-child combinations of treatment when the therapist used a "structured," as against a "permissive," approach. In the former, the procedures were somewhat similar to those stressed by Ellis (1962), Eysenck (1960), and others; that is, the therapeutic intervention was relatively direct and deliberate, and the therapist was more active in structuring behavior and using daily schedules and explicit plans. In the permissive cases, however, the therapist activity was slight, characterized by a wait-and-see attitude, the absence of suggestions, and an emphasis on "warmth and understanding" and interpretation of the patient's feelings. Phillips found that the structured approach was rated more favorably by parents and tended to be shorter.

In a report on 37 studies of child therapy, Levitt (1957) concluded, as did Eysenck, that psychotherapy with children fails to produce consistently good results. More recently Levitt reaffirmed these findings in an additional evaluation (1963). However, most of the child-guidance cases in his follow-up, as with Eysenck's review cases, were provided by clinics or therapists that used what were essentially conventional (little structured) therapy practices. Other studies of follow-up, which were of more behaviorally oriented therapy, generally suggest advantages for the more structured and specific approaches. While Hood-Williams's reply (1960) to Levitt makes a cogent point about the adequacy of a "base line" for the evaluation of outcome, basic change in the attitudes and practices of therapists will undoubtedly be needed before the success rate in diverse therapy populations improves significantly.

Working with currently high attrition rates and the prevailing differences between therapist and patient evaluations of outcomes of therapy which is not behavior-oriented, it is doubtful whether satisfactory evaluation of outcome is possible. Perhaps no therapeutic method which deals mainly with indirect or internal processes can yield generally accepted results.

Therapist Factors

Although the data are still incomplete, the beginning behavior of the therapist in *any* therapy appears to have a substantial effect upon the outcome of treatment. Apparently, each therapist has a sort of "cognitive map" of all previous patients, against which he compares each new patient. Often he is preoccupied with covert, internal-state variables, so that it is difficult for him to maintain a flexible attitude and to perceive his patients and therapy in the perspective of the environment outside the interview office. He also has difficulty in evaluating the patient at the end of therapy—as already discussed—in a way that is consistent with the patient's expectations and evaluation.

Even though the therapist is subject to human preconceptions and biases, he can deal in cogent, objective ways with specific variables if he chooses to. Specific practices that will solve problems can be made clear to the patient, especially in shortened therapy (see the studies of Shlien et al., Phillips and Johnston, and Stieper and Wiener). Under structured conditions the patient appears to move faster toward whatever goals are practicable and desirable for him. Most therapies do not seem to be attempting to provide the patient optimal opportunities for efficient behavior change.

An interesting twist to this theme appears in Boileau's article on brief psychotherapy (1958). His approach, termed "need-integrative therapy," is the opposite of Ellis's; Boileau thinks that the patient is not mistaken or a victim of misunderstanding but, rather, that he has normal needs and that his neurosis is an expression of normal inclinations. He states that a neurosis represents the best effort the patient can make under the circumstances. However, the differences between Boileau and Ellis appear to be chiefly semantic. Ellis stresses the *changes* that are needed to produce integrated behavior, not the possible motivation for the change. Boileau may be right about what the patient's needs are.

Although their work was not concerned with short-term therapy per se, Stieper and Wiener (1959) found that the length of therapy is determined more by the therapist than by the patient. In their comparison of short-term with interminable cases (2 to 10 years in an outpatient clinic), they found no differences among either patients or results. However, they found that it was possible to predict who the long-term *therapists* would be and concluded that the ". . . 'long-term' therapists failed to adequately formulate therapy goals, and to impersonalize the therapeutic relationship."

A problem which first began to be documented in the late 1950s lies in the fact that relatively few of the persons who come for therapy remain long enough to finish in a way acceptable to the therapist. In a study by Rosenthal and Frank (1958), it is reported that of those who applied for outpatient psychiatric help, one-third refused the help when it became available and that 75 per cent of those who began the therapy terminated it prematurely. The cause of this attrition could have been the length of waiting lists and the fact that the applicants found they could cope with their problems or redefine the situation. Also, when therapy did begin, it may have been unsatisfactory.

In their study of this closely related problem of attrition—that of patients who drop out too early to receive much benefit—Lorr, Katz, and Rubinstein (1958) found that early terminators were likely to be less well educated, of lower social-class standing, and less dissatisfied with themselves than remainers. Later the same authors (Katz, Lorr, & Rubinstein, 1958) found that predictors of "stayers" in therapy did not correlate with ratings of improvement, a finding similar to the one cited in the Kirtner and Cartwright study.

Haddock and Mensh (1957) described another facet of the attrition problem. They studied approximately one thousand therapy cases in three settings—a university student health center, other medical divisions in the university, and a Veterans' Administration mental hygiene clinic. About two-thirds of these patients were in treatment for less than 5 hours. Even in the relatively sophisticated university population, a high percentage of cases dropped conventional therapy very early in the process.

Current literature suggests a correlation not only between length of therapy and the therapist's activity and persuasion but perhaps also between length of therapy and the therapist's personality structure. Although the complex of variables in therapist behavior has had little study, it is probably highly instrumental in helping the patient toward a good start. The little research that has been done on therapist behavior (there are some examples in Strupp, 1960a; Strupp, 1960b), however, is weakened by the fact that it involves an arbitrary choice of variables about what therapists do in therapy. A movie or a record of a therapy hour, stopped at various junctures so that listeners (therapists) may be asked what they would do under particular conditions, may bear no resemblance to actual therapist behavior with the patient.

One author (Krasner, 1962) believes that therapist behavior can be predicted somewhat by his learning-theory position (if any). However, an inefficient therapeutic method, or a therapist operating inefficiently from any persuasion, may well produce a large number of premature terminators or many relatively long-term or interminable cases.

Not only should efficient therapy be able to interest and accept a higher percentage of applicants for help but it also should produce greater gains in less time than presently is the case. This would seem to be the most worthwhile goal within the psychotherapeutic domain. Moreover, it can be pursued from an operant or reconditioning standpoint (or from other vantage points) as effectively as from the standpoint of interpersonal or traditional therapy, or perhaps more effectively.

In the latter approach, the choice of variables would have to be solidly defined and anchored to produce objectively validated results. This is not likely with such conventional variables as the amount of talk by therapist and patient, the way in which the transference was handled, whether emotional excesses were cathected or drained, and whether the therapist acted as a buffer for the patient or helped him gain insight.

Behavior-change Emphasis: General Reports and Theory

An awareness of the value of behavioral variables and behavioral theory in psychotherapy has developed quite slowly. Although some influence can be traced back to Watson, Pavlov, Jones, and other pioneering psychologists, the trend toward developing behavioral theories applicable to psychotherapy has quickened only in the last few years. In stressing a variety of learning-theory bases for psychotherapy, Bandura (1961), Pascal (1959), and Eysenck (1960; 1961) not only proffered new conceptual dimensions for psychotherapy but also suggested new empirical leads for clinical and laboratory applications.

In an article on learning theory and psychotherapy, Bandura (1961) stresses the fact that the serious application of learning theory in psychological treatment would stimulate a wider variety of methods. He writes that, in the extensive development of schools of psychotherapy, some of the older studies by Watson, Jones, and Eysenck on behavior change have been overlooked, together with their implications for present-day therapy:

> While it is customary to conceptualize psychotherapy as a learning process, few therapists accept the full implications of this position. . . . If one seriously subscribes to the view that psychotherapy is a learning process, the methods and treatment should be derived from our knowledge of learning and motivation. Such orientation is likely to yield new techniques of treatment which, in many respects, may differ markedly from the procedures currently in use.

Like Wolpe's, the work of Frankl (1960) is based on behavior-centered therapeutic intervention; that is, he attempts to get the patient to assume attitudes and practices diametrically opposed to previous, fear-ridden behavior. This kind of confrontation, direct and focused as it can be in skilled hands, seems likely to help the patient to a constructive regard for his own problem-solving potential and to shorten therapy. The relationship between Frankl's procedures and other techniques of intervention needs further study.

Most criteria of personality and behavior change in psychotherapy have been based upon self-reports by patients (Zax & Klein, 1960). Although process changes within therapy are also commonly studied, overt changes of external behavior have been little used. More attention to all measures of change, especially overt behavior changes, could help to define psychotherapeutic goals more clearly and to increase efficiency. The relationship among the beginning, the process, and the outcomes of therapy would inevitably become more distinct.

In one study, Zolick and Hollon (1960) had a clinical psychologist rate 23 applicants for brief therapy on 16 scales presumably related to outcome. The result was three small groups. The "nonbeginners" either refused the therapy or dropped it after two interviews; the "brief-therapy" patients had 12 to 30 interviews; and the "long-term" patients had 40 to 95 interviews. The second and third groups were similar in some psychological characteristics, but both felt more self-conscious and inadequate than the nonbeginners. Of the two, however, the short-term cases tended to have more guilt feelings and more awareness of conflicts, with less overall pathology. They also appeared to be more ready to undertake therapy, were more responsive at the outset, and established a working relationship more quickly.

There is a marked trend toward experimenting with direct methods of influencing, interfering, and desensitizing. Five examples of reports on this trend were published within a recent 2-year period. Heckel, Wiggins, and Salzberg (1962) conditioned against silences in group therapy settings. Jensen and Yanagi (1961) used direct methods in treating closed-ward schizophrenic patients. Rachman (1961) used aversive conditioning with sexually disturbed male patients. Salzberg, Clark, Drennen, Hamilton, Heckel, Long, and Marr (1962) employed "multiple therapists" to help overcome a delusional system. And Finney (1964) used "partnership therapy."

Perhaps the attraction of the earlier "schools" of psychotherapy (Ford & Urban, 1963; Harper, 1959; Munroe, 1955; Stein, 1961) will wane as the therapist becomes more resourceful in dealing directly with problems and disruption through a variety of conditioning, counterconditioning, or reconditioning techniques. Innovations will be stimulated which will apply to specific situations and settings, testable for their relative effectiveness in solving specific problems.

Behavior-change Emphasis and Somatic Complaints

Psychosomatic problems have often been regarded as refractory in psychotherapy; that is, the physical symptoms are considered an additional layer atop the psychological problems, which, in turn, rest upon anxiety and repression and control the original stimulus to pathology. It is generally believed that therapy cannot reach psychosomatic symptoms directly. The very word "psychosomatic" is, at best, a loose semantic attempt to bridge the mind-body dichotomy, to acknowledge that mental and physical phenomena are interrelated. One might wonder why they were separated in the first place via the philosophical tradition, beginning with Descartes. The term also suggests a more holistic basis for psychotherapy. Out of this tangle of theory, semantics, and treatment regimens, it is not surprising that little clarity in methods of treatment has developed. New directions toward more behavioral treatment of psychosomatic problems are developing, however.

Ever since the mid-1940s there have been various reports on behavioral (or quasi-behavioral) approaches to psychosomatic problems. For example, Seitz (1953) used brief psychotherapy on 25 patients with an excoriation syndrome. Treatment was based on a limit of 12 interviews; 12 discontinued prematurely, but 12 of the remaining 13 obtained a symptomatic cure (skin clear) and remained clear at a 3-month follow-up. After a six month follow-up, 6 or 7 cases were still clear; however, after one year there was evidence that the treatment had not been permanent. Such brief therapy attempts could be followed by more frequent "reinforcer" treatments. This is an important theme and will be discussed later.

A psychoanalyst, Saul (1951b), reported on two interviews with a hypochondriacal woman of 30. She was alleged to have had her symptoms for as long as she could remember. Saul states that the patient was completely free of symptoms in two interpretative interviews, but points out that another patient might require a different therapeutic procedure.

Opinions about the use of psychoanalysis in the case of peptic ulcer vary, as reported by Stine and Ivy (1952). They questioned all 368 members of the American Psychoanalytic Association and obtained reports of only 17 cases of treatment for peptic ulcer. Seven of these proved suitable for follow-up; five improved, and two did not. Eighty per cent of the analysts polled failed to report having treated a single case of ulcer.

One report on the use of brief psychotherapy in psychosomatic problems (Grinker, 1947) emphasizes the presumptive precipitating factor. Grinker's view is that this factor and the individual personality both have an influence on the psychosomatic problem and on therapeutic shortcuts. Frank (1946) cautioned that although symptomatic treatment may be beneficial, it should be used with full awareness of its limitations.

The effect of brief psychotherapy on *diabetes mellitus* was studied by Daniels (1944) and reported in the *Proceedings of the Second Brief*

Psychotherapy Council, Chicago Institute of Psychoanalysis. He also discusses the outcome of brief treatment on patients who were suffering from asthma and from various gastrointestinal disorders.

Enuresis is sometimes considered a psychosomatic complaint, but it may equally well be included under a "habit-disorder" category. Although the studies of enuresis are numerous, a typical method of direct psychological treatment that showed excellent results is that of Mowrer (1939). All the children in the study not only overcame the symptoms but were free of it in the follow-up period.

Other studies report a high percentage of improved cases from direct behavior treatment, exceeding the usual 60 to 70 per cent found in general psychotherapy cases (Levitt, 1957; Phillips, 1961). Although a number of different therapeutic approaches are represented, each used a direct method of retraining in the habit of urinary control (Baller & Shalock, 1956; Grandall, 1946; Harris, Firestone, & Wagner, 1955; Phillips, 1961).

But the belief persists that only indirect, depth, empathetic, or permissive approaches can "really" cure—even in the problem of enuresis. For example, English and Pearson (1963, pp. 272–273) write of the treatment of enuresis in a male child: "Treatment therefore will be directed toward the amelioration of his fear of his own sexual self in relation to persons of the opposite sex. It will not be directed toward the stopping of the enuresis, which after all is only an incidental part of the problem. . . ." And further: "What is called for is intensive psychological treatment that will rid him of his fear of the opposite sex, and in our opinion this is best accomplished through a psychoanalysis, which will take a long time and will certainly have to be continued long after the bedwetting itself has ceased."

These indirect methods of diagnosis and treatment, if not outmoded, are at least unnecessary. Certainly, the prospects for overcoming enuresis are now more encouraging using short-term psychotherapy than long-term treatment. Nevertheless, Yates (1960) (as reported originally by Eysenck, 1957) reports that not a single child-guidance clinic in England was found to be using any of the available direct treatment methods for enuresis. (By now this situation may have improved.) What the exact situation is in regard to direct behavioral methods of treating enuresis in the United States currently is unknown. However, it seems likely that it resembles the situation in England.

In 1963, in a symposium of the Eastern Psychological Association, Carr (1963) reported on the use of brief psychotherapy with 26 neurodermatitis patients (12 weekly sessions). The therapeutic emphasis was on current life experiences, particularly on the expression of anger. He reported good results. The report of Schoenberg and Carr (1963), of which the symposium report of Carr (1963) was an outgrowth, also dealt with brief psychotherapy with neurodermatitis cases. In 12 of 13 patients who completed a 12-session regimen, the symptoms disappeared. The motivation of patients who responded to short-term therapy may have been greater than for the others.

In a thorough 5-year review of the effects of direct intervention on physiological responses, Barber (1964) found that direct as well as indirect suggestion could influence a wide variety of such responses in awake as well as hypnotized subjects. These physiological effects included allergies, deafness, cardiac acceleration and deceleration, urine secretion, and many others.

Behavior-change Emphasis with Psychotics

Although the problems of schizophrenia are not a major focus of this discussion, they will be mentioned in connection with selected studies that show how direct behavioral-change methods can be of benefit even in this population, which is generally considered refractory to psychotherapy.

In a study on the effect of habit-training regimens on 10 schizophrenic patients, Bennett and Robertson (1955) found that, compared with 10 controls, the patients were more alert, attentive, and cooperative, although these effects decreased within a 2-year period. When external therapeutic pressures were relaxed, there was generally some decline in the adjustment and integration levels achieved by seriously disturbed patients. Here again, there is apparently a need for a renewal and reinforcement of learned improvement over an extended period of time. Reinforcement through follow-up "practice" is often necessary to maintain improvement, even in simple skills that are not pathologically interfered with by the rest of the patient's behavior repertoire.

Fairbairn (1952) believes that even psychoanalysis is beginning to focus less on exploring the past and more on examining the current problems of the patient through the patient's unconscious motivation. The work of Rosen (1947; 1953) illustrates such an analytic effort to look for the unconscious meaning of schizophrenic behavior and for ways of controlling it currently. The more behaviorally oriented therapist, however, prefers to bypass problems of the unconscious and deal more directly with overt behavior that can be manipulated.

Some of the most recent literature in the field describes some promising attempts to restructure psychotic behavior using behavior-change techniques, for example, the work of Ayllon (1963); King, Armitage, and Tilton (1960); Cowden and Ford (1962); Ferster and de Meyer (1961); and Salzberg et al. (1962).

Of what significance is the therapist's activity level in handling psychotic behavior? In determining outcomes of treatment with schizophrenic patients, Whitehorn and Betz (1954; 1960) investigated the role of the therapist. They report that the therapist who focuses on psychopathology and who is relatively passive and permissive obtains poorer results than the one who functions oppositely.

Money has been used as a reinforcer in some of these studies on direct treatment. Peffer (1953) found it useful as a reward for healthy behavior in rehabilitating psychotic patients. Ayllon and Haughton (1962) also used food and "tokens" as tools in modifying behavior.

Two other intriguing examples of the use of direct methods with psychotic patients have been reported recently (Fine, 1963; Philpott & Boyer, 1964). Fine worked in fairly simple and straightforward ways with long-term psychotic patients in a mental hospital to get them to perform more activities in the hospital and to do more for themselves. He taught them to make file boxes and other paraphernalia that were of use at work. (This has some relationship to the Montessori method of educating children through the "direct experiencing" and handling of materials.)

Although treatment was relatively brief compared with care of previous, desolate years, these patients showed good results. They were able to move out of the back wards and into gainful employment—in the hospital cafeteria, the laundry, and other hospital functions. Fine stresses the importance of simple, gradual steps and of specific behavioral tasks that he could control. He says, for example, that although even the simple effort required to drive a nail or to paint a small file box seemed to overwhelm his patients at first, through patient, persistent, and carefully directed effort he got them over this initial block, so that they eventually developed more spontaneous activity.

Another interesting study is described in a recent informal report by Philpott and Boyer (1964). They worked on an outpatient basis with psychotic patients using some of Wolpe's suggestions but extending the direct manner of treatment. Through their method of direct, aversive conditioning, they were able to improve the withdrawn behavior of catatonic patients, the depressive withdrawal of involutional patients, and the anxious, agitated behavior of anxiety-hysteria patients. Their methods were also effective in treating alcoholics.

They point out that since the patient must be relaxed before these aversive reconditioning methods are used, such techniques should be directed toward the treatment of anxiety. If a phobic reaction is to be reconditioned, the aversive methods should be used early in the therapeutic contact, perhaps at the very beginning. On the other hand, if an anxious or agitated patient is to be reconditioned by aversive methods, he should be calmed and receptive first; otherwise his agitation may be exacerbated.

This distinction as to where the anxiety may reside in a given symptom formation seems to have been previously overlooked. The therapist tends to regard anxiety as a distinct unity, and has failed to distinguish the existence of subtypes, with subconditions. Some reconditioning methods may actually ignore the presence of anxiety and thereby undermine what might otherwise be an effective technique for gaining a foothold suited to changing the patient's disturbed behavior.

These studies show how drugs and relaxation methods were used to relax the patients, thereby making them more amenable to conditioning. Philpott and Boyer also found sleep useful in relaxing the patient in preparation for this aversive reconditioning.

Certain Problems in Brief, Structured Therapy

The use of short-term and behavioral methods presents its own special problems. As already discussed, the first attempts at short-term therapy were not undertaken to answer theoretical questions but as a practical resort, to relieve chronic and persistent problems. Once the use of shortened, structured therapy is accepted as a practical concept, the special problems and issues related to it can be studied in perspective. Some of the problems having special theoretical significance are discussed here; they may serve as guidelines in the theoretical reorganization that is needed.

If the idea is accepted that shortening therapy is important, regardless of the type of treatment that is used, perhaps the first important issue is that of learning "without awareness." This idea is gaining wider acceptance—and it alone forces reconsideration of traditional theory and traditional methods of treatment. Another problem is that of determining the significance of cognitive variables as, for example, in Rogers's work (and most other therapies). Third, the effectiveness of structuring applied to current problems needs to be determined (as a substitute for developing, displaying, and understanding the past history of the patient). Probably one of the most fundamental questions to be answered is whether short-term therapy will create basic change or minor adjustment.

Behavior without Awareness

The problem of awareness (and its complementary clinical state, "unconscious" behavior or motivation) has long filled the clinical literature. The problem is too broad theoretically to consider in much detail here; however, it has clinical implications which are significant and which can be reviewed briefly. Recent data suggest that many viable new notions are emerging on how subtle and indirect behavior change can be and on the many ways in which it can be influenced.

Obviously, awareness is frequently lacking in behavior. Almost everyone has bruised a leg, smiled, or raised his voice without realizing it until it was called to his attention. However, much of learning is intended, in the sense that the person who is learning is aware of cues, of the arrangement of elements in a manner designed to produce a given result, and of rehearsing intentionally as in memorizing. In other words, learning is likely to be associated with an effort to be aware.

In daily life, most behavior seems to occur and to be learned without this awareness. Generally, awareness has only a small role, though frequently an important one, to play in behavior and learning. Until the young child reaches the point where he has gained facility in labeling, his learning seems to occur almost entirely with limited awareness or none at all. The behavior of animals probably takes place without any state comparable to the adult human state of awareness. Obviously, behavior modification does not depend on specific and direct labeling or on awareness. In its most important role, awareness may permit the amalgamation of large chunks of experience and the storing of this as information under appropriate labels for future reference. In this sense, it may also permit conceptualization and organization, or rearrangement, upon demand. But even so, there remains the unaware element, such as the hidden assumptions in a logical sequence or the implied relationship between the premises and the conclusion in an argument.

Learning without awareness underlies many facets of behavior change (Adams, 1957; Bullock, 1960; Bullock & Brunt, 1959; Greenspoon, 1954; Krasner, 1958; Rickard, Dignam, & Horner, 1960; Weiss, Krasner, & Ullmann, 1960). As these studies indicate, rather than being a great reservoir of unconscious motivation and effect, the "mind" may not actually organize or conceptualize all behavior. Or it may do this inconsistently, may misunderstand, or may label incompletely. Biologically, it would be uneconomical for any one part of the body to act as a computer, constantly pyramiding all possible permutations of ideas, concepts, and relationships, and such a possibility is unlikely. To do this in a controlled way would require a process similar to that of playing all the notes of a piano in all combinations as rapidly as possible, in one sequence after another. The nature of adjustment and behavioral selectivity in the environment demands that many organizational or influential elements escape awareness.

The process of learning without awareness may explain why the therapeutic relationship may suddenly change, why the patient may display unexpected behavior, or why the patient and therapist may disagree on results. There is some evidence that the patient in nondirective therapy, for example, may not acquire a deep-seated reorganization of his "self," as the therapist may believe, but that instead he may gain verbal facility—a more facile conversational interaction that is not demonstrated later in his behavior outside the therapy sessions.

It is not necessary that the locus of the effects of learning without awareness be placed in the psyche of the individual. It can be conceived of more usefully in the complex, subtle, and highly variable interaction between the patient and his environment, including the therapist. The notion of unconscious motivation and interaction in therapy, which has fostered this concept of an internal locus, now can be described in behavioral terms. Interpersonal and situational influences can then be specified and studied in a behavioral context.

Personal characteristics of the therapist may, for example, affect the patient's subtle learning (Krasner, 1958; Krasner, 1962). These interpersonal effects have been studied as specific conditioning variables, such as sex, status, and physical characteristics of the therapist (Binder, McConnell, & Sjohlern, 1957; Ferguson & Buss, 1960). The list of reinforcement techniques possible through interpersonal effects is virtually endless—for example, saying "mmm-mm," shaking one's head, smiling, scowling, making specific comments of approval, making gestures, or assuming a particular stance (Krasner, 1962, pp. 71–72).

The "Greenspoon effect" (Greenspoon, 1954; Greenspoon, 1955) suggests the extent of such subtleties in the matrix of therapist-patient interaction. The possibilities of steering or shaping the patient's behavior loom even larger if the multitude of approaches that exist for influencing behavior are considered—even aside from the distinct characteristics of patient and therapist as individuals.

The therapist needs to know how these subtle influences in learning can be directly useful in shortening and sharpening therapy. Variables can be highly mobile and manageable, and the resourceful therapist can manipulate their conditions and effects to the great advantage of the patient. Into this complex matrix of interaction he can bring renewed and extended possibilities for influencing behavior. The entire enterprise of changing behavior can be lifted from the barely accessible and unverifiable processes of the mind to the social plane that lies more clearly in the view of the therapeutic participants (Ayllon, 1960; Ayllon & Michael, 1959).

In searching for manipulable variables that will permit a more direct confrontation with the scientific and practical problems in psychotherapy and behavior change, Skinner's (1953, p. 31) comment on their location is pertinent:

The practice of looking inside the organism for an explanation of behavior has tended to obscure the variables which are immediately available for a scientific analysis. These variables lie outside the organism, in its immediate environment and in its environmental history. They have a physical status to which the usual techniques of science are adapted, and they make it possible to explain behavior as other subjects are explained in science. These independent variables are of many sorts and their relations to behavior are often subtle and complex, but we cannot hope to give an adequate account of behavior without analyzing them.

Cognitive Variables in Therapy

Cognitive or phenomenological variables may be considered to represent a "cognitive scheme," based on experience and experiencing (English & English, 1958, pp. 93, 387). The terms "phenomenological" and "cognitive" here refer to internal, self-perceived events rather than to external data that are objectively observable. Cognitive theories generally designate significant variables "inside the head." Such theories may be based upon experiential or neurological variables—hypothetical or real—or upon some other, inferred, internal process. As Rogers (1954) has long emphasized, therapy may produce changes in self-ideal references with changes in the self-ideal moving from a pre-therapy state of noncongruence to a post-therapy state of congruence.

In the past, much of the patient's change, particularly from the point of view of phenomenological or cognitive therapists, could be conceptualized in terms of the subtle influences of the uncontrolled interaction of the patient and therapist.

The use of the Q Sort in measuring therapeutic change (Rogers & Diamond, 1954; Shlien, et al. 1962) illustrates this commitment to cognitive variables. In their study, Phillips, Raiford, and Batrawi (1965) sought to replicate Rogers's reported movement in therapy, using the Q Sort, on 79 cases of high school and college students who were receiving help at a university psychological clinic. In a similar study by Ends and Page (1957), various therapy regimens were used in several groups of patients. However, neither study corroborated Rogers's findings. Here, the cognitive structure of the individual, hopefully viewed as a source of change, appears not only to show no change but also to be once removed from behavioral significance.

What takes place with re-sorts of the Q deck? Perhaps there is some subtle learning by the patient of verbal cues that are somehow embedded in the very nature of the relatively passive, reflective, self-searching ther-

Table 1   Comparison of Ideal-Self Q Sort Correlations from Three Studies (Ends & Page, 1959; Phillips, Raiford, & Batrawi, 1965; Rogers, 1951, p. 319)

Study	N	S_1–S_2	S_1–I_1	S_1–I_2	S_2–I_1	S_2–I_2	I_1–I_2
Rogers	1	0.15	0.18	0.00	0.70	0.81	0.71
Phillips et al.	79	0.49	0.53	0.42	0.45	0.59	0.60
Ends and Page	63*						
Learning	16	0.34	0.31	0.17	0.14	0.12	0.54
Client-centered	15	0.48	0.33	0.32	0.30	0.40	0.44
Analytic	15	0.40	0.18	0.16	0.31	0.32	0.56
Control	17	0.53	0.36	0.26	0.28	0.27	0.60

* The Ends and Page study included a total of 63 cases, subdivided into the four populations indicated, according to the type of therapy utilized.

apy of Rogers and his students. And the relationship of these changes to overt, external behavioral change is vague.

Rogerian therapists have found repeatedly that their "best" client is the introspective one. The Rogerian approach is most likely to build upon and enhance this introspective tendency, which may cause the kind of shift that occurs in the verbal-report scores.

Current Structuring versus Historical Analysis

In an efficient approach to short-term therapy, topics should be selected from current problems in living. Because of the time limitations, the details of the patient's background simply cannot be explored and discussed at length. Therefore, behaviorally oriented therapy begins with presenting complaints and attempts directly to modify these specifiable and observable problems through verbal or nonverbal means. Whatever his theoretical position, the therapist must minimize historical analysis if shortened treatment is the focus. Instead, he must begin directly to concentrate on current problems and their restructuring and control.

There is, however, an important distinction between the assumed *therapeutic* value of analyzing and "reliving" past history and the *diagnostic* value of recording the past history of persisting problems so that the therapy with current problems may be handled more efficiently. The second process may be useful in facilitating current behavior change.

Szasz (1960; 1961; 1964) is one of the most vigorous critics of the traditional methods of diagnosis and the consequent treatment of psychological disturbance. Orlansky (1949) could find no relationship between the early life history of an individual and any subsequent emotional or personality problems or characteristics. Other attempts to relate infantile experiences to subsequent behavior yielded few positive results (Stevenson, 1957). This conclusion was also supported by King (1958) when he examined a similar problem in the behavior of animals.

Once the therapist feels free to intervene in the current situation, he can develop new theoretical leads. He can decide what aspects of the pathological behavior might best be interfered with and the best manner in which to interpose, or he can select another method of regulating or producing the change.

Although "directiveness" previously has had negative connotations, a growing number of therapists are now recommending purposeful and direct intervention to modify behavior pathology. Among them are Ellis (1962), Krasner (1962), and Rotter (1954), who are active interventionists, and Garner (1960) who recommends a "confrontation" technique.

Even the temporary "exploration" of the personality seems certain to have an effect on the course of therapy different from the effect generated if the therapist starts directly to attempt to change behavior in specific ways. As Bordin (1955) observed, the degree of structuring may affect topics discussed in therapy; the therapist's "set" also affects the behavior of the patient. If the therapist is reflective or passive, he seems less likely to elicit problem-solving behavior from the patient than if he actively solicits it.

Some therapists maintain that they are not trying to change external behavior but, rather, are exploring the patient's feelings, attitudes, and motivation in the hope of changing his outlook, which will then automatically change his external behavior. Nevertheless, these therapists are pleased when specific behavior changes appear—and particularly so if the changes fit the therapist's theory or bring more successful action outside therapy. Whatever the theoretical justification for adopting a particular therapeutic technique, there are many opportunities to make therapy shorter and more productive by specifying goals and behavior and by working directly toward them.

Laboratory-based Behavior Change

There is evidence in the work of eclectic, psychoanalytic, and nondirective therapists, as well as in the work of therapists who adhere closely to learning-theory models, that there is a close relationship between shortened therapy and the emphasis on direct behavior change. There are those in each persuasion who believe that direct behavior-change efforts can make therapy fruitful. Even among therapists who rely solely on verbal exchange, there is a trend to react less passively to the patient and to develop various methods for getting the patient to act in his own behalf.

Not only has the approach in verbal therapy become more active, but there is also renewed interest in the studies of conditioning techniques of more than a generation ago by Jones (1924a; 1924b), Watson and Rayner (1920), and Watson and Morgan (1917). And although the influence of learning theory on psychotherapy has been sporadic, inconsistent, and highly selective, out of this meandering development of theory has come a substantial unity of viewpoint. During the past decade, there has been a growing acceptance of operant conditioning; its relationship to such molar behavior problems as programed learning is of particular interest.

Many believe that more rigorous and effective methodologies can be found by applying learning theory and laboratory techniques in both verbal and nonverbal form to behavior-change efforts. Although this belief is based partially on a broad view of laboratory techniques, it applies not only to therapy and behavior change as proposed here but to the study of clinical problems as well.

It may be that the movement to apply laboratory methods in the clinic will match the reform efforts from within clinical practice. Although molecular problems and solutions of the laboratory often appear trivial and meaningless to the clinician, the clinician's fuzziness in theory and practice often seems unscientific and careless to the experimentalist. There is an urgent need to begin to broaden the former and to sharpen the latter, for the common goal of making all behavior-change efforts more effective.

Excellent surveys of recent progress in relating laboratory and learning theory to clinical problems have been reported by Bandura (1961), Eysenck (1960), and Krasner (1962); in a more limited way by Pascal (1959); and in very broad ways by Ullmann and Krasner (1965) and Krasner and Ullmann (1965). It may be useful briefly to generalize their findings here and to cite some of the outstanding conditioning studies that relate to clinical problems.

In general, laboratory studies of behavior change allow more specific control in testing methods and results as compared with verbal therapy, even though verbal therapy can produce very specific changes. Of course, laboratory methods can be derived from clinical approaches to behavior change, as is illustrated by the Lang and Lazovik study (1963), to be discussed. While these clinical approaches are centered on laboratory methods, the problem does not wholly determine the method. It is method that is being studied and applied first to one clinical problem, then to another.

The laboratory methods that have been applied to clinical problems are derived primarily from the background of operant conditioning, as well as from classical conditioning. In the clinic, the choice between operant or classical conditioning to attempt behavior change may depend on practical considerations. Operant methods, however, appear to be the more resourceful, ingenious, and relevant. These differing methods will be discussed in the next chapter.

The use of more precise behavior-change methods encourages the therapist or investigator to set up a specific plan for behavior change and to work in concrete steps to carry it out. A good example of this process is the study reported by Lang and Lazovik (1963), which used methods of desensitization to overcome a phobia.

Although desensitization methods have been used in quasi-laboratory and verbal therapy settings by Wolpe (1958), a less verbal and greater laboratory emphasis was used in the study in which Lang and Lazovik attempted to overcome a snake phobia. In setting up the specific plan, they constructed an anxiety hierarchy. This was a series of situations involving snakes, each of which was rated by the subject (patient) according to the degree of anxiety it provoked. The items in the hierarchy were rated differently by every subject.

After a training period during which the subject was taught deep muscle-relaxation methods and was encouraged to practice these methods at home, he was given a series of 45-minute "systematic desensitization" periods to teach him to relax in what was previously an anxiety-provoking situation.

This prepared the subject for the reintroduction of the anxiety hierarchy under conditions of utmost relaxation. The subject was asked to imagine himself at the farthest point on the hierarchy and then was moved progressively and cautiously from this smallest measure of anxiety toward more anxious conditions. These states were repeated gradually until the patient could report that he was no longer disturbed by a given stage; that is, the ". . . goal of treatment is the presentation of the item originally ranked as most frightening without impairing the individual's calm state. At this point a new response (relaxation) has been attached to the imagined representative of the fear inducing stimulus. . . ." (Lang & Lazovik, 1963, p. 520)

Despite the lack of control cases, the plan may serve as a useful model since it illustrates how to prepare a precise plan for behavior change. And what were the essential steps in planning such a change?

1. A specific aim was delineated: overcoming the snake phobia.

2. Specific means were provided: desensitization through relaxation techniques to overcome the anxiety or phobia associated with the potent stimulus.

3. Each step was taken gradually in logical sequence, and each stage was checked for its validity and relevance.

4. There was a follow-up to evaluate the usefulness and persistence of what was learned.

As a fifth step, the effectiveness of the plan could have been more fully confirmed scientifically had a control group been established to ensure that the outcome was not the result of chance, environmental events, or experience—or that it was not an instance of the "placebo" effect, that is, having the problem given any attention at all.

The period of therapy was short—there were only 11 therapeutic sessions—and there was no time spent in historical analysis. As Lang and Lazovik write (1963, p. 25):

> It is not necessary to explore with a subject the factors contributing to the learning of a phobia or its "unconscious meaning" in order to eliminate the fear behavior. . . . The form of treatment . . . does not lead to the symptom substitution or create new disturbance of behavior . . . it is not necessary to change basic attitudes, values, or attempt to modify the "personality as a whole." The unlearning of phobic behavior appears to be analogous to the elimination of other responses from a subject's behavior repertoire.

What is the learning process in this type of reconditioning? It may be called "emotional reeducation," "eliciting response alternatives," "behavioral tutoring," "interference with aberrant behavior," or the "restructuring of behavior." What variables are used? Only those subject to manipulation, directly or indirectly, in an experimental regimen. There was no need for an historical résumé, no need to explore (unconscious) motivation, no need to take the personality as a whole into major consideration. In fact, any attempt to do this would have obscured—and perhaps have defeated—the practical therapeutic goal.

Another example of conditioned behavior change is described in a case study by Brady and Lind (1961). The choice and manipulation of variables in this study were even more austere. The patient, who had been hysterically blind for about 2 years and had not responded to traditional psychotherapeutic treatment, was treated by a method of operant conditioning in a hospital setting.

First, the authors established a type of stable behavioral performance suitable for operant conditioning. After an interval of from 18 to 21 seconds the patient was to press a button located in front of him. If he responded correctly, that is, within 18 to 21 seconds, he was reinforced through praise and approval. If he pressed the button in less than 18 or more than 21 seconds, he received disapproval. The treatment lasted for 63 sessions; each session lasted for $\frac{1}{2}$ hour, and sessions were held twice daily, 5 days a week. Objective data were plotted to show the percentage of correct responses in 3-second intervals that progressed as follows: 0 to 3 seconds, 6 to 9 seconds, 12 to 15 seconds, 18 to 21 seconds, and 24 to 27 seconds.

As the patient's response in each of these successive time intervals was established, an unobtrusive light outside his direct line of vision was introduced. This light was a visual cue designed to assist him in responding accurately to the 18- to 21-second interval, for it came on only during this interval. This cue was introduced in the second phase of the experiment, that is, from the seventh through the sixteenth sessions.

The data showed some temporary instability in the patient's performance when the light was introduced, as well as some secondary and "defensive" reactions to its presence. However, except for the decision as to when to alter the amount of illumination from the light, the entire treatment process was virtually automatic and involved no human interaction other than reinforcement (approval or disapproval) at the end of each conditioning session. The treatment could probably have been made completely automatic if the reinforcement had been given without direct human intervention.

This study was similar to that of Lang and Lazovik in that it introduced a specific aim (overcoming the hysterical blindness) at the start, as well as a specific means (operant-conditioning technique) that involved only a minimum of human interaction. The means to the end involved gradual steps (the method of successive approximation from Skinner's operant-behavior procedures), as well as a stable reactive characteristic of behavior (motor response), in bringing about the new responses needed (visual discrimination) and changing the old behavior (hysterical blindness). The outcome was substantial change that remained stable during the follow-up period of 13 months.

The therapy required no analysis of history, feelings, or motivation. It involved only the means to overcome the pathology through a well-constructed program of "response alteration" or "emotional reeducation," in the most precise meaning of these terms. Yet, at the same time, what more traditional therapy terms "dynamic" indexes of behavior or personality change were present; that is, the patient made spontaneous comments and metaphorical statements about his vision, his reactions to highly conflictive situations, particularly when the light was apparently first noticed and recognized as a threat, and, increasingly as therapy progressed, his anger and resentment toward members of his family.

Operant-conditioning techniques have been used in similar studies that involved other sensory modalities and other hysterical conditions.

Examples are studies by Walton and Black (1958) on the treatment of stammering; another study by Walton and Black (1959) on the treatment of chronic hysterical aphonia; and studies reviewed by Krasner (1962), Rachman (1963), Eysenck (1960), Ullmann and Krasner (1965), and Krasner and Ullmann (1965).

In fact, studies on the general technique of conditioning are proliferating so rapidly that special bibliographies are necessary to document them (Orlando, 1964) and special journals are being founded (for example, Eysenck and his group's *Behavior Research and Therapy*, entering its third year of publication, and the *Journal for the Experimental Analysis of Behavior*, an outgrowth of Skinner's work).

Some Problems of Follow-up

Although the problem of exporting the results of these operant-conditioning changes is significant, this aspect will be developed later in a chapter on synthesizing learning and cybernetic formulations. Often, reconditioning is regarded as somehow incomplete, and although the desired behavior change has apparently been stabilized, the attitude may prevail that conventional therapy is still necessary or desirable (Brady & Lind, 1961, p. 339). Does the conditioning therapist lack faith in his work, so that he must seek corroboration and assurance in more conventional approaches? The study by Wiener et al. (1963) provides a clue, since it indicates that long-term outpatient users of tranquilizers did as well off as on the drugs. Nevertheless, when the experiment was over, almost all the patients were put back on drugs for no discernible reason. Perhaps the therapists lacked the initiative or skill to terminate the treatment or the alternatives necessary to translate the change to new habits outside therapy.

In reconditioning techniques, therapy can be viewed as using both proximal and distal variables. After the immediate variables are placed in an orbit of behavior consonant with the overall progress of the patient, the more distal variables begin to assume more importance (such as long-range job adjustment, better integration of family living, or completing an education). There is no logical reason, however, why the more remote variables cannot be brought into the same specific, highly structured focus as the closer ones. Perhaps this cannot be done as reliably outside the laboratory as in it, but it can certainly be consistent with laboratory conditions and with principles of learning and cybernetics.

Although there are few reports of long-term follow-up of reconditioning therapy, such information is being accumulated and may be available soon. Nor are there many published reports on the results of any other type of follow-up on therapy. If the reconditioning process is fundamental, it may bring lasting changes that can be maintained without supplemental reinforcement, although this seems doubtful. Of course, any follow-up on therapy would be profitable if it served as a long-range reminder to the patient that he is in a transitional period, in a sense, and must therefore be alert to maintain his self-control and direction and his newly achieved behavior. Reconditioning therapy alone might so modify a person's attitudes and interactions with his environment that such changes would be maintained—or even enhanced—with time. A man who has learned to handle fear, whether of dogs or of his employer, may well move on independently to new successes.

It is not yet known whether reconditioning methods carried on in the laboratory or in the clinic can transfer automatically to other areas of living. The application of improved behavior to life situations outside the laboratory may constitute a larger (but continuous) learning and therapeutic problem (see Chapter 10). Some people who stop smoking or drinking apparently cannot afford an occasional lapse for fear of reconstituting the full force of the old habit. Perhaps the discriminations and prohibitions against drinking and smoking were not sufficiently learned and can be maintained in the relearning situation only with continuous effort, ad infinitum. Even this alternative is far better, however, than remaining the victim of destructive practices. After a once strong and destructive habit has been eliminated, relearning may remain precarious. However, good follow-up data on this point are lacking, as they are on all forms of psychotherapy.

Follow-up research can be posed as a specific challenge here, however, because in highly specific restructuring therapy it is possible to establish means and ends for definitive control of problems. Traditional long-term therapy does not so readily permit an examination of this problem because it does not formulate specific steps in a formal structure.

In the newer efforts, the approach to the patient is in terms of his overt behavior and employs principles of learning and conditioning. There is no agreement, however, on which principles of learning and reconditioning are most useful, or on how they can best be applied in specific situations. Regardless of which ones are used, however, they help to clarify the solution to therapeutic problems and follow-up since the results can be tested more precisely.

The Length of Short-term Therapy

How short is short-term psychotherapy? An exact number of hours cannot be set; various figures are used in different studies, and any number selected is arbitrary. The studies described here represent some of the common definitions, however.

A generation ago, Taft (1933) mentioned the importance of single interviews, although she did not document their relevance or productivity in statistical terms. Allen's work (1942), arising from the same context as Taft's, also pointed up the importance of brief therapy, particularly in contrast to Klein's analytic work (1935), which ranged into hundreds of therapy hours with children who had common neurotic and parent-child difficulties.

More recently, Wolpe (1952; 1954) began to report on his "reciprocal inhibition" therapy, producing as high as 90 per cent improvement according to his estimates. He reported on 70 cases having from 4 to 125 interviews. In his second population of 122 cases, he reported similar findings based on clinical impression and test-retest findings as well as other indexes. These cases, too, ranged from very few interviews up to about one hundred sessions.

In comparing time-limited therapy with nonlimited therapy, and using Rogerian client-centered and Adlerian approaches, Shlien et al. (1962) noted that all groups showed gains between the seventh and the twentieth interviews. The results obtained in time-limited therapy were as good as those obtained in nonlimited therapy; moreover, the gains were achieved in about half the time. This and many other studies on short-term therapy suggest that a relatively small number of interviews will show whether there will be a change. Thus it can tentatively be assumed that only a relatively few interviews will indicate whether benefits will be achieved.

An experience of one of the authors is relevant here, involving preparation of diagnostic workups on 20 patients whose psychoanalysis had extended from approximately 300 to 1,500 hours and from 2 hours a week for 3 to 4 years up to 4 or 5 hours a week for 4 to 6 years. These cases were evaluated only incidentally as part of an administrative process. In all 20 cases, however, the administrative decision to be made posed questions about the patients' potential stability for job-assignment purposes or for assignment to posts under stressful conditions. Twelve out of twenty persons studied reported no noticeable gains from their therapy; six felt some gains had been experienced; and only two reported sizable and lasting gains. In all 20 cases, the MMPI findings at the end of therapy—and, in some cases, several years after termination of the therapy—showed from one to six substantial elevations (above T scores of 70) among the nine original scales. Most of these cases, psychometrically at least, looked as if they were ready to begin therapy, not as if they had already had intensive treatment.

All these persons could have been candidates for short-term therapy, as it is defined today by a growing number of therapists, for all were employed and had been vocationally stable. Moreover, all were or had been considered neurotic, not psychotic (none had been hospitalized for even episodic psychotic conditions), and nearly every one was the head of a family that was relatively integrated. Not one had ever been fired from a job because of emotional problems. Short-term therapy was not likely to yield poorer results, and focus upon specific problems with modern behavior-change methods might well have produced better outcomes. Surely this possibility would be worth testing in a similar situation—at perhaps one-tenth the cost of the therapy that was used here.

In therapy to overcome enuresis, Lovibond (1963) reported on 36 child subjects with whom he used several different signal systems. All but one overcame the enuretic habit in between 14 and 30 reinforcement sessions. On follow-up 2 years later, 50 per cent of those who responded to treatment had remained dry; the others showed varying degrees of return to the old habits. Of course it cannot be assumed that reconditioning methods need not be reinforced periodically to become firmly established in life outside therapy. Such follow-through seems to be necessary for most forms of therapy.

The outcome of 126 cases of behavior-change therapy was reported by Lazarus (1963). After a mean of 14 interviews, he found that 62 per cent had "markedly improved" or "completely recovered" according to several psychometric instruments and ratings. In a larger population of 408 patients, which included the above population, he reported that 78 per cent of the patients showed substantial benefit from short-term treatment.

In using reconditioning methods with a group of approximately forty adolescent delinquents, Schwitzgebel and Kolb (1964) paid the offenders to talk into tape recorders, as a part-time job, about anything they wished. In 25 sessions this treatment brought about dependable behavior in performing this "job" promptly. Over a 3-year follow-up period, there was a reduction in severity and frequency of crimes in the population studied, compared with a control group of matched pairs. Other studies similar to this are also reported by Bandura (1961) and Krasner (1958), who describe the use of operant conditioning in changing limited segments of behavior.

Under the general rubric of "behavior therapy," the new journal *Behavior Research and Therapy* has published numerous articles on the treatment of specific symptoms or problems through some type of short-term conditioning. Some of those most recently described are the use of faradic aversion conditioning in transvestism (Blakemore, Thorpe, Barker, Conway, & Lavin 1963); the use of stimulus satiation and food to reinforce behavior in a psychotic adult (Ayllon, 1963); and the use

of systematic desensitization of a patient suffering from monosymptomatic phobia (Clark, 1963b), a patient suffering from hysterical
spasms (Clark, 1963a), a patient suffering from a so-called disaster
phobia (Ashem, 1963), and another patient suffering from stammering
and phobic symptoms (Walton & Mather, 1963b). Other cases include
the successful use of behavior-change methods to treat encopresis in children (Neale, 1963), obsessive and compulsive states in acute and chronic
stages of illness (Walton & Mather, 1963a; Walton & Mather, 1963b),
hysterical spasms and agoraphobia (Clark, 1963a), and bronchial
asthma (Cooper, 1963). Also described are the value of verbal conditioning with psychiatric patients (Beech & Adler, 1963) and of aversive
methods in treating homosexuality (Thorpe, Schmidt, & Castell, 1963),
overcoming a phobia of travel (Friedman, 1950), and overcoming childhood phobias (Lazarus, 1960).

These topics represent a broad but not exhaustive selection of significant approaches in the experimental and behavioral treatment of specific symptoms. Experience is rapidly accumulating for those who are
interested in formulating a broad theory of behavior change and
psychotherapy.

In all these studies, the emphasis is on techniques of behavior
change. In each one, the variables for treatment are drawn from the
behavioral matrix at hand, not from the psyche or from the biographical
history of the individual (Azrin, Holz, Ulrich, & Goldiamond, 1961).

What is needed next is an organized theory of psychotherapy and
behavior change, in terms of a broader, more comprehensive approach
to the problem than is represented by the specific methods and concepts
now used by the experimenter-researcher-therapist. Although any sketch
of such an organization here is necessarily tentative, it may stimulate
new therapeutic measures and theory refinement. Since this emphasis
is largely generic, perhaps this sketch can later be expanded as more
comprehensive concepts of behavior change are developed in the clinic
and the laboratory.

4 Learning Theory, Behavior Change, and Psychotherapy

Early History

Psychotherapeutic phenomena have been analyzed in terms of learning theory for several decades. Although Burnham (1924), Holt (1931), and Willoughby (1938) attempted to apply experimental, objective, and learning-centered concepts to what today is called the "clinical situation," it was a Yale group that made the most stimulating and penetrating of these attempts to relate laboratory psychological science to psychotherapy. The outstanding work of Sears (1936; 1943), Dollard and Miller (1950), and Dollard, Doob, Miller, Mowrer, and Sears (1939) on frustration and aggression (1939), as well as some of the early work by Mowrer (1939; 1948), contributed to a learning-theory paradigm for psychotherapy.

These experimentalist authors, stimulating as their work was in the 1930s and 1940s, had chosen, however, to work within a psychoanalytic context. They accepted, with whatever reservations, psychoanalytic concepts of what must transpire in psychotherapy before the patient could benefit. In spite of the difference between the laboratory findings and those described in the clinic, they accepted the psychoanalytic version of such clinical phenomena as repression, unconscious motivation, abreaction, and catharsis. At the same time they were beginning to search for a more precise understanding of how psychotherapy really functions.

Much later, Shoben (1948) was to write about catharsis and extinction as defined in the laboratory and applied to clinical phenomena. His ideas were much like those of Dollard and Miller and other psychologists who have followed essentially the Hullian learning-theory model in analogizing to psychotherapy. Shoben (1960, p. 73) believed that

> *Catharsis will be effective when it involves* a) *the symbolic reinstatement of the repressed cues for anxiety,* b) *within the context of a warm, permissive, non-judgmental social relationship.* Under these conditions the situation is ripe for counter-conditioning to take place whereby the patient learns to react non-anxiously to the original stimuli.

So far, the basis for integrating the work of the psychotherapist with that of the learning theorist has centered on the role of the original stimulus; the importance of stimulus generalization, extinction, and reinforcement; and concepts, such as reactive inhibition, that relate to the notions of drive, motive, or conflict. A recent book by Pascal (1959), although remarkably objective and experimentally oriented, is still based chiefly on a limited selection of variables and concepts from Hullian learning theory as they apply to the problems of changing behavior.

Most previous attempts to explain psychotherapy through learning theory (usually Hullian theory) have put the major emphasis on the stimulus. The stimulus becomes central in understanding the original conditioning, traumatic or otherwise, which more or less determined the subsequent pathological course; the stimulus, it is suggested, is the basis for later generalization, which, in turn, explains the patient's present difficulty. The problem has presumably generalized from past stimulus situations involving various interpersonal complexes, such as between parent and sibling and with authority figures. Failure to differentiate between the original stimulus situations and similar, but realistically different, current stimulus complexes has greatly influenced measures adopted by the clinician in trying to help the patient change his behavior. As Pascal has expressed this problem: "Failure to identify the pertinent stimulus situation results in a 'hit-or-miss' approach in behavior change" (1959, p. 88).

He says further: "Failure to define the stimulus situation related to the deviant behavior not only results in variability in efforts to change behavior but also makes it impossible to gauge the effects of laboratory procedures calculated to change behavior" (1959, p. 88).

As for the problem of defining deviant behavior inside and outside the laboratory, to redintegrate this stimulus complex, his position is that ". . . the stimulus is all we can manipulate" (1959, p. 89).

The role of the stimulus, then, is in this view crucial in an attempt to get the patient to reconstruct his past; that is, in both classical learning theory and psychotherapy, it is necessary to reactivate the response to the original trauma or pathological experience in order to provide a basis for extinction of the pathology, mainly through catharsis or abreaction. The original feelings associated with the original stimulus are reactivated, but through permissive or analytic therapeutic handling—instead of the previous punitive, repressive, or otherwise traumatic handling—the patient gradually extinguishes his originally acquired problem (of which anxiety and repression are important components). Thus the patient is led to believe (perhaps "insightfully") that the contemporary situations are different from the original ones, or at least he comes to a new understanding, based on partial stimulus differentiation. He then extinguishes his old behavior through catharsis and abreaction and arrives at a point where he can handle the problem—by *not* reacting in a disturbed way to prepotent stimuli and by learning to distinguish the current stimuli from the old. In a sense a new stimulus generalization is learned in the extinction process; this process also implies a considerable reduction of the anxiety felt in the previously disturbed situation.

The main therapeutic effort might be said to be designed to root out self-defeating behavior, before problem-solving behavior is taught for the critical situations. This is a long and arduous therapeutic route, as Shoben observes (1953, p. 138):

> All this squares with the time that effective psychotherapy seems to require. Repressions cannot be lifted and therapeutic goals attained until the relationship has reached a sufficient degree of strength to elicit comfort reactions which are stronger than the anxiety released by the verbalization of the repressed cues. This means that the process of interpretation must proceed slowly; otherwise the patient develops a kind of intellectual glibness about himself or discontinues therapy.

Such older learning-theory–psychotherapy formulations can be put in terms of Woodworth's S-O-R formula, where S refers to the stimulus; O refers to the organism (cognitive states, central processes, feeling states, or phenomenological events); and R refers to the response. If the Woodworth statement were rewritten to fit the learning-theory position just cited, it would include a large S:

$$S\text{-}O\text{-}R$$

If Rogerian therapy were translated into the same statement, it would emphasize the O:

$$S\text{-}O\text{-}R$$

These are not discrete classifications, however, since in psychoanalytic and early learning theory, the obscurity of S and O variables often leads to their apparent interchangeability; moreover, many present O variables are the vestigial remains of earlier S conditions.

The point here is that Rogerian therapy depends upon the capacity of the individual client to arrive at his own solutions to problems, given the proper kind of permissive and understanding relationship (Rogers & Diamond, 1954, pp. 44–68). It emphasizes process, and it has relatively little interest in the original stimulating conditions or in the conditions of response; moreover, the external product (behavior change) receives little attention, compared with internal changes.

Both Rogerian and psychoanalytic therapists attempt to answer the question: "What makes him do that?" seeing causes in the antecedent stimulus or organismic ("internal") conditions. Pascal (1959, pp. 84–85) makes this viewpoint explicit:

> Knowledge of the past history of the individual should result in some sort of catalog of the expectancies specific to the individual. Survey of the stimuli impinging on the individual should result in a decision concerning the expectancies being frustrated at the time of the investigation. The most helpful principle in discovering these frustrated expectancies seems to be stimulus generalizations. The implication here is that those current stimulus situations which are on a similarity continuum with previously experienced stimulus situations which resulted in frustrated expectancies are suspect as being currently stressful. Thus a young man with a history of frustrated expectancies directed towards a father now thrown into close contact with an older man may be reacting to the older male with stress. The amount of stress experienced will be a function of the position along a similarity continuum with a father.

Thus Pascal puts the stimulus in a central role in therapeutic intervention. In the last sentence, he places the present situation of stress into a hypothetical prior condition of stress in relation to the patient's father, and this relationship is made explicit on the basis of a "similarity continuum" or, in learning-theory terms, on the basis of stimulus generalization. In such an approach the patient's situation is somehow "locked in," and the only way to unlock it is to refer back to the presumed original stimulus.

In the history of psychotherapy, few therapists have systematically attempted to deal directly with the *response* capacities of the organism as a primary instrument of change (Harper, 1959; Munroe, 1955). In fact, psychotherapeutic theory has for several decades sought a locus for pathological experiences ever more remote in the patient's history. In this sense, Freud was outdone by Rank, and Rank by Jung, in focusing on ever-earlier events in the patient's life. Jung, with his "racial unconscious," would be hard to predate, although in recent years Hubbard, who is less accepted professionally, and his dianetics movement have emphasized preconception pathological conditions.

Significantly, in all these historical theories the notion was implicit that the earlier that causal events could be identified and uncovered, the better; and also that the more pathological the current condition, the more likely the causes were to have occurred early in the development of the patient's personality. However, since "amount" or "depth" of pathology has never been clearly defined, the assumption has been to equate "remoteness" with depth and to proceed accordingly.

More Recent Developments

For a long time, Skinner's experimental work was ignored as having little significance for clinical psychology and psychotherapy. However, many clinicians, and experimentalists also (considering the Hullian-based learning theorists who devoted much effort to analogizing with personality, psychotherapy, and other molar behavior), were overlooking some important signs, by the late 1940s, of the beginnings of a response-centered psychotherapy and behavior-change theory (largely independent of Skinner). Such signs appear in Mowrer's work (1939; 1948; 1953), as well as in the work of Rotter (1954), Kelly (1955), Salter (1949), Wolpe (1956; 1958), Ellis (1958), Phillips (1956), Herzberg (1941; 1945), Cameron (1947), Shaw (1946; 1961), and Lehner (1954), and in the early and generally neglected writing of Meyer (1948; 1958). Clinicians have only very recently developed greater interest in Skinner's operant-conditioning views.

But few of these therapists seemed wholly aware of the possibilities of changing behavior through response-centered variables. Even today, the focus of Rogers and his followers, and of the psychoanalytic groups, on stimulus and central process or organismic variables is widely accepted. It seems likely that the shift in emphasis from these variables to response variables will come at first through the work of experimentalists, rather than that of clinicians. Clinicians appear to be less likely to initiate radically different views.

Theory making and innovating in psychotherapy still tend to be far removed from general psychology, and further yet from cybernetics and general systems theory. They are too deeply rooted in impressionistic and intuitive techniques and theories, such as free association, projective study, unconscious meaning, and vague notions about feelings, to be likely to change widely soon.

There are some signs of change, however. There is the venturesome work of such theorist-therapist-researchers as Eysenck (1952; 1960) and his group in England, appearing in the new journal *Behavior Research and Therapy*. Others exploring the emerging rigorous techniques are Franks (1958; 1964), Lang and Lazovik (1963), Ayllon (1960; 1963), Raymond (1956), Shah (1963a; 1963b), Lazarus (1960; 1963), Ayllon and Michael (1959), Rachman (1959; 1961; 1962; 1963), Krasner (1962), Ullmann and Krasner (1965), and Krasner and Ullmann (1965). Ten years ago few therapists could have been classified as "response-centered." Today there is a trend toward response-centered therapy, toward developing experimental attacks on clinical problems, toward shortening therapy, and toward a synthesis of these emphases (reviewed in Chapter 3).

Discussion of behavior change in the clinic through a response-centered position should distinguish between learning theory and behavior theory (especially regarding Skinner) and should consider the meaning of this difference for therapy (Rogers-Skinner debate, 1962).

Conventionally, especially as interpreted by Hull and Tolman, learning theory uses many variables outside the context of behavior, usually "intervening" variables. Hull offers internal or hypothetical concepts that are physiologically oriented; Tolman favors cognitive concepts.

Although most learning theories utilize intervening variables, Skinner's operant conditioning eschews explanation and intervening concepts and depends instead on a descriptive account of behavior. In this sense, Skinner's operant methods are closest to the preference expressed in this book for response-centered concepts for the whole clinical domain. The work of Guthrie on one-trial learning is perhaps a partial exception to this difference between learning theory and behavior theory.

The influence of conventional learning theory on psychotherapy through theorists like Hull and his followers has centered on the original conditions of the learned problem behavior and has encouraged the positing of internal states and intervening variables. To develop more behaviorally oriented therapy requires the development of a more descriptive, Skinnerian, response-oriented theory, or of a set of principles or rules, for general guidance in the clinical situation as well as for guidance in specific therapeutic behavior change.

Conventional learning theory did seek more operational statements of the concepts of clinical theory and practice, and it did stress the importance of verifiable hypotheses and of laboratory testing of clinical notions. But this influence from learning theory also directed interest to original stimuli responsible for the disturbed behavior, making it especially congenial from the start with psychoanalytic formulations. A response-centered therapy as envisioned here does not provide a convenient marriage of learning theory with psychoanalytic theory.

Another distinction needs stating: that of the role of the stimulus, as described in Skinner's operant conditioning. Skinner emphasizes the stimulus more than seems necessary for clinical purposes. As yet, fundamental stimuli cannot be identified for therapeutic use. Clinicians seem inevitably to accept and build upon hypothetical original stimuli as if they were fundamental truths. The use of traditional concepts built around the importance of the stimulus is a continuing source of rigidity in therapeutic practice.

Behavior may be put under stimulus control from a Skinnerian viewpoint (behavior at a traffic intersection is an example), but the significance of this control is judged in terms of the responses. The stimulus itself commands little attention unless it can be related to discriminatory responses. In the clinic, and in any attempt to change large segments of behavior, the primary need is to discover what can be done to modify response. The therapist will find the responses far more accessible and useful if he does not manipulate only the stimuli. When stimuli are important, they are usually obvious, so that their relevance in response modification does not have to be sought in obscure recesses of the mind, but may be established more readily in the concrete present.

In response-oriented therapy, the relevance of stimuli and other conditions is defined in the matrix of behavior, when the responses are observed. Knowledge of the response is essential before the therapist can decide what to control, what to manipulate, or what other conditions may be relevant for change (Phillips & Mattoon, 1961).

The Response-centered Position

Response-centered variables are valuable for manipulation in psychotherapy for several reasons:

1. They are more easily observed, measured, and controlled for scientific evaluation than variables located in the patient's internal state or in his remote past.

2. They are more easily checked against both experimental and clinical data and allow greater coordination between theory and practice.

3. Most unwanted behavior is already described in terms of responses—stereotyped behavior, persistent maladaptive behavior, various diagnostic syndromes, response-deficient behavior, and objectively measured anxiety and tension—so that internal states need not be posited as causes.

4. Their use facilitates greater alignment between clinical behavior theory and other, more precise areas of scientific knowledge, such as cybernetics, general systems theory, and experimental branches of general psychology.

5. Since the rationale for the clinician's practice is to change responses, economy of operation dictates seeking the most direct path to the goal.

The modal training for clinical psychologists, psychiatrists, and social workers, however, continues to emphasize the motives behind disturbed acts and other reference points in the internal state. Murray (1938; 1963), for example, has written of the "irrelevance of actones" and has urged personalogists and clinicians to be wary of purely behavioral descriptions. The clinical student is taught to look *behind* the manifestations of behavioral acts and tendencies.

In commenting on this bias, Frank (1950a; 1950b) observes that "metaphysical interpretation" is one in which there is "a search for reality behind the (observed) phenomena" (1950a, p. 62). A metaphysical *explanation*, on the other hand, is one that tends to "offer explanatory concepts which cannot be checked by the agreement of their consequences with experience" (Phillips, 1959, p. 1).

If the therapist can curb his tendency to explain observed phenomena other than in terms of additional observable phenomena, he should be better able to accept external behavioral acts as central to a conceptual schema, at molar, clinical, or social levels. Making hypothetical explanations not based on observable events has diverted psychology away from behavioral explanations for many years (Broadbent, 1961).

But what difference does it make to the choice of working variables and to the therapeutic process if S-centered and O-centered variables are replaced with R-centered ones? Although there are no good proofs yet, some tentative answers are possible:

1. There would be less interest in the presumptive origins of a patient's difficulties, that is, little effort to find the original stimuli for the problem.

2. The client would be taught to develop new responses to troublesome situations by manipulating his behavior, his environment, or both. He often states his objectives in simple terms, such as "to control my temper," "to overcome sexual impotence," "to feel happier," or "to stop changing jobs so often." Since the therapist may not agree with the objective as stated, in response-centered therapy the therapist and the patient would then seek agreement upon an objective and upon steps to attain it.

3. Other people would be involved where needed to aid the patient—wherever they were able to act as change agents—in addition to, or even in lieu of, the patient where he was too young, handicapped, or otherwise ineffectual or uninterested.

4. There would be less need to depend on verbal-talking-insight therapy, either partially or totally, if more effective means were available. Many other techniques exist—including reconditioning, and restructuring the environment—which are discussed elsewhere in this book.

5. Any problem-solving responses would be identified and encouraged. The means to this encouragement could be as pervasive and inventive as the client and therapist could contrive.

6. Undesired behavior would be prevented from occurring whenever possible, rather than being allowed to occur or studied in the hope that the analysis of it would "cure" or automatically produce behavior change. The extinction process through analysis appears, at best, to be a weak method of changing behavior.

7. The general task becomes that of finding and instituting new, desired behavior in place of the problem behavior. Since the new behavior is to be set up for reinforcement, the situation must be structured accordingly. In restructuring a situation for reinforcement purposes, the therapist has many procedures available, including simplifying the choices available, reducing external stimuli, and putting the individual on various schedules to ward off undesired behavior. Restructuring is essentially an experiment; as in experimental control, it must hold unwanted variables in check and allow other variables to operate to reinforce the desired behavior.

8. The solution to most problems would be approached step by step, and not by depending upon "insightful" bursts. These gradual steps would be scheduled, with more specific ordering of behavior, setting of limits, blocking of self-defeating behavior, and similar structuring. At times the solution will appear hesitant or tentative, in the way that most habits develop.

9. Corrective behavior, whether it is only a simple act or a large response system, would be considered to occur only on a very specific basis. The behavior that directly opposes the problem-bearing tendency would be identified and promoted through such methods as desensitization, operant conditioning and reconditioning, and aversive stimulation. Specific corrective measures could be forward-looking; they would deal with what is needed to solve the problems *now*, not with what may have caused them originally (although the original causes are probably similar to the causes of the present problems).

10. Clinical terms and descriptions, such as anxiety in most of its uses, complexes, unconscious motivational states, and most diagnostic

classifications, if they are used at all, would be reduced to behavioral descriptions and discriminable responses. There would be no need for a separate, esoteric clinical language or explanation. Clinical modules are preserved, if at all, only for convenience, rather than because they are irreducible entities (Skinner, 1953; Wiener, 1954).

Planning Behavior Change

Learning-theory formulations centered on response increase the therapist's resources for changing behavior. As Krasner (1962) suggests, the psychotherapist may also operate as a "reinforcement machine," but there is a still more general and strategic position, which is to focus upon the therapist as the "architect of change."

Throughout these pages, the basic intent has been to develop the case for, and to describe, behavior-change methods that are optimally short-term, effective, and efficient. This is best done not only through the individual's own efforts under conventional, but limited, therapeutic tutelage and through experimental situations that are often tidy and convincing but also through the use of all (other) relevant and available instruments and environmental resources and through structuring any useful situations by withdrawing, rearranging, and interjecting variables. The therapist can even act or increase his impact *in absentia*. He need not confine his skills either to the consulting room or to the laboratory. His skills can be made much more broadly usable than they now are. And his arena for action can be greatly expanded.

Change Plan. The therapist begins with a change plan, which is a statement of what behavior has to change, how the change may be brought about, by whom the change can be wrought, and other tactical and strategic considerations. In general, the change plan is based chiefly upon rules derived from principles of behavior theory and cybernetics. As previously discussed, the special approach to changing behavior by emphasizing R variables provides a set of rules.

Change Object. In addition to the change plan, there is the change object. This is the client, or it may be several clients, for example, a classroom of disturbed children. It is ordinarily assumed that the patient must want to change, must be "motivated" to get help, although "resistance" or waning determination may dilute his desire to change his behavior. In the latter case, the patient may no longer be his own change agent, even though he remains the change object.

Change Agent. Much confusion about therapeutic success seems to arise over the question of how much the patient (the change object) is his own change agent. The change agent is the vehicle, that is, the person, condition, social arrangement, or even laboratory condition, through which the change is accomplished. It is not necessary that the change agent be the change object too. For example, the parent or teacher and spouse can be the change agent and bring about changes in the patient through their actions. It may often be better, particularly at first, with a reluctant patient, if the change object is changed by (and has recourse to) a change agent other than himself. "Motivation," as it is commonly conceived, is thus no longer a prerequisite, although it may help to prepare for change, as relaxation, desensitization, or operant reconditioning can. In this case, environmental conditions or circumstances play the role of the first change agent, however momentarily, manipulated by the therapist-experimenter (the architect of change), in helping the patient develop the improved behavior necessary for his recovery.

The best candidates for conventional psychotherapy are those who are most motivated to change and most willing and able to sustain their efforts, that is, those change objects (patients) who are their own best change agents. Whatever the therapist's persuasion and therapeutic tactics, the outcome is likely to be successful when he treats one of these patients.

But what of the patients who are less amenable to direct—or any other—change efforts? What about those who are coarctated; who are (sometimes) psychotic; who act out their distress on or against others, instead of introspecting; who only demand and never give; who must always dominate or win? In conventional practices they are usually dismissed under the label "inaccessible to change." But it is possible to characterize them as having "extreme response inadequacy," instead, and to teach them more effective responses.

For most therapists, the best patient is the one who is ready, willing, and able to profit from orally delivered analysis, counsel, support, or empathy. The basis of successful conventional therapy is the treatment of people who are already capable of acting in their own interest. No wonder that the record of most current therapy (Eysenck, 1952; Levitt, 1957) is so discouraging, when the change object is not fully willing or able to act as his own change agent. In these cases conventional therapy is virtually at an impasse.

Ordinarily, therapy can involve several change agents: the patient himself and others close to him or having an impact on, or control over, his life, such as parents, siblings, teachers, and employers. The broader the change plan and the more these change agents act in concert, the more likely the change object is to change.

It is possible that the change agent may reside in a situation, such as a certain type of classroom environment or "therapeutic milieu" (Haring & Phillips, 1962). The change agent may also reside in an experimental regimen to overcome some unwanted behavior, where the therapy follows a laboratory, operant-conditioning model (Brady & Lind, 1961). Or the change agent may reside in restructured social conditions, such as those which minimize family or neighborhood influences. For some problems, perhaps the broadest and most ambitious of current change agents will be necessary, as in the "war on poverty" program.

To generalize: *any person, condition, or situation that can purposefully be conducive to bringing about behavior change can be considered a change agent.* The fundamental question the therapist must ask in a behavior-change enterprise is: "Who or what can best be the change agent?" This question should not be answered casually or rigidly, for the change agent must be specific to the response sought if the change is to be brought about most efficiently.

Classical and Operant Conditioning, and Behavior Change

The emphasis on response orientation as the economical route to behavior change may be usefully compared with therapeutic relationships in classical and operant conditioning.

Classical Pavlovian conditioning has served as an extinction model for psychotherapy change (Phillips & Mattoon, 1961); that is, the therapeutic exchange between patient and therapist seeks new or different responses to old anxiety-provoking stimuli. The intent of this effort is to reverse the original conditioning in which the troublesome stimulus was somehow paired with the nonnoxious stimulus that caused anxiety-dominated behavior.

The classical model is also used currently in desensitization studies. First, the noxious or anxiety-provoking stimuli are presented so gradually that they do not dominate the patient's responses; their potency is thus reduced, so that they no longer greatly disrupt the patient's behavioral economy.

The operant-behavior model, on the other hand, identifies responses in terms of their consequences in or on the environment, since the stimuli may be unknown or essentially unknowable (English & English, 1958, p. 37). The key element is that the responses have an effect on, or consequence in, the environment for the responding organism. Even though it is mostly response-oriented, then, there are developments in operant-behavior therapy that depend on "stimulus control" and on "constant stimuli" or "deprivation variables" (Goldiamond, 1964b).

The emphasis on response modification in operant-behavior work is compatible with response-oriented therapy; the latter also utilizes formulations (see Chapter 5) which appear to stimulate even more viable techniques of response modification.

The choice may seem inconsistent, since stimuli, or "input" notions, are emphasized, but they are used in another context for current and response-centered purposes and are not analyzed for historical significance or primary current manipulation. The behavior changer can begin his work without knowing the historical significance of stimuli. The unwanted, disrupting behavior is the "given." His task is to change the damaging behavior without necessarily knowing how the system got to its present state; for example, there are no validated stimuli to account for a functional condition such as hysterical blindness. Therefore, there is no known stimulus, Pavlovian style, to pair with other stimuli to produce "sightedness." The superficial resemblance between classical conditioning and clinical-therapeutic operation, in terms of traditional learning theory, can be misleading.

The Architect of Change and His Work

The architect of change is willing to design or plan for behavior modification, using all reasonable resources in specific, structured ways. His role is not passive, interpretative, or aloof. He may be an experimentalist who devises reconditioning studies to overcome clinical problems; a sociologist who develops and carries out plans for economically stricken or high-delinquency areas of a city; a psychologist-educator who develops special programs for emotionally disturbed, delinquent, or underachieving students; or a member of a hospital staff who uses work therapy as a means of behavior change (Fine, 1963). In broad theoretical terms, the architect of change applies the principles of behavior theory, or cybernetics, to devise concrete action directed toward the solution of specific individual and social problems.

The architect of change should be trained in behavior technology, but he also needs general scientific training. He must have a broad view of behavior-change principles. He may be able to operate as a talking therapist in the consulting room, but, more importantly, he may act as a *contriver* of special change conditions in the clinic, the laboratory, the hospital, the school, or the community.

When the architect of change operates in this manner, his skills can be spread over a wider area. More people can be helped, and many more types of behavior problems can be solved. Not only can he operate as a "social reinforcer" in the one-to-one setting, but he can also abstract his skills and knowledge and apply them through others into more distant situations. As an example:

Mrs. T. sought help for her 9-year old daughter, who was a soiler (encopresis). This problem had existed for several years, but had worsened over the months just prior to referral. The child was scholastically able, with an IQ in the range of 120 to 125 according to school-administered group tests. She was accepted socially by her peers except when her odor was strong, and she had generally good relations with adults and school authorities. The child was the oldest of three children, all of whom seemed free of serious psychological problems. Recognizing the stubbornness of her problem, her parents sought help from their pediatrician. Mild laxatives and suppositories did not help, and physical examinations furnished no solution. The parents alternately scolded, cajoled, and ignored the child, without success. The child responded by being alternately contrite, impervious, or angry. However, she soiled only at home, during play inside or out, and never at school so far as was known. Since the child sometimes hid her soiled clothes, the soiling might be discovered 2 minutes, 2 hours, or even 2 or more days after the fact. Even though she was made to wash them upon discovery, this had no effect.

Upon questioning, the mother revealed that she had tried, without success, to get the child to sit on the toilet a few minutes after breakfast; but since the mother was easily discouraged, she had soon abandoned this tactic when it was unsuccessful. Finally, when no organic or dietary pathology could be found, the parents were advised that the child would "grow out of it."

The hypothesis derived by the therapist, based on his discussions with the mother, was that the child was too busy playing to heed the cues related to defecation. Being unable to suppress all related physiological movement and excretion, the child "let go" to a small extent, thus allowing herself to continue to play uninterruptedly and to reduce somewhat the internal pressure at the same time. She accomplished in this truncated bowel movement two purposes, it was hypothesized: taking off sphincter pressure and continuing to play. Since she had relatively poor elimination habits, the bowel was usually overly full, and since she was a very active child, there was continuous opportunity to maintain her encopresis. The habit, therefore, continued. The parents were never able to stop the individual instance until it was too late.

The therapy was direct and specific. The parents were told that they should not mention the habit, but that the mother should tell the child that she was to sit on the toilet a few minutes after each meal. If, after 10 minutes, there was no bowel movement, the parent was advised by the therapist to say nothing, but to have the child come back after about 1 hour of play and sit on the toilet again. The child was to do this each hour until there was a movement. Then the child was to be free to play without another "sitting" that day unless continued observation showed that a second or third movement appeared to be necessary or likely.

In the second interview, 3 weeks later, the mother reported that the child had become symptom-free after 2 days of this regimen. In the next follow-up conversation, 1 year later, she reported that the child had had only one relapse, that otherwise the problem had disappeared, and that the child was continuing in a normal fashion with school and other activities. The mother said, "Well, I guess you trained *me* first and the child second, but it certainly worked!"

As an example of how the architect of change can operate, it is important to note that the therapist did not interview, test, or even see the child in this case. However, it was necessary for him to decide whether the parent-child relationship was sufficient to carry out the proposed scheduling without raising other problems. This is the kind of judgment that the clinician, operating as the architect of change, must be able to make, as soon as he is satisfied that he has enough data to propose a plan for change. In this example, the therapist was the architect of change, the parent was the change agent, and the child was the change object.

In this case, change object and change agent were not the same, which is not the case in conventional psychotherapy.

What was the change plan? Essentially, it emphasized response modification. Specifically, it stressed the manner in which the responses were to be changed—through a scheduling of trips to the toilet, to deal with the problem or unwanted condition—as well as the peripheral ways in which the parents were to avoid creating other problems, such as by not talking uselessly about the soiling and not blaming anyone or acting guilty about their present efforts or previous failures. The efficiency of this plan contrasts sharply with more conventional alternatives, for example, consulting pediatricians further, considering the child as organically damaged in some obscure way, or diagnosing the problem as a severe emotional disturbance and recommending extensive therapy for child and parents, with the child in play therapy and the parents in psychoanalysis (Klein, 1935).

A somewhat similar change plan is described in an early study of Mowrer and Mowrer (1938). Not for many years did further reports of similar therapy appear, for example, in the studies reviewed by Krasner (1962) or in reports by Wolpe (1961) and Salter (1965).

In this approach, the present is emphasized rather than the past. Instead of calling the presently observed problem a "symptom," and thereby denying its relevance to immediate therapeutic strategy, a direct solution is proposed to a specifically labeled problem. The present and future resourcefulness of the patient is developed by teaching him certain new behavior, rather than allowing him to continue some undesired behavior. This therapy depends on setting specific, direct, step-by-step goals, rather than on working vaguely toward "character reorganization" or "major psychic surgery" or on assigning such other broad goals that they cannot be given common meaning.

The change plan has other implications. At the outset of therapy it aims to answer the question: "Who is the best change agent?" For without a change agent there can be no behavior change, except by accident. In conventional psychotherapy the patient must be his own change agent, when he is in fact often unwilling or unable to function effectively as such or is at best relatively inefficient. In developing the change plan described above, the therapist must specify not only the change object but also the change agent. In fact, as this therapeutic regimen progresses, in many cases now considered intractable or unmotivated, the therapist will have to use others as change agents and may also have to use others as additional change objects. In complying with the change plan, the parents in the case discussed above acted as change agents as well as change objects counseled in relation to the child.

These change plans are also significant in an interpersonal theory of psychotherapy. At present such theory speculates largely on interpersonal stimuli early in the patient's life which make him as he is today, and it has little to contribute to present theories of behavioral change.

Even though a specific change plan may have to be altered, if it is functional at the outset the alterations can be made promptly, logically, and economically. To illustrate, with the above-described case of the 9-year-old girl, suppose that the mother had become ill. How would this have affected the change plan? It would have been necessary to find another change agent somewhat comparable to the mother in influence. Perhaps the father could have so served; the fact that his role was less direct than the mother's might have lengthened the therapy, but would not have changed its nature significantly. If neither parent could have served as the change agent, it would have been necessary to work out other roles or find a parent surrogate.

The use of a human change agent might even have been unnecessary, or at least subordinate, if some mechanical device, comparable to the warning systems used in enuresis cases, could have been found. It has been successfully demonstrated that mechanical assistance, or a mechanical change agent, can supplant humans, just as the teaching machine for programed instruction can be more effective than the classroom teacher in helping students learn certain educational matter.

In conceptualizing behavior change at a higher level of abstraction and efficiency, the change plan and its implementation are placed in a broader perspective no longer restricted to the therapist-patient paradigm. In this context, such problems as describing and classifying symptoms, hunting for etiology, and uncovering hidden motives can largely be set aside. When he serves as the architect of change, the therapist becomes a strategist in designing new behavior and solving behavior problems. When the issues of behavior change are placed in this context, the therapeutic process is spared the circuitous waste of effort and time spent in defining traits, discovering distant causes, overcoming defenses, and performing many other adjunctive tasks long considered basic to the theory and practice of psychotherapy.

The Problem of Control of Human Behavior

Questions may properly be raised about whether the freedom and integrity of the individual are being violated in this therapeutic system—whether it somehow involves an insidious manipulation of people. Since our society, and the authors, are firmly opposed to authoritarian approaches in directing or changing human behavior, this area needs careful clarification.

The problem of authority in changing behavior has its counterpart in the political environment of a democracy, that is, the problem of how to choose and control leaders who nonetheless can represent and help people to achieve their desired social and political goals. The leaders must be chosen freely, they must represent their constituents well, and they must be subject to direction, control, and recall by those they represent. Precisely the same relationship should—and can—prevail between the architect of change and his clients, or "constituents."

But the history of medicine, as of nearly all science, is studded with the inevitable criticism of most innovations. Surgical techniques and inoculations were, in their time, widely labeled inhumane, too experimental, or dangerous. Rarely has there been a significant advance in scientific knowledge that has not precipitated a struggle to overcome strong moral, religious, ethical, and other objections.

It is to be expected that one criticism of objective new methods will be that they "lose sight" of the individual. But any measure that produces good results with human suffering; that is open to study, verification, and consequent modification; and that is encompassed by the democratic process should meet all reasonable objections.

Scientific findings and observations must be differentiated from mere fads and nostrums. Before the consumer can be educated in how to make this distinction, he must be introduced to, and acquire an understanding of, the criteria of improvement which measure this crucial difference and which are necessary to ensure reasonable critical judgment by the client.

Why should it be considered debasing to the human being to be treated according to the same principles of learning and behavior that are used in treating animals such as the rat, the pigeon, and the chimpanzee? Such animals have been found useful in other research on living organisms, and clinicians support this research. Nor does the psychologist who is sympathetic to subjective approaches usually question the insight that comes through research on chimpanzees (when dynamic interpretations fit theoretical predilections). The psychologist who is reluctant to apply findings from (other) animal research to human beings faces a worse dilemma in the developments in cybernetics (an even more inhuman spectacle), in general systems theory, and in computer simulation and analysis of behavior phenomenon (Tompkins & Messick, 1963).

Not only is the behavior-change psychologist of today interested in all animal research as it applies to psychological problems, but he is also learning constantly that nonliving systems offer worthwhile prototypes useful in creating new concepts about human behavior. For example, the principle of feedback has its origins partly in biology, but its greatest impetus came from the study of nonliving systems (see Chapter 5). Wiener believes this is a semantic question. He writes (1954, p. 31):

> I want to interject the semantic point that such words as life, purpose, and soul are grossly inadequate to precise scientific thinking. These terms have gained their significance through our recognition of the unity of a certain group of phenomena, and do not in fact furnish us with any adequate basis to characterize this unity.

When the precise meaning is sought of terms such as "ego," "self," "abreaction," "ideal self," "complex," and a host of other common clinical terms, it is obvious that, as Wiener notes, the professed unity of these concepts cannot be realized. The careless clinician, in his ready use of such general terms, presumes to have a focus on behavioral phenomena. But since these global terms cannot be reduced to behavioral referents, such behavioral referents must be sought elsewhere. The consequence is a behavioral system—not a system of personality.

Similarly the clinician's choice of variables can be questioned. A more rigorous way of choosing variables and of finding conceptually more powerful notions in cross-fertilization with other sciences is through research on animals and on nonliving systems, as well as on gross human behavior.

The use of the word "manipulation," which to some suggests the work of an insensitive or arrogant experimenter, is sometimes misunderstood because of its moral rather than scientific connotations. In the behavior-change context, a child who is being forcefully taken to school or forced to stay in classes is being manipulated with general agreement that is "for his own good." Nor is any patient with any therapist entirely free of manipulation in the sense of being limited or influenced unwittingly as well as wittingly—by the example of the therapist or by his tone of voice, at least.

In short, it is not a question of whether to have some manipulation or none, but of the kind and amount of manipulation, whether it is relevant and is used judiciously and whether the subject (or his proxy, such as parent or guardian) still has absolute final control, is aware of it, and exercises it.

The purpose of control, or manipulation, in therapy is to overcome a problem reasonably and without injuring a participant (Krasner, 1955). In behavior theory, no method should be used that will damage the economy of the individual or violate the integrity of the system. While there may be a temporary pain when one is operated on by a surgeon, the end is generally assumed to justify the means, for without the operation, one may die or become much worse. The choice about how to interfere in behavior will depend on the alternatives, as is true in any decision.

Control and manipulation should not be avoided on the a priori grounds that they are authoritarian or inhuman. On this basis surgery, too, might be rejected. Manipulation of the person or his environment is not necessarily undemocratic and harmful. The patient or his proxy is still free to quit the process, and he can judge the results for himself, always assuming, of course, that the therapy meets a basic democratic condition: that the subject is informed as fully as possible of what is going on and why.

If manipulation and control were harmful as therapeutic methods, the results should by now be evident in work with such perennial problems as enuresis in children. Or, if compulsion itself in education were harmful, the damage should be seen and corrected by now. Even though commitment procedures for the emotionally disturbed have been abused, they are not condemned as totally unnecessary or amoral; they do require more safeguards of the type discussed above.

The process of control and manipulation described above appears to have one outstanding benefit, since the patient and his problems are not neglected—or damaging alternatives ignored—to the degree that may occur in permissive, inactive, or history-centered therapy. This benefit becomes obvious when the countless "dropouts" from community clinics, school centers, and private therapy are considered, where patients report that they received no definite recommendations on such crucial issues as whether treatment was needed, whether it should be continued or modified, and what the outcomes were likely to be. In such instances, the patients were actually seeking the firmness and clarity of a therapeutic situation to help them evaluate and solve their problems and decide among alternatives. Even maintaining the *status quo* can be stated as an alternative. The clinician who strives to be neutral and noncommittal in order to encourage the patient's independence can find that this neutrality has the opposite effect on patients, making them even less capable of modifying their behavior.

Diagnosis versus Problem Solving

Does the behavior-change clinician treat merely symptoms? The tendency to divide a problem into cause and symptom stems from the context of medicine, and this concept fits an explanatory mode that is least useful in behavior science (Eysenck, 1960; Yates, 1960). Although the term "symptom" is avoided in studying behavior directly, it is occasionally used here, in a limited sense, to refer to aspects of a problem or to the effect of a chain of events open to observation (see Chapter 5).

When behavior is observed that is unwanted, deficient, or defeating, it is conventionally labeled a "symptom" of a more fundamental process, without objective verification. The psychotherapeutic effort is then directed toward a strenuous search, beyond the manifest behavior, for the remote, but "basic," cause of the symptom. Most psychotherapeutic theory includes opinions about what causes to look for or what must be uncovered.

On the other hand, if the observed and observable behavior is regarded as *the* problem, the therapist searches directly for a solution that can be tested. But the "observables" (Yates, 1960) in behavior must first be brought into focus.

This divergence of views is underscored in the following comments by Colby, a psychoanalyst. Compare these two statements with the next two: "The goal of psychotherapy is to relieve the patient of distressing neurotic symptoms or discordant personality characteristics which interfere with his satisfactory adaptation to a world of people and events" (1951, p. 3). "The goal is further circumscribed by the aim of therapy to deal only with those areas of the personality producing major disturbances. Aspects of the patient's character which are egosyntonic and which he wants to keep are better left alone unless they are inextricably bound up with his neurotic symptoms" (1951, pp. 3–4).

These are fairly acceptable as behavioral descriptions (except for the "ego-syntonic" reference), although they are not as specific, precise, and useful as could be derived from a wholly behavioral context. However, compare them with the following: "In theory, the goal of psychotherapy is to produce a favorable change in the disturbed balance of a conflictual wish-defense system, thus allowing a fuller gratification of the wish or at least a more suitable compromise" (1951, p. 7). "The therapist's task is to help the patient understand himself by bringing unconscious ideas and memories into his consciousness through the verbalization of them" (1951, p. 23).

Wolberg also tries to go both ways. Compare his statement of goals in the first sentence with the behavioral point of view expressed in the second: "In reconstructive therapy, various strata of the unconscious may be explored, from topical spontaneous unconscious manifestations to those that are so deeply repressed that they require mobilization through the dissolution of repressive barriers" (1954, p. 429). "Were we . . . to attempt the definition of a practical goal in therapy, we might say that it is the achievement by the patient of optimal functioning within the limitations of his financial circumstances, his existing motivations, his ego resources and the reality situation" (1954, p. 554).

It is common for therapists to state similarly uncertain and mixed goals, problems, orientations, and processes that may appear at one time to be wholly consistent with behavioral goals and yet another time represent classical views, opposing in principle and theory the behavioral position advanced here.

It is hard to acquire a logical, empirical, and consistent set of guidelines for psychotherapy and behavior change through the examination of conventional writing on psychotherapy. Theories such as have been quoted here have made it difficult for many therapists to pursue practical goals with their patients, focused on the patient's problems outside the interview office. Thus a patient who says he cannot afford intensive, probing therapy may be classified as "resistant"; his loss of anxiety about going deeply into debt in therapy may be termed "developing a positive transference"; or his eagerness to make more money to pay off his debt incurred in therapy may be considered "gaining maturity."

The most parsimonious approach to this problem, scientifically and practically, would seem to lie in trying to find a solution on the basis of the financial realities as they conflict with the patient's desire to achieve certain goals in life outside therapy. If irrational or unwanted behavior then develops in the patient, it may be dealt with in the perspective of the realistic situation and problem.

Choices, alternatives, expectations, values, and judgments—all and more are involved in the therapeutic situation; but at the center should

be the patient's observable behavioral problems in his life outside therapy, not the therapist's techniques or his dynamic formulations about
life inside therapy.

A View of Responsibility

The behavior-change therapist must decide whether responsibility
should be part of a behavior-change model and, if so, how to fit it in.
Both Skinner and Mowrer are advocates of learning formulations; however, they are near opposite ends of a responsibility continuum. In the
opinion of Mowrer (1963), "sin" (that is, a "responsibility for and sense
of wrong doing") is one of the vital molar concepts in behavior change.
Skinner, on the other hand, limits his concept of responsibility to the
reinforcement history of the individual.

Can responsibility be defined in behavioral terms? Can it be considered a focus of reinforcement toward establishing a good reputation,
or can it be considered part of a highly structured situation where, at
first, the child is taught specific and pointed responsibilities through behavioral acts such as returning purloined objects, taking turns, and ful-
filling promises? In any case, it would appear possible to select or devise
events open to reinforcement (that is, to manipulate behavior) to
achieve responsibility.

It may be that the answer here depends on how we define responsibility. The therapist must choose whether to try to change the specific
responsibility characteristics of the individual in the same way that other
goals are selected in therapy. Responsibility would not be considered
separately from its behavioral referents, as an isolated moral concept.

The problem of responsibility looms so large in psychotherapy that
methods of teaching it need serious attention. Herzberg (1941; 1945)
assigned tasks to patients between psychoanalytic sessions for this purpose. The more recent practices by Ellis (1962), Stevenson (1957), and
Phillips (1956; 1961) are in a similar vein. The keeping of an appointment is, itself, a responsible act, which the therapist "assigns" and re-
inforces. How far the therapist needs to go in assigning responsible acts
to accomplish his purpose can be determined empirically.

Some believe that the teaching of responsibility in psychotherapy
cannot be simply a hortatory process (Snyder, 1958). This view suggests
that some patients will accept responsibility for previously neglected behavior if the desirability or necessity of these acts is confirmed or if
the therapist provides some social reinforcement, as well as selectivity.
Most scheduling, prescribing of behavioral acts, and setting of limits in
the therapeutic relationship is probably hortatory, at least at first. This

need not diminish the importance of the teaching processes otherwise, nor does it take initiative away from the patient. The therapist can seldom suggest goals not already perceived, at least partially, by the patient. He plays his more vital role when he helps to control the behavioral acts by which the patient can reach these goals.

The process of teaching responsibility—through specific behavioral aims and requirements—is so essential to the achievement of many other goals in therapy that it merits serious attention and effort.

The emphasis in this book is on the need to enlist any useful change agent rather than to depend upon the change object's own desire to change. This view opens a wide range of opportunity for the therapist to act to increase the probability that the patient will learn the desired behavior. The more active the therapist can reasonably be in promoting given behavior in patients, the more quickly and heuristically the patient can test the adequacy of the therapy and the more readily he can assume and demonstrate responsibility behaviorally for his own welfare and self-direction (Ellis, 1962; Dinoff, Richard, Selzberg, & Sipprelle, 1960; Stevenson, 1957).

In short, responsibility is essentially to be taught. In selecting ways to teach it, there is no intention of rejecting ethical or moral standards; however, each moral and ethical problem in the patient's behavior and views is examined as carefully and objectively as any other problem such as enuresis, job hopping, wife beating, or temper outbursts. In its simplest form, the meaning of responsibility distills down to the behavioral significance, the circumstances involving the behavior, and the therapist's resourcefulness in structuring events that will lead to the desired behavior change.

The Role of Catharsis

The final problem to be discussed in this chapter, in the light of learning theory and behavior change, involves catharsis. This problem has special relevance in comparing classical theories of personality change with the concepts now emerging on changing behavior by more direct means.

In classical learning theory and psychotherapy, some reexposure to the original or to a simulated original stimulus situation is usually required (Shoben, 1948; Shoben, 1960). As a therapeutic aim, this return to "repressed" material presumes that once the repressed has been identified and discussed, a therapeutic effect occurs through abreaction and catharsis. Moreover, without this cathartic release, the patient's problems and residual emotional tendencies presumably will not be dispelled, and he will not improve, at least fundamentally. It does not seek primarily to foster new responses to the original, traumatic stimuli to overcome anxiety. In the words of Shoben (1960, p. 56):

> Anxiety is allayed by some anxiety-reducing symptoms; if the symptomatic behavior is somehow eliminated, the anxiety returns. On the basis of this notion it is possible to define a neurosis or a maladjustment in terms of behavior which serves to reduce anxiety directly *without altering* the conditions which produce the anxiety.

Later, Shoben (1960, p. 57) reaffirms this opinion:

> In summary, then, one might say that clinical cases share in common (a) anxiety touched off by (b) unverbalized, unsuccessfully repressed impulses to act in ways that have met with punishment, and (c) persistent non-integrative behavior of many kinds, which reduces the anxiety but does nothing about eliminating its objective causes.

The question remains as to what constitute the objective causes of neurotic behavior. The original stimulus (which must be uncovered, re-examined, and redintegrated) is the basic cause, Shoben and others say. This is part of the traditional learning-theory interpretation of psychoanalytic psychotherapy. In catharsis, the original stimulus is discovered, examined, and handled. To be effective, it is said, catharsis must allow not only for the redintegration of the stimulus but also for the necessary emotional release, in the reexamination and redintegration of these formerly traumatic experiences. This is the traditional viewpoint.

In fact, the catharsis hypothesis is a vague one, for it does not permit predicting whether the cathartic effect will operate one way or the opposite way (Yates, 1960); that is, will catharsis reduce or aggravate aggressive symptomatology under specified testing conditions? Studies of Maier (1949), Feshback (1956), and Thibault and Coules (1952) yield an equivocal answer.

In their review of literature on aggression, Bandura and Walters (1963) point out that catharsis does not fit the Freudian notion of aggression as the "liberation of affect." The "letting out" of emotion, which ostensibly is the therapeutic role of catharsis, has little support in studies of child and adult behavior. As Bandura and Walters (1963, p. 406) point out:

> If conclusions were to be based on studies of children alone, the catharsis hypothesis, in all its forms, would have to be discarded. Findings from studies with adult subjects are much less

clear cut. Generally speaking, participation, direct or vicarious, in aggressive activities seems to increase the incidence of subsequent aggression, both in the same and different stimulus situations, for most groups of non-angered adult subjects. . . . For angered subjects, participation has, under some experimental manipulations, resulted in a decrease in subsequent aggression . . . but in no case can this reduction be certainly attributed to catharsis.

Nor was there support for the theory of the "drainage" effect of catharsis, put forth in the earlier reviews by McClelland (1951) and Allport (1954).

Overviews: Modifying Behavior through Cybernetic Innovations

An attempt has been made to trace the influence of traditional learning-theory formulations on psychotherapy and behavior-change views and to sketch the practical inefficiency, and often ineffectiveness, of the contribution.

In practice, the application of the Hullian type of learning theory to psychotherapy has had disappointing results, nor have other attempts to find, in the laboratory, support of traditional psychotherapeutic measures been any more encouraging.

It appears likely that psychotherapy and behavior-change efforts can best be improved by basing methods and theory justification on a response-centered approach, regardless of whether the analysis of behavior change begins with such variables as punishment, reward or reinforcement, alternative behavior, or extinction. The response-centered emphasis helps to avoid the complexities and ambiguities that follow in attributing behavior change to such elusive states as analysis of unconscious motivation, reduction of defenses, recovery of original stimuli, or catharsis. Such an emphasis holds out the promise of a conceptual and practical union at the clinical level.

A kind of simplicity is sought that will not only facilitate the researchable and heuristic statements of problems but also forge a connection between clinical-molar behavior-change problems and the more rigorous laboratory work of response modification. Such a union appears to be more readily available in a response-oriented context.

A similar emphasis on the importance of learning and behavior-change practices such as reconditioning, desensitization, negative practice, and operant behavior is expressed by Bandura (1961). He believes that laboratory-related methods will modify many of the practices of clinicians, particularly the frequency and number of therapeutic visits or sessions, the amount of time taken in the therapy hour, the massing and distribution of times for therapeutic sessions, and other details of behavior-change efforts.

Other critics of traditional learning theory and psychotherapy are searching for new directions in cognitive theory and motivational theory and for combinations of these two. Although learning-theory models from the 1930s and 1940s have offered many useful leads, response modification seems likely to provide for more valid and robust use of behavior theory in psychotherapy (Lawrence & Festinger, 1962).

The response-centered position is significantly similar to operant-conditioning methods and fits in readily with cybernetic formulations. While operant-behavior theory is very useful, there are important ways in which cybernetic notions may be more viable for behavior change.

The exploding field of operant-behavior research and its application to a great variety of behavior-change problems must impress the alert psychotherapist today. To focus on primary behavior problems and attempt to solve them most economically is the hope held out by operant-behavior research. However, when one is confronted with a patient with, say, five or six definable and pressing problems, cybernetics would seem to provide better "rules" for interfering constructively and priority systems for the architect of change to use. After the therapist enters the matrix of problems via a cybernetic analysis, he still might want to examine the reinforcement contingencies when dealing with a number of specific behavior-change issues.

While some cybernetic notions will be discussed in the next chapter, operant or other learning-theory methods are not to be passed by. At present, however, any more precise approaches to behavior change should be examined wherever they seem appropriate. Operant and cybernetic notions may be quite similar (especially in instances such as reinforcement, as used by operant analysis, and the notion described as "controlling the effects," often encountered in cybernetics), and the choice between them at some points may simply be a matter of convenience.

The fact that cybernetics affords an opportunity to study "systems in operation" has a strong bearing on the behavior problems of the individual, as well as those of groups and societies. To solve one problem of an individual may have a counteractive effect of worsening another facet of his behavior; here a systemic approach seems necessary. The same may be said about the problems of interrelationships between groups or about the individual as he exhibits different roles in different settings.

Cybernetics is even more important than behavior theory for clinical study, for its many facets suggest new dimensions in instrumentation, conceptualization, and practical application in behavior-change therapy, some of which will be examined in the next chapter.

5 Cybernetic Concepts Applied to Psychotherapy and Behavior Change

The field of cybernetics is relatively new, having become prominent about the time of World War II. Although it is rooted in many scientific disciplines such as physics, electronics, biology, and mathematics, its more recent application to behavioral sciences has been somewhat more tentative.

In its modern role, cybernetics (which comes from the Greek word meaning "steersman"), which has been shaped largely by Wiener (1948), is generally considered to be the study of control and communication in human beings and in machines. It has significant applications in communication theory and information theory.

Just as learning theory early, and behavior theory later, expanded the approach to psychotherapy and behavior change, so does cybernetics promise to affect the direction and dimensions of both theory and practice in these areas. Even though the influence of cybernetics is just beginning to be felt in clinical psychology, it has for many years affected such other areas of psychology as human engineering and human factors analysis, which are most susceptible to a systemic approach (Pask, 1961; von Bertalanffy & Rapoport, Vol. I, 1965; Vol. IV, 1959).

Cybernetics has also excited the imagination of social planners. Ford (1964) points out that in Russia there exists a national cybernetics program which is intended to "engineer" social change on a massive scale. The Soviet program was initiated in 1959 and has grown steadily since, comprising a major section of the Presidium of the Academy of Sciences, U.S.S.R.

One part of this section is termed "applied cybernetics," which is intended to engineer social change throughout the country by molding children's character and development, inculcating ideologies, and establishing social patterns.

Some ways in which cybernetic thinking might apply to the macrocosm, the social order, are highlighted in Chapter 10. In the present chapter, problems of behavior change of a more limited type (in the clinic laboratory) will be discussed. One can hope only to suggest the enormous potentialities of cybernetic thinking, whether applied to limited behavior change or to the entire fabric of society.

It may be considered that cybernetics is still too abstract a science to be of value in psychology, that it has mathematical aspects which cannot be operationally specified or made useful at clinical or other molar levels because of insufficient clinical knowledge, or that the form is not generally compatible with the disrupted, or perhaps any, human being. However, Tomkins and Messick (1963) try to show how cybernetic thinking may be highly useful to the psychological clinician, and that approach will be pursued here.

Since it emphasizes *control* and the manner in which systems operate, cybernetics can be of great value to a theory of behavior change. At the turn of the twentieth century, when psychology was in its infancy, it acquired much from biology, particularly from the theory of evolution and species adaptability to the environment. Psychologists were concerned not only with ways of adapting evolutionary theory specifically to behavior but also with its lessons and with the new questions and new meaning that this theory brought to psychology. The early school of functionalism and the later emphasis on learning theory derived largely from this influence of biology.

It has taken several decades for psychologists widely to accept and utilize the concepts of statistics and of individual differences. There are many other instances of the slow adoption of notions from cross-fertilization among the sciences today. The principles of cybernetics are already making research in psychology more productive. Some promising applications to special domains of clinical practice and behavior change have been already published (Adler, 1961; Ashby, 1958; DeLatil, 1957; Greniewsksi, 1960; Maruyama, 1963; Pask, 1961; Wiener, 1948).

In putting cybernetic principles to work, the psychotherapist must select the useful variables, for cybernetics is primarily a response-centered system. As will be discussed later, its application is more clearly response-centered than learning theory generally is, even more pronouncedly than in Skinnerian operant-behavior theory. The outstanding characteristic of the systemic approach to behavior change is not the emphasis on prior conditions, the discovery of original stimuli, or the process of the particular stimulus generalization. Instead, it deals with a cycle of events which need not have a discernible beginning or end but which can be controlled and regulated. This cycle of events (typically a "loop") may be influenced at any point to "open up" or "explain" the subsequent observations.

Basic Cybernetic Concepts for the Psychotherapist

In cybernetics, the first and fundamental concept is that of *control.* As Pask (1961, p. 12) writes: "A great deal of cybernetics is concerned with how stability is maintained with 'control mechanisms.'" The main question might be: "How can the observed events be controlled?" taking self-defeating behavior as the pivotal point. The purpose, as in Skinner's "behavior shaping," is to overcome obstructive and unwanted behavior. The concepts of stability and the maintenance of control in cybernetic theory would largely replace those of habit and motivation in learning theory.

Another important cybernetic concept is that of *entropy,* which refers to the degree of disorder in a system, or to the tendency of the system to "run down." The tendency of variety in a system to diminish has been discussed by Ashby (1958, p. 136). This concept is relevant to the common idea that systems tend to disintegrate or to become non-differentiated. Systems must be worked at to be maintained, for order does not automatically maintain itself.[1]

When the product of a change cannot be maintained reliably, the process is called "entropy." When behavior is changed or when new behavior is learned, but the change is not maintained, in traditional therapy it is assumed that the therapy has not gotten to the root of the problem. Instead, the difficulty can be stated in terms of how to maintain the new order reliably and permanently. In learning theory, the failure to maintain order may be caused by a delay in reinforcing the original learning or by the timing of the intervals of reinforcement (Lawrence & Festinger, 1962).

[1] The basic question of "ultrastability" of the organism (Ashby, 1958, pp. 244–264) is beyond the scope of this discussion.

There are forces such as contingency, determinism, and positive organization which tend to counteract entropy, as DeLatil (1957) points out. These forces are part of the techniques available to the resourceful therapist in the behavior-change effort. The therapist may mobilize these forces in maintaining order and in overcoming entropic influences. The cybernetic approach emphasizes the need to overcome entropy and to maintain order. The effort to change behavior requires dealing with whatever elements are present that produce disorder or that obstruct or oppose efforts to introduce a different order.

What traditional therapy regards as the patient's "resistance" or "lack of motivation" to change, the cybernetic approach regards as evidence that the patient's disturbance is, itself, a kind of order. That is, the patient's disturbed behavior may represent a smaller orbit of influences (a loop within a larger loop) similar to the condition that exists when cancer is considered as a kind of smaller system of order within the total body economy, creating "disorder" in the total organism. The embezzler who systematically withdraws funds from the bank for his own purposes is another example of a smaller system of order that brings disorder to the larger system—the bank.

The entropic influence of one system on a larger system is described clinically as a kind of gain, or satisfaction, in traditional psychotherapy. To the learning theorist, this indicates the presence of some reinforcement or tension reduction that enables the individual to escape facing certain facts about himself—to avoid obligations he dislikes, for example—so that the symptoms protect him from these unpleasant realities. However, these are not symptoms in the traditional medical sense, but are events in a smaller orbital (or conflict) system, which is generally entropic within a larger system.

An example of a symptom, interpreted in the usual sense, would be the anxiety of the student who "freezes" from nervousness before a typing exam or playing for a large audience. The nervousness impairs control or coordination and spoils the performance—that is, the tense and perspiring fingers fail to strike the typewriter or piano keys properly—or it leads to premature retreat.

An individual with these symptoms may be considered to have serious doubts about himself and his adequacy—perhaps in situations far beyond the one in question—arising out of earlier problems, so that he "uses" the symptoms to avoid embarrassment, as an excuse for not doing well, or as a way to escape and yet save face. These symptoms are said to be the person's unconscious protection or defense mechanism against more fundamental anxiety about himself.

But the anxious, vitiating behavior can be explained in different terms—terms that are not only simpler and more manageable clinically but also less hypothetical. The cause of the anxious behavior may be any one of a host of circumstances. Indeed, anxiety may—and often does—have a variety of behavioral causes. One's effort to do well is often accompanied by tension and a strong attempt to please, and is admired. One loop could be described as follows: desire to please—strain in muscles used in performance—muscle strain leading to sweating—sweating leading to poor finger coordination—poor performance—defeat in the desire to please. The performer may redouble his effort to please, retrace the self-defeating loop, and become trapped in a vicious circle.

Conversely, a series of factors can be programed to produce better performance, illustrated by these factors in a loop: practice—improved skill—encouragement—more practice. But this larger loop may be vitiated because of interference from the first, smaller loop, so that there is a negative result from a positive effort. The negative result of the smaller loop interferes with, or acts as an entropic influence on, the larger loop—the skill essential in typing or playing the piano. The latter skill may still be of high order when there is no tension. Like cancer, the negative result of the smaller loop may grow and affect the larger loop adversely. In time, apprehension in a test situation may grow so great that the person may for this reason alone fail the tests required to move ahead. The circumstances of the current entropic behavior must be discovered to correct the entropic influence of the smaller system on the larger one. This is information far more relevant than knowing the origin of the pianist's or typist's problems. What is actually needed is only the knowledge of how to enter and control the smaller orbit, for example, how to prevent tension from destroying the pianist's presence or coordination, or how to control the embezzler's tendency to purloin funds. The change plan in structured therapy must coordinate the two loops, so that the smaller loop will not destroy the larger one. The forces that tend to amplify or counteract possible deviations in any loop will be discussed later.

Probably the best-known concept from cybernetics is that of "feedback," which may be implicit in the concept of entropy. In one excellent discussion of feedback, DeLatil (1957, p. 6) defines it as "a device which makes an effect act back on one of its causes, thus enabling this effect to carry out its given aim." Learning-theory concepts of retroactive or proactive inhibition or facilitation bear some resemblance to feedback.

The concept of reinforcement in learning theory is relevant here despite the facts that it is essentially animal-oriented—in examples such as the satiation of thirst or hunger, the escape from discomfort, and a signal of "well done" or a high grade as a reward for work—and does not suggest the context of an entire system, as feedback does. The concept of feedback implies a loop whose parts act in sequence or in a specific relationship to one another, representing a more systemic connection of these elements than is present in reinforcement.

Also, the concept of feedback concedes that one element may belong to two or more different—even conflicting—loops. Moreover, a given type of behavior (an element) may be reinforced in one loop and not in another, and an ability to predict or understand specific behavior may not even be possible from the standpoint of specific reinforcement.

In yet another sense, the concept of feedback is more inclusive than that of reinforcement. A system may run amuck in spite of—or even because of—elements that are effectively reinforced, for example, a runaway car, an uncontrolled furnace, or a successful person who pushes a good thing until it destroys him. In an institutional loop, the stock market may build up to the point of a crash because of the reinforcement of separate elements, placing the whole system in jeopardy. If each person's "gain" is observed in the stock market, the concept of reinforcement might suffice, but when the elements of gain pyramid to a disastrous loss, a more powerful concept is needed.

Not only may behavior mean different things in different loops, but much behavior to be taught in overcoming disturbed or unwanted behavior or in changing behavior is, in a sense, already present in the organism's behavioral repertoire (Gagne, 1962, p. 85). The problem lies not so much in learning or teaching behavior as in *installing* behavior into a given loop; that is, the behavior to be inserted in the loop is already present and available, and it needs only to be applied in a given context. This is another advantage of short-term therapy, since often what the patient needs to do is to insert or to apply known behavior effectively, rather than to search for novel solutions to problems.

Stated another way, behavior change can be promoted by structuring the context and supporting a class of behavior from a larger setting of which it is a member. For example, to make employees more productive, distractions in their work environment may be reduced, materials may be made more readily available, or their duties may be posted in easily observed places. Any of these efforts to structure the context of the employees' behavior and reinforce their ability to concentrate and to read, in a new loop, can lead to greater productivity. Similarly, the behavior and educational accomplishment of children in a classroom may be measurably enhanced by inserting certain elements into their behavioral loops (Haring & Phillips, 1962).

In a cybernetic sense, then, behavior elements are shifted from one loop to another. The therapist may try to shift the behavior of the patient from one locus to another, to switch behavior highly appropriate in one setting in order to solve problems in another setting. A parent may be firm toward the child when it comes to setting limits about bedtime, for example, but be too lax in setting limits around eating habits. In this case, switching behavior is presumably based less on the reinforcement of elements (although this may occur) than on fitting elements into a loop differently, in a way more compatible with the organic whole.

Special Aspects of Feedback

Further distinctions important to behavior change and psychotherapy can be specified by using the notion of feedback. The concepts of *deviation-amplifying* and *deviation-counteracting* mutual causal processes (Maruyama, 1963) are fruitful results. Maruyama differentiates between deviation-counteracting mutual causal processes or feedback loops, which are dealt with in what he calls the "first cybernetics," and deviation-amplifying ones. His use of the term "deviation-amplifying processes" (commonly called "vicious circles") refers to such phenomena as mental illness, international discord and conflict, or what he calls the "second cybernetics."

An example of deviation-amplifying feedback processes might be the weathering of a rock, Maruyama observes. At the outset there is a small crack in the rock in which some water collects. Freezing water enlarges the crack, the crack collects more water, eventually soil is deposited, and perhaps plants begin to grow there, further enlarging the split. A tree may sprout, the roots of which enlarge the crack still more. The point is that at each juncture, there are deviation-amplifying processes in operation.

Behavior problems may develop similarly. A child is scolded for some misbehavior; other children tease him about his scolding; he becomes tense and less in command of himself; he errs again, this time to be ostracized perhaps as well as scolded; and so on, to the point where he gains a reputation for misbehavior in the eyes of peers and adults. Or a small misunderstanding may occur between two people. One party reacts to the dispute by withdrawal, whereupon the other party is angered or offended and likewise withdraws, leading either to a spoken or a tacit break in communication. In this way, an "offended" person in a group may eventually become isolated from much of his social environment.

Concepts are needed that will span diverse processes in natural and man-made systems—that will help to order the processes involved and point to ways of intervening to alter the direction of a stated process. Within the concept of deviation-amplifying feedback processes, one can speak of "steering" the system into different directions.

DeLatil (1957, p. 21) explains this concept of steering in his discussion of "synthetic animals":

The tortoises of Grey Walter are machines which move freely about and have certain attributes of an independent life. (We are not speaking of the exterior attributes of life, which, naively enough, are associated with the automata of old.) They "feed" on light which they seek and transform into electric currents. This current charges an accumulator. When their stomachs are full (or, if you prefer, when their accumulators are charged) their behavior changes. They no longer need a bright light on which to feed, but a soft light on which to "repose." In their search for rest, they run down the batteries of their motors, so that they are soon "hungry" once more and set off again to hunt for "food." In the same way an animal divides its life between a search for food, and periods of rest.

In this passage there is ample evidence of learning, of reinforcement, and of behavior change. Here is a way to deal with concepts of order and control that enlarge the understanding of behavior and behavior change through reference to other systems.

Integrating Concepts

How can these cybernetic principles of control, entropy, feedback, and specifically, deviation-counteracting and deviation-amplifying feedback loops be applied to the theme of this book? How can meaningful behavior-change applications be derived from them?

Take the case of a bed wetter of any age. Here is a system that has a certain order, or predictability; at the same time, this system is inimical to the larger system, called "maturity," or responsibility. In a cybernetic sense, the order of the smaller system must be steered to make it compatible with the order of the larger system—which is the whole behavioral economy of the individual.

In terms of entropy, the bed-wetting habit may grow and injure aspects of the larger system; it may destroy self-confidence or restrict social activities severely. The smaller system (the bed-wetting) exerts an entropic influence on the larger system, so that the larger system may "run down." Presumably some kind of feedback process is operative.

Figure 1 shows two ways to look at the feedback loop in bed-wetting. On the left side of Figure 1a, element A (some fluid in the bladder at bedtime) acts through B and C to counteract A. This is a deviation-counteracting loop, which is to be preserved, or established if it is not

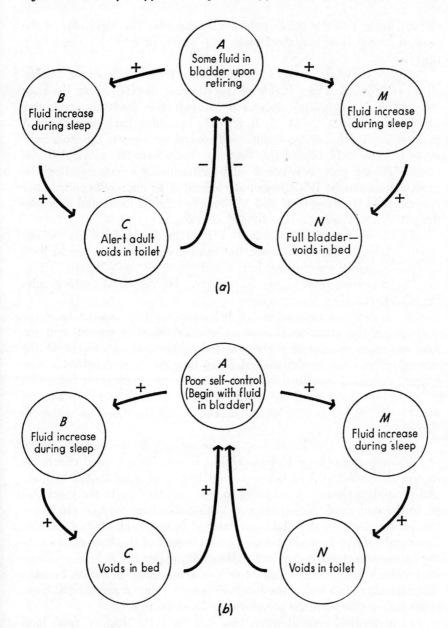

Figure 1. Two ways to view feedback loops in bed-wetting.

already present in the child's behavioral economy. The right side of the same drawing, however, shows how the "same" process can also empty the bladder.

Figure 1b, while similar in many ways to Figure 1a, puts the emphasis on self-control. The left side of this drawing illustrates how the poor self-control is magnified—increased through the deviation-amplifying process shown in elements A, B, and C—by acting back on element A to increase it (that is, to reduce self-control or worsen the poor self-control). The right side of this drawing shows how this original deviation-amplifying process is corrected by introducing a counteracting element at element N. What began at element A as poor self-control later is corrected via elements M and N; thus the original unwanted or inadequate behavior is mitigated, corrected, or reduced.

In Figure 1a, with "reducing the fluid in the bladder" as the criterion, both systems would work, but in different ways that would have an opposite effect on personal habits and problems, as indicated in Figure 1b. In moving from Figure 1a to Figure 1b, the social problem-solving criterion finally comes into focus.

In this cybernetic analysis of behavior, several considerations are underlined: the criterion change to be established is named, and the kind of order or control to be inserted in the system to achieve the desired effect must be determined (note how the "same" behavior may operate differently—with different consequences—in different loops).

The two systems, of bed-wetting and of voiding in the toilet, can also be diagramed as two loops, one containing the other, as shown in Figure 2.

In Figure 2, the larger loop is the mature behavior (self-control and self-respect) obtained by the child who has been trained effectively in regard to voiding. The behavior loop begins with voiding at bedtime and progresses through awakening to void and voiding in the toilet and on to the end result of self-respect. Within this loop may be envisaged the smaller loop of the child not trained in such self-control. In this latter and smaller loop can be seen each element of the loop abcd working in tandem, in a redundant, self-defeating process, where elements b, c, and d work back to a and return to the unwanted behavior. Perhaps the feasibility of entering the feedback loop at any of several junctures is one reason that there are so many theories of therapy.

In a practical clinical sense, how can the child "escape" from loop abcd to loop ABCD through any one of the junctures? In a cybernetic sense, any route open can be used to meet behavior-change objectives. Note that the therapist does not need to find the cause of the behavior to be changed, any more than he needs to find the cause of the desirable behavior, in order to keep the latter operating stably.

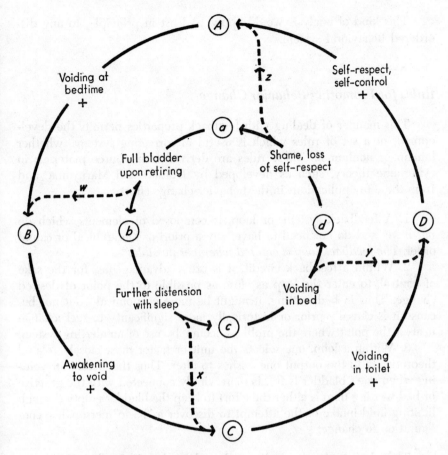

Figure 2. Comparison of efficient with inefficient loop in bed-wetting.

In the psychotherapeutic or behavior-change effort, the therapist needs to transfer the patient from the smaller system to the larger one. The smaller system is entered wherever possible—at one or more junctures in the deviation-amplifying system. With a given individual, it will be easier to enter one juncture than another, and all possible junctures may not and need not be known to insert an effective change.

Note that throughout this analysis there has been no concern with the history of the disorder, the motivation of the individual, or his perceptions of the situation. Instead, effort is directed toward *rearranging* or *reordering the system as it is presented.* There is a complex set of variables, but the most cogent, simple, and heuristic alignment of these variables is what is of concern in the development of an effective method of behavior change.

This kind of analysis would apply, at least in principle, to any disordered behavioral system.

Rules for Promoting Behavior Change

This manner of dealing with feedback properties permits the development of a set of rules which is useful in correcting systems, whether human or nonhuman. These rules are derived from source materials in cybernetic theory, such as developed by DeLatil and Maruyama, and from these to applications in the behavior-change effort:

1. A feedback system, or loop, is composed of elements which do not have, and do not need to have, any a priori or hierarchical or causal order. *The feedback loop is entered wherever possible.*

2. Within a feedback circuit, it is often advantageous, for the sake of control, to enter the loop as close as possible to the point of desired change. Thus in bed-wetting, it might be more economical—but not because it is causally prior or historically more significant—to seek change nearest the point where the problem occurs, by use of an alerting system.

3. Within a loop, one selects the unit or factor most closely related theoretically to the output one wishes to alter. Thus the "habit" of voiding when one's bladder is full is more vitally connected with the practice of bed-wetting than is either the effort to keep the bladder empty through limiting fluid intake or the attempt to discover a "basic" personality configuration to change.

The above rules are subsumed under what DeLatil (1957) calls "controlling the effects." With nonhuman systems taken into account in studying human behavior, tangential issues are eliminated, such as the cognitive or motivational states of the individual, and the practical alignment of the variables under theoretical guidance is promoted.

Within the cybernetic framework, although not unique to it, variables are selected and regulated in the feedback chain which are most amenable to manipulation and control. In structured therapy elusive causes are not sought that might operate to produce a disordered system; the therapist goes directly to the element (information) in the feedback loop that has a meaningful coefficient of efficiency in maintaining the loop, and he proceeds immediately to try to insert the change.

The above rules are readily applicable in making therapy more efficient. As discussed earlier, short-term therapy and behavior-change methods have been used by therapists of different persuasions. The available data must be organized and integrated, however, and cybernetic concepts help greatly to provide conceptual clarity. If a cogent behavior-change plan is prepared in this way, therapy seems likely to be significantly shortened and improved.

From this kind of analysis, behavior-change theory can be put to work in other crucial and direct ways. For example, if Meehl's (1962) views on the biological aspects of schizophrenia prove to be correct, they would furnish the behavioral scientist with a more adequate rationale for direct intervention, perhaps using drugs, shock, or aversive conditioning, as well as with positive feedback controls, in a deliberate logical effort to alter the behavior (feedback loop) of a schizophrenic patient. Or the limitations of some behavioral analysis of schizophrenia might be revealed, so that new elements in the behavior system could be conceptualized as a basis for more effective intervention. Patient behavior might be retrained or rescheduled on the basis of larger loops of interconnecting elements (and not by means of such simple rewards as candy for very limited problem-solving efforts). Whatever the future may bring in the study of schizophrenia, it seems likely that a feedback analysis that will apply to neurological functioning as well as to molar behavior will be a rewarding one (Wiener, 1948; 1954; 1964).

The Operation of Feedback Loops

Now that relationship of change principles to behavior has been described, applications can be discussed in detail. The "positive" and "negative" nature (direction) of elements in the loop will be of concern here.

Positive elements in a loop can be thought of as directly facilitating another element. Positive elements are deviation-amplifying. Thus the more courses a student takes, up to a point, the more credits he earns; or the more money a person puts in the bank, the more interest he draws. A negative element is one that operates in a direction opposing another factor; it is deviation-counteracting. For example, the more time a student puts into studying, the less time he has for recreational pursuits; the more money a person spends of his earnings, the less he has to invest.

Positive and negative loops may be interwoven with respect to a similar set of conditions. Any factor that changes the direction of the loop (or the direction of any factor in the loop) is, by definition, negative. A negative factor, leading to a negative loop, will reverse the original direction of the loop (see Figure 3).

In Figure 3, both the positive and the negative loops begin and end at the same point, but with different meaning. Loop *ADEFA* begins positively but ends negatively; loop *ABCA* begins and ends positively.

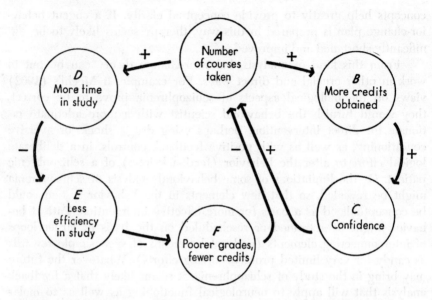

Figure 3. Comparison of efficient with inefficient loop in studying.

Loop *ADEFA* ends with a counteracting influence on the initial state *A*, the number of courses taken. In contrast, loop *ABCA* ends with an amplifying effect, when more credits and increased confidence permit increasing the number of courses taken. Loop *ABCA* may end negatively when it reaches a state of no further increase because of a limit on the number of courses allowed. Thus, under differing circumstances, the same behavior can lead to the opposite outcome.

Loop *ADEFA* in Figure 3 operates in this way: The more courses taken (*A*), the more time needed to study (*D*), the less time available for recreation and overcoming fatigue (*E*), and the less efficiency in meeting requirements (*F*), leading to a reduction in effort and in courses mastered (*A*). This is a "negative" loop because it ends with a counteracting influence from *A*, through *D*, *E*, and *F*, back to *A*. A loop with a negative influence, as in this example (loop *ADEFA* actually has three negative influences or elements: *E*, *F*, and *A*), is deviation-counteracting. In this example, *A* is reduced by acting through three negative or counteracting elements, *D*, *E*, and *F*. One negative or counteracting influence would, however, have changed the loop.

This condition is familiar in everyday clinical situations: the patient who says "The harder I try, the further I seem to get away from my goals. So why should I try anymore?" People who try too hard often disrupt their own efforts or direction; they introduce negative or counteracting elements in the loop that otherwise has a positive direction.

On the other hand, the positive loop *ABCA* in Figure 3 is deviation-amplifying—that is, each element in the loop amplifies the next. Thus the number of courses increases, bringing about an increase in the credits earned and leading to increased self-confidence on the part of the student, all of which acts back on the original element by increasing the number of courses taken, with successful students allowed to take additional ones up to a limit. All loops have some kind of limit, obviously.

A "success pattern" in life may be interpreted in this way: The more one accomplishes, the more skill he develops; the greater skill places him in demand; the greater the demand, the more he strives to meet it. Success begets success. Following the loop analysis, practice increases practice, acting through other mutually amplifying processes, and a circle of success is thereby produced. Conversely, a vicious circle of failure can be considered in the same way.

If a loop has all deviation-amplifying factors, it is a positive loop. As soon as one negative factor is introduced, the direction of the loop is changed, and it becomes a negative loop. The introduction of more than one negative (counteracting) factor into a loop increases the likelihood that the loop will be negative, in relation to its original direction. With the help of Maruyama (1963, p. 177), these characteristics of a loop may be described:

1. A loop whose elements all point in the same direction is deviation-amplifying.
2. The introduction of a counteracting (negative) element will change the direction of the loop.
3. An element may be positive in one loop and negative in another, depending on the influence of the element on the total loop.
4. The elements in a loop have no hierarchical or causal priority.
5. The presence of more than one negative factor in a loop may only strengthen the counteracting influence on that loop.

In these generalizations, it is assumed that the elements or factors in loops are of equal strength, are equally likely to occur, or are of known differences in strength or probability, so that the effect of their introduction into a loop can be calculated.

Finally, when elements in a loop are to be manipulated, one more principle must be kept in mind:

6. To change the direction of a loop, one or more of the elements need to be altered. This alteration may consist simply of changing the direction of the element (hence the loop); or by increasing or decreasing the time-lag; or by making one element or factor prepotent in a way that reverses or counteracts its influence on another element.

While the logic of feedback loops, especially overlapping loops, is more complex than will be discussed here, the present analysis should suffice to explicate some principles of feedback as they apply to behavior change; it is not intended to develop a complete rationale for feedback loops.

Practical changes in the behavioral loops are being sought here in propitious, effective ways. If the architect of behavioral change seeks to alter loops by all reasonable means, he may well find that several loops in a given individual's behavioral economy can be changed.

In ordering or reordering elements in a patient's behavior, the change comes about through manipulation of such variables—now including one person, now another. Whether the patient makes the change for himself or whether it is made through others depends on the nature of the experimental or structured condition. In traditional psychotherapy, most of the change effort has used only one modality, talking, to one end—the analysis and reworking of causes presumably to be found in significant past events, through the medium of two persons, the patient and the therapist.

What, then, is the "root" of a behavior problem? Since no scientific answer to this question is yet possible, perhaps the wrong question is being asked for current therapeutic purposes. If the interconnections of factors and the ways in which they relate through feedback can be analyzed, many common traditional problems can be avoided and behavior problems can be placed into a more meaningful context. This viewpoint is inherent in another feedback concept, "initial kick" (from Maruyama, 1963, p. 165).

Initial Kick and the Development of Problems

In the initial kick, the direction of deviation amplification is less important than in a deviation-counteracting feedback system (Maruyama, 1963; Myrdal, 1957; Myrdal, 1964).

A slight kick may start a boulder rolling downhill, loosening other particles of rock and earth, breaking down plants, and overrunning animals, until finally a thundering landslide may result. This is an example of a series of deviation-amplifying contacts. The influence the boulder has on all the elements in the environment is not determined by the intensity of the initial kick, but by the deviation amplification of these elements. And since none of these elements is deviation-counteracting, the effect is large. A small blaze from a lighted cigarette may cause a forest fire of enormous proportions, or a small leak in a dam may cause a catastrophic flood for hundreds of miles.

The concept of the initial kick may be usefully applied to many mental health problems. An individual gets off to a bad start, falls behind in some endeavor, makes a poor work record, loses interest and reduces effort, and finally gives up. The poor start might not have been serious enough to account for the end result, and the instigating conditions (initial kick), even if they could be accurately determined, would be mistakenly held accountable for subsequent problem behavior. Nothing in psychological science, in biological science, or in cybernetics suggests that this initial kick can be held accountable for the results that eventually follow.

In conventional psychotherapeutic procedures, the deviation-amplifying process has been largely overlooked—an omission of the greatest significance for today's therapist.

Effects of the initial kick frequently remain unexplained coincidence. In the same way that discovery or settlement of new lands may have been directed to a particular spot by many irrelevant circumstances, such as navigational error or the direction of wind or tide, so may behavioral outcomes be determined by chance elements or relationships. If one is in a large crowd, his contact with others will probably be largely accidental, but the eventual outcome of the contact may be friendship, marriage, or even bitter enmity.

From the field of possible choices, a relatively chance event may have enormous and unpredictable consequences; that is, given a set of deviation-amplifying processes which concatenate events, an enormous growth may ensue unpredictably from the initial kick.

To put the example in another context, it might be said that the initial kick does not contain much information. Even the knowledge of how a complex process began would help little in predicting end results and so could not be used to understand or to change the results. In traditional psychotherapy, the initial event (the original stimulus situation) has been studied as if it were almost entirely responsible for the disturbed behavior, although the initial event is of slight importance in the cybernetic context; by contrast, it is the deviation-amplifying feedback process that determines whether the initial event leads to later problem behavior.

The initial kick and the deviation-amplifying feedback process may also explain why a given behavior will not improve, while another does. Often, the therapeutic effort falters in an attempt, against seemingly unsurmountable odds, to change behavior. In the cybernetic sense, such a therapeutic effort to search for the origin of the behavior is nullified by deviation-amplifying or deviation-counteracting processes.

It is considered unlikely that a young man whose behavior is unreliable, antisocial, and wasteful (a "character disorder") will change to any degree in even intensive conventional therapy. Any progress that might be made in the consulting office will ordinarily be reversed by the deviation-amplifying process—that is, his tendency to drink excessively with his buddies, carouse with available girls, borrow money from others, and avoid all work and responsibility. His problem behavior will remain untouched by nonintervening therapy because such behavior is constantly being reinforced.

The therapist who fails to exercise some control over the continuing choices and actions of such a patient is unlikely to create any change in his behavior. If these important deviation-amplifying processes are overlooked or if they are treated as symptomatic of a more basic problem, the therapist will waste his basic tools and resources.

A young student like the one referred to above was seen when on the verge of expulsion from school because of his irresponsible and wild behavior. When he consulted a therapist who tried to treat his problem behavior from this learning-theory–cybernetic viewpoint, the student felt that the therapist was overlooking the "real" problems in his past. Consequently, after six sessions with this therapist, he transferred to another therapist to get "deep" therapy. Two years later, at the midpoint of a semester at school, the youth reappeared and asked to resume with the original therapist. He had spent 2 or 3 hours a week for nearly 2 years with the second therapist, during which time he had been dismissed from school and told he could reenroll only after he had worked outside school for a semester to show some evidence of stability. In explaining why he was returning to the first therapist, he said he had "learned all about how he got the way he did and how the problems arose in his life, but not how to get over them." He was again asking for help to change the same old current behavior problems.

Further conversation suggested that while this student was in "deep" therapy, few if any of his self-defeating patterns of behavior had changed; that is, his behavior with schoolwork, friends, and carousing were still the same, although he had learned their presumed causes.

He also added that in his learning about the origins of his problems, he had really found out nothing new about his current problems—he still knew that he refused to do inconvenient things, that he would not study if the assignment appeared difficult, and that he was too concerned with immediate pleasures to put up with the inconvenience of weighing his actions or living up to his promises.

He admitted that he had been directed to these things in the original therapy sessions but that he had not acted to change them because he thought he needed to find out what was causing them—at least he preferred that pursuit, with its implication of painless, effortless change and sympathy, rather than the strenuous efforts his original therapy called for.

Upon returning to his original therapist, his therapy was directed toward identifying the deviation-amplifying processes in his life. The therapist helped him to identify these processes and to bring them under control. First, a study schedule (a deviation-counteracting element) was developed as part of his daily schedule, which was to be followed up in detail. This daily schedule called not only for avoiding certain of his self-defeating friendships and absenting himself from their haunts and temptations but also for limiting his recreation to very carefully selected activities, and then only after the completion of his scholastic duties. After 6 months of this therapy (18 interviews), he was able to report marked progress: no drinking for the last 4 months, no carousing after the first month, a better scholastic record, and increased self-confidence through his progress in getting off the probation list.

In his original treatment, this young man had argued, as many do, that he had suffered wrongdoing at the hands of his parents, such as too much pressure from them for accomplishment and too many admonishments to come in nights at a reasonable hour so that he could meet the next day's obligations. It was his conviction that he had to locate, relive, and "work through" traumatic orgins of his behavior before he could improve. He had been disappointed when the therapist rejected this approach to his problems. The initial kick in his life, in the judgment of the original therapist, consisted, instead, of indulgence, laxity, and ineffectiveness on the part of the parents, which had eventually led the youth, through deviation-amplifying experiences, to the point where he believed his own thoughts, feelings, and actions were unassailable and that he was helpless to control and direct his life effectively. In his eyes, the blame for his difficulties lay with his parents and their past treatment of him, and this allowed him to avoid any responsibility for changing his behavior.

The common technical problem in this young man's therapy, as is true to some extent with most patients, is that the implication of deviation-amplifying events was overlooked, when their *control* was vital if behavior was to change.

One final comment about the initial kick. It has already been noted that the amount of information in the initial kick is very small in comparison to the amount of information that exists in the deviation-amplifying feedback process. This concept of the amount of information is a crucial one.

The information needed to understand and predict adult behavior should be derived, in the cybernetic sense, from the amount of information in the feedback process at each crucial juncture in the development of the organism. In genetics, for example, manipulation of the embryo, as in grafting and interfering with normal development, is generally considered to furnish more knowledge about the development of the embryo than an attempt to retrace this history from data about the adult.

In other words, the information supplied at the point of interaction of parts and processes is the information that is needed to accomplish change. In the loop, the closer each juncture is to some end state, or to some arbitrarily determined observational point, the more relevant is the information it contains. The process is directed forward. Each new point chosen provides an up-to-date statement of the information needed to learn the direction of movement and change.

In studying molar behavior, the necessity of gaining information about the junctures the patient faces becomes clear. What are the relevant units of information at the following choice points: To study or to seek recreation? To marry or not? To take the additional drink or forgo it? To blow up or constrain oneself? To tell a lie or the truth? At these junctures the choice can seldom be predicted from general developmental facts or from remote "causes." Yet many theories and methods of psychotherapy rest squarely on this tenuous latter proposition (for example, Dollard & Miller, 1950; Pascal, 1959).

Changing Deviation-amplifying Loops

This examination of the deviation-amplifying feedback process has attempted to show how deviation-counteracting loops can be introduced to interfere with ongoing self-defeating processes.

In the case of the young man who returned to the structured, behavior-oriented treatment after his experience with more conventional therapy, the structured therapy interfered with his self-defeating behavior. The therapist introduced a change plan which called for a deviation-counteracting process in a deliberate effort to interfere with problem-creating behavior. This technique has its counterpart in Skinner's emphasis on the use of schedules as a powerful technique for control of behavior.

These questions need continually to be posed: "What are the alternatives to the present unwanted behavior?" "How can these alternatives be set up?" "Who should set them up?" "What means can be used?" "How and by whom will the alternatives be carried out, in whole or in part?" At the same time that desired alternatives to the unwanted behavior are being developed and used, the therapist tries to reduce the likelihood of occurrence of the undesired behavior. Some behavior is blocked, and some is facilitated, on a carefully chosen selective basis. It is never assumed that effective behavior will occur spontaneously.

Great importance is attached to introducing the deviation-counteracting process as early as possible, rather than trying to analyze etiology first and hoping to replace the problem behavior later with more desirable behavior. The client should not be continuing to practice the unwanted behavior in the meantime.

In his emphasis on reciprocal inhibition, Wolpe makes a similar point, for there is also an immediate effort in his reconditioning techniques to "knock out" the unwanted behavior. In other reconditioning methods, too, as soon as the unwanted behavior is eliminated, reinforcement of the desired responses follows immediately.

Once the defeating behavior is constrained, is no longer practiced, and is not exposed further to uncontrolled and often far-reaching reinforcement or amplification, it is possible to supplant it more adequately. Various reinforcement or amplification methods can be designed to move the organism toward successful behavior. This may be done through a "successive approximations" method, through inserting an existing behavior loop in a new context, or even through programed learning. In any case, this reconstructive effort can employ operant conditioning to change or replace small behavior elements at one end of an interference continuum, or at the other end, very large segments of molar behavior.

These deviation-counteracting elements act directly to restore a larger order in the organism's behavioral economy or to restructure behavior to achieve some desired end. For example, instruction in study habits may be introduced to the failing student as one useful method of entering the deviation-amplifying loop of his self-defeating behavior. The patient is taught to schedule his time, to take notes on choice points in his daily living that clarify alternatives for him, and to help to identify problem areas in his daily life that can be brought into the behavior-change plan.

6 Synthesis of Theory and Practice: Models and Applications

Behavior-change models and therapies are beginning to appear today with increasing frequency. In several years, perhaps, a few with superior accuracy and stability in solving human problems will establish their preeminence among competitors. The future development of behavior theory may follow that of the physical sciences, toward models initially of limited comprehensiveness but of greater specificity and usefulness than broad but vague current theories of "personality" provide.

In this chapter, some tentative models for behavior change will be discussed relative to the clinical situation. Variables must be selected, and a rationale developed. This is not formal theorizing in a hypothetico-deductive sense, but constructing working models that can serve to relate behavior theory to cybernetic formulations, on the one hand, and to clinical phenomena, on the other.

The Choice of Variables for Change

There are a number of possible choices of variables from historical, medico-biological, cognitive, and learning areas. The latter is chosen here, and from this choice cybernetics is considered an enlargement and extension of behavior theory.

The distinction between static and manipulable elements should be stated. Static variables refer to states, historical events, traits, and other personality measures not directly manipulable. Behavior-theory variables, on the other hand, are accessible to direct manipulation under conditions that can be specified.

The probable degree of change over time also needs to be assessed, at least in the limited sense of the difference between a "state" change and a "process" change. For example, a person who overcomes the drinking habit shows a state change, but the particular choice of variables and the manner of manipulating the variables in the change involve a process change. In a conventional view of process change, the focus is generally on the internal workings of the organism, rather than on the external, observable behavior of the individual in his environment. The notion of process may also refer, however, to a hypothetical internal state said to underlie the observed behavioral change.

Since traditional psychotherapy has been a conversational affair between patient and therapist (compared with behavior-change therapy, which need not involve talking at all), the variables with which the therapist could work have been largely forced on him at the outset. But the behavior-change therapist can choose his variables from a far wider field than verbal exchange provides.

Readiness for therapy is a difficult and poorly understood problem. It has been referred to earlier in discussing whether the patient (the change object) must be his own change agent. In traditional therapy, it has been assumed that the patient's voluntary presence before a therapist is requisite to his changing. This assumption is unnecessary, however, when variables can be utilized which change behavior in spite of the fact that subjects are resistant or do not come to therapy voluntarily.

To illustrate, a surgeon may display great skill in operative techniques. If the patient or his proxy will not permit the surgeon to operate, the surgeon's skills are useless, but good patient motivation is not necessary—only his presence is essential. The surgeon has the skill to succeed if the person is available.

Similarly, the patient in psychotherapy can be helped simply if he is available for behavioral operations. Many patients come for help and quit; the attrition rate is very high where therapy depends upon voluntary cooperation. Not only does the limited choice of variables for the change process produce disappointing results, which lead to therapy dropouts, but dependence upon the patient's interest or enthusiasm puts an unnecessary strain on the situation, with adverse consequences.

If the variables selected for change effort give the patient a measure of control over his difficulties immediately, the attrition rate is likely to be lowered. In addition, such an approach takes the burden of being interested or enthusiastic off the patient and charges the professional practitioner with the responsibility of being inventive.

How best to prepare the patient to change his behavior in psychotherapy has not been extensively considered. It is an important technical problem, not solved on a large scale simply by selecting or depending upon the patient and his initial attitude. For one thing, many patients who apparently wish to change want to dictate the conditions for change, even when they are not qualified to do so. Or they enter therapy with distorted notions about how to solve problems with little or no work. If the therapist is no better qualified than the patient to direct this relevant preparation, the patient may quickly be lost to treatment or a successful outcome may become impossible. It is not enough to assess the personality or to study other characteristics of potential patients in an attempt to predict who will be an early terminator or a dropout if the variables to be used in therapy are not likely to be relevant to producing behavior change. For example, to say that lower-class, less well-educated, less anxious, and less self-critical patients will quit and that those who score higher on these variables are more likely to remain may be an accurate *ad hoc description* for a nebulous therapy in general, but it ignores crucial pressure points which could produce change. A central aim of this book is to show how to improve the methods of psychotherapy, not how to choose those who will respond to severely limited conventional methods.

Quitting therapy prematurely or staying in it should devolve upon the same choice of variables that provides for the behavior-change process itself. The effectiveness of these variables in predicting any such outcome would appear to hinge initially on the capacity of the therapist to work with the patient on the relevant dimensions of the behavior change as soon as possible after the start of therapy. Specifically, this is done by teaching the patient the control and direction he will need if he is to break with his self-defeating behavior and to perform the necessary effective behavior. The sooner this effort begins, the more effective the therapy should be in producing desired results.

From the host of variables available, the therapist should select those which will accentuate the behavior-change effort and work most efficiently for the patient. These variables, already described as response-centered, have been discussed in the previous chapters on learning, behavior change, and cybernetics. If the therapist is continually mindful of the response potential of the patient, he can move most effectively toward desired behavior change. The following schema illustrates the behavior-change operation.

In Figure 1, the behavior-change effort begins at O and moves toward effective problem solving through a stepwise progression. Therapy could start any place along the line OP, but would risk activating more undesired behavior than necessary. The more efficient and effective the therapy, the more nearly vertical the line will be (line OB is more efficient than line OA). Effectiveness is seen as an orthogonal line to prob-

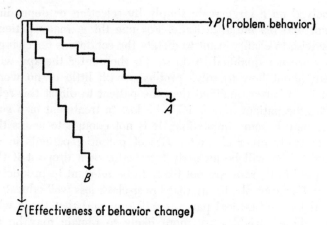

Figure 1.   Sketch for determining effectiveness of behavior change.

lem behavior. The moment therapy begins, rather than etiology, provides the 0 (zero) point. This avoids an activation of any more unwanted behavior than is absolutely necessary to define the problem. Problem solving is defined as reversing the unwanted, self-defeating behavior.

There are many ways to follow this model of behavior therapy. For example, in operant conditioning the very first problem-solving steps may be set up in advance and reinforced immediately; later there may be a changeover to a periodic reinforcement schedule. During this process the unwanted behavior is screened out, so that when the desired behavior occurs or is evoked, it is more accessible to reinforcement. The undesired behavior is never studied for its own sake, but instead is prevented from occurring, if possible, so that the desired behavior can immediately be reinforced.

This model would represent any therapy that focuses on the present behavioral description of the patient as its starting point. Wolpe might focus on the patient's unwanted behavior more in terms of a hierarchical description of anxiety-ridden situations than an operant-conditioning therapist would, but Wolpe would focus on current problems. One need not describe all the patient's pathology in following the above model. The point is that the behavior therapist is intent upon teaching effective responses to the patient, not in reviewing in therapy the full extent of the disturbance.

As line *OB* in this model indicates, there would still be some movement in the unwanted direction, since problems beyond the presenting complaint will almost inevitably come up. Also, as the organism learns to discriminate between wanted and unwanted behavior, there will be some juxtaposition of these two directions of choices. For example, the individual who is overcoming a phobia or a drinking habit may make hesitant movements toward a fear response or a drink before he realizes it; then he stops and finally performs the discriminating behavior.

Implicit in this model is a redefinition of self-defeating processes. Concepts of anxiety, dissociation, defenses, and complexes become secondary in such therapy. Instead of attempting to apply clinical classifications, the therapist tries to move the patient in the direction of the desired response as surely and swiftly as his knowledge and skill will allow. His task is not to decide what is wrong in terms of disease or hidden meanings, but always to search for ways to teach the new response. It is where the patient is headed, not where he has been, which is the primary objective.

Another version of this model is shown in Figure 2, where the emphasis is almost entirely on the pathology rather than on the new behavior, which is not taught specifically, but is expected to develop somewhat spontaneously. In this conventional model, the depth therapist works between existing, observable, or reported undesired behavior (right side of this model) and past instances of adverse experiences that are presumed to account for the patient's current condition. Problem A in the present "requires" an exploration of the alleged cause, A' in the past; and by working through B and B', and so on, the patient is presumably helped to more effective behavior. Thus the direction of the therapy is sideways, between A and A' and B and B', not directly toward E (effectiveness).

The disadvantage in this model is that, as this effort is expended in conventional therapy, the effective behavior that would act as an antidote to the unwanted behavior usually comes about not by design and specific effort but under conditions of much lower probability.

The conventional depth model for psychotherapy is a restrictive one, with prescriptions concerning the number and frequency of interviews,

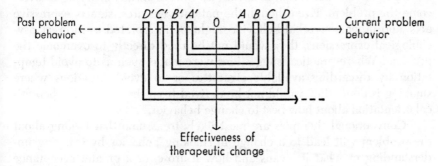

Past problem behavior ← — — — — — — — D' C' B' A' 0 A B C D → Current problem behavior

Effectiveness of therapeutic change

Figure 2.   Sketch of effectiveness of the depth therapy process.

the use of free association, uncovering the past, and analyzing unconscious motivations and symbolism. In contrast, there are relatively few restrictions in behavior therapy, and they concern the handling of the structure or the interrelationship of the variables held responsible for behavior change. The following discussion of various ways of handling the problem of smoking may illustrate this distinction.

An Example of Application

There is very little scientific literature on effective ways to stop smoking. The many pamphlets and articles on the subject are practically never founded on solid research. Suppose a depth therapist were to try to help an inveterate smoker (or a drinker, a socially anxious person, or an underachiever) to overcome his problem. What variables would he select? He would not be likely to choose for specificity and direct control, but would use broad aggregates of variables. They would probably include history of smoking habit; circumstances under which smoking began, such as in emulation of older siblings, friends, or parents; and the meaning the smoking has to the individual, for example, in terms of hostility toward parental ban or overcoming feelings of inadequacy and becoming a "big shot." Many other factors, such as oral gratification, fixation, or displacement, might also be considered important.

Instead of the variables mentioned above, the nondirective therapist might select those which were inherent in the therapeutic relationship, such as unconditionally accepting the patient, showing a sincere desire to help him, making empathetic verbal comments on the patient's statements, making a studied effort not to judge him, or showing a special concern about facilitating the expression of his feelings.

Probably most therapists would proceed on some such verbal, social-interaction, oral-discourse basis. That is, the therapist would use words, not overt, nonverbal behavior, as a major means of trying to overcome the problem. Even though the patient's gestures, stance, expressive acts, and other nonverbal behavior might be interpreted as indirect psychological expressions, they would not be used directly to overcome the problem. Where practical suggestions were made, such as to avoid temptation by discarding available cigarettes or to avoid situations where smoking is done, they would not be derived from the therapist's theoretical orientation about how best to change behavior.

Conventional therapies are most likely to assume that talking about the problem will lead to a change in smoking behavior by bringing understanding of what it means and how it arose, or a greater acceptance of its undesirability, by reducing the psychological "need" for it, or by solving other, presumably more basic problems. The specific routes that the therapy was to take would be left open.

If presumably more important problems were to be the focus, the choice of variables would become primary; some specific residue of experience from the individual's past would be assumed, probably hinging on some aspect of the "oral" phase of development, although the specific interpretation would differ from one therapist to another. When smoking is considered not the *real* problem, but a symptom, and thus not directly accessible to permanent change (or if so, only to be displaced by another symptom), the problem of smoking would be redefined, as a different problem. The therapy would then focus on this redefinition, not on the problem of stopping smoking as initially presented.

But there are other alternatives. The reconditioning approach would begin by pointing up aspects of, and moving directly to, the smoking habit itself. If aversive conditioning were used, there would be an early choice of the noxious (unconditioned) stimulus, which would be paired, in closely regulated temporal proximity, to some aspect of the smoking habit, such as unpleasant inhalation.

The use of conditioning in discouraging smoking is only one of many direct approaches. The therapist may use hypnosis; habits that compete with, and substitute for, smoking can be reinforced; systems of social rewards, supports, and penalties could be mobilized; or broadened positive alternatives could be developed and implemented where desired effects would conflict with those of smoking, for example, athletic prowess, saving money, or skill in playing wind instruments.

Care should be taken not to enhance the smoking habit. What the therapist does may defeat the therapy from the start. The right variables need to be chosen to succeed in the reconditioning approach. The effect of punishment or noxious stimulation, for example, depends upon the total stream of stimuli or activity and upon how the noxious condition fits the whole situation (Church, 1963; Solomon, 1964). One of the outstanding advantages of a reconditioning approach is that whether or not it is going to be successful should become apparent quickly.

In choosing an unpleasant stimulus, should a taste or olfactory stimulus be paired against the tactile, taste, and olfactory sensations of smoking? Should the unconditioned stimulus complex be matched for sensory modality against the conditioned stimulus complex for best behavior-change results? Or will any well-controlled noxious stimulus be equally effective? Consider, for example, the choice between sound and light. There are few data on the effectiveness of cross-stimulus conditioning, though it may be an important problem in behavior-change efforts. If sound were selected as a noxious stimulus, new problems could arise. What is the optimal number of presentations of such a stimulus needed to effect behavior change in a habit like smoking? Should the noxious and unconditioned stimulus be presented in a series of bursts or for longer periods of time? Is the "rise time" in a stimulus of a given intensity of some importance in avoiding results that are harmful but effective? Would still other stimuli have a more permanent effect?

As the field of behavior-change therapy increases in scope and intensity, it is likely that many challenging and heuristic problems will present themselves. Behavior-change efforts offer a chance to break new ground in a more fundamental, far broader sense than is possible in the ordinary limited clincial situations.

Criticisms of this approach imply the variables held important by other therapists. For example, the objection that the reconditioning approach might make the patient worse implies not only the risk of exacerbating symptoms but also the possible disruption of the total behavior economy. In the case of smoking, it might be considered that smoking fulfills a deep-seated need and that the abrupt denial of this source of vital gratification might result in other, perhaps more damaging behavior. Or the entire reconditioning approach may be considered a superficial problem, not worthy of clinical time and effort.

Thus the choice of variables is markedly different in the different therapeutic approaches. The manner in which the variables are put into operation in the quest for problem solutions is also strikingly different. In the structured behavior-change approach, therapy moves as directly as skill and knowledge will allow.

Sundberg and Tyler (1962), in their comprehensive and well-integrated book on clinical psychology, indicate some of the other conditions or variables emphasized by various therapy theorists: strengthening the patient's motivation; catharsis; encouraging the patient's potential for growth and releasing his powers; changing the patient's habits; changing the patient's way of feeling and thinking (loosely called the "cognitive structure"); increasing the patient's self-knowledge; and improving the patient's interpersonal relations.

But are these techniques and conditions really not a mixture of variables, theories about origins, identification of desirable outcomes, and administrative concerns? Such practices as Sundberg and Tyler mention can be useful at times to almost any therapist and would seem to refer to other, more fundamental concepts. A successful reconditioning approach which set about to accomplish or utilize them for a stated purpose could do so in the same degree as any other form of therapy.

How does the therapist who is careful, selective, and purposeful in his choice of variables actually identify a cathartic episode? How does he know when the patient's potential for growth is being released? In learning-centered and response-centered therapy, the therapist has many indicators that he can use to choose variables, measure outcome, and identify processes most effective in accomplishing the desired goals.

The more specific the pursuit of goals, the more successful the outcome of a behavior-change effort seems likely to be. Fear-ridden, failing, badly structured, or badly organized behavior is to be replaced with problem-solving behavior that is capable of coping with environmental demands and achieving the desired changes.

Better methods of teaching control will probably always be sought in behavior-change therapy. A behavioral approach does not seek simply to eliminate the unwanted behavior but to restructure the important variables to allow for greater control. The greater the degree of control that can be developed for goal achievement, the greater will be the personal, social, attitudinal, and other creative rewards to the individual. The likelihood of obtaining such benefits would seem to be greatly enhanced by the initial selection of proper specific variables for study and manipulation.

The broad considerations of therapeutic changes and goals, described by Bergin (1963), Murray (1963), Truax (1963), and Shoben (1963), can be encompassed within the province of behavior change and psychotherapy as envisaged here.

Behavior Change and Basic Behavioral Science

Another potentially productive outcome of a behavior-change position is a ready relationship to basic behavioral research. In the pursuit of new knowledge, basic science, in behavioral as well as in other sciences, proceeds by developing and testing hypotheses without regard to immediate practical consequences. But the ways in which a problem is generated and studied constitute an issue separate from applications. As understanding of scientific phenomena increases, more fundamental ways arise to test theory and to pose questions. "What will happen when. . . ?" is a basic query. Any practical question should first be considered in the light of basic knowledge, but once the question is properly posed, the origin of the question becomes unimportant. Newton's understanding of what later became the law of gravitation arose from an exceedingly modest, perhaps unsophisticated, question that had little theoretical sweep. Archimedes' "Eureka" experience and Poincaré's solution, while asleep, of a mathematical problem are similar examples.

Basic research and theory development have not usually come from the clinic, although they can and hopefully will. As clinical practice becomes more solidly rooted in basic behavioral science knowledge, there will be greater opportunity for fundamental questions to be derived from the clinic, especially when the clinician is able to translate his problems into researchable variables. Such a translation has, of course, been tried before—as in Dollard and Miller's efforts to put psychoanalytic concepts into learning-theory terms—but not as systematically, precisely, and clearly as is possible today.

In effecting behavior change, the experimentally minded clinician should always consider new parameters or variables. As he actively creates and utilizes a variety of behavior-change acts, he is more likely to contribute to fundamental scientific knowledge, rather than being only a broker or consumer of fundamental knowledge.

The clinician can make another major contribution to basic behavioral science knowledge because of his special stake in sustained behavior changes. Not much is known about the parameters of maintaining change. In the laboratory, studies of learning phenomena have so far been typically short-range to fit experimental resources and interests. But the human-behavior changer can broaden the basic scientist's scope by his interest in the conditions of sustained change, an inviting, basic—and little understood—phenomenon today.

Change has to be maintained if therapy is to be fully effective. But the techniques of maintaining change are not yet known, except for certain roughly identifiable schedules of reinforcement. In exporting behavior-change methods from the clinic or laboratory to community living, should the therapist search for variables in the home or community that seem to match those identified in the artificial laboratory or clinical environment, or should he fashion the variables available in the outside world in the manner of successful laboratory or clinical examples? In either case, what rules or procedures for exporting change are available by which to make appropriate decisions and take relevant action? And how can the long-term effectiveness of change efforts best be judged?

As discussed in Chapter 5, the problems that are related to generalizing or exporting behavior change into wider terrain have just begun to be faced because concrete results are only now beginning to be demonstrated. Given some rewarding examples of behavior change, how can the components of change be identified so that systematic can be differentiated from random change? These and other intriguing questions can be posed which relate basic knowledge of behavioral science to more limited, but heuristic clinical evidence of change.

Freedom—or Constriction—through Structure?

Behavior change through such direct and specific means as conditioning, programing, and restructuring the environment has been said to have a possibly deleterious influence on creativity and resourcefulness. Experience to date, however, suggests that students not only may learn subject matter better in programed instruction but also may launch out into more learning on their own, adapt the learning to new tasks, and show other forms of initiative (Anderson, 1962; Ferster & DeMyer, 1961; Goldiamond, 1964a; Goldiamond, 1964c; Komoski, 1963).

The therapist should be alert to side effects and unwanted behavior alteration from any source, though this topic has not received systematic attention in a psychotherapeutic context. Although more research is needed in this area, its absence may be due to the lack of untoward results as well as to the lack of interest in public examination.

Another criticism of highly specific behavior-change therapy is that too much formalization or overorganization may in itself deter growth. However, even redundancy may serve a useful purpose in complex systems (Pierce, 1964). If the complexity of the human organism is compared with that of sophisticated computers, the importance becomes apparent of having part systems overlap and capable of taking over functions when there is a failure anywhere in the system. On the other hand, if efficiency is overformalized, the generality of the system with regard to broad objectives may be constricted. A system could, in principle, become too efficient in a limited way and be disrupted by a breakdown of an independent element not compensated for in another part of the system.

At present, there appears to be no great danger of overformalization, especially where unwanted behavior needs to be overcome. The problem of self-defeating behavior can logically even be considered a special case of overcontrol; that is, some redundant elements are so prepotent that they dominate the system and preclude change. In fact, pathology can be defined precisely in these terms: the overcontrol of the whole system, or a large part of it, by some part system, where the latter acts in ways prejudicial to the larger system. In this sense overformalization could, indeed, push efficiency to the point where it would preclude resourcefulness and thereby act as an influence toward pathology.

One way to overcome the problem of overformalization is to recognize the fact that it is not some ideal state of "ultrastability" (Ashby, 1958) that is being sought but, rather, control of the system in a way that facilitates learning to achieve predetermined goals. In cybernetic terms, what is being sought is the development of "loops" that have an ever-increasing orbital possibility (Pask, 1961).

Beer (1956; 1958; 1960) has discussed the problem of overformalization with an example using industry as the system. Industry strives to maintain integrity and identity in the midst of environmental flux. The organism behaves similarly in the presence of flow, and the behavior-change process can be characterized in a like way as attempting to maintain control and stability despite flux. In behavior change there is no single optimal growth index; the goal is not a static, wholly stable, nonredundant condition.

The student of cybernetics does not fear automation or the domination of men by machinery. Nor is cybernation or programing likely to replace the therapist. Such fears depreciate man. Systemically oriented thinking can elevate concepts of man, emphasizing his capacity to act as a self-organizing system and to free himself from a robotlike role in industry and in society. The parallel with psychotherapy and behavior change, following Beer and Pask, is striking; the conventional therapist is usually one who follows a set of procedures automatically, between narrow lines representing mostly mystique, which dooms the therapist and the patient to enacting roles that vaguely grope toward indeterminate goals. It is this concept which violates the concept of man as the master of his environment.

To enhance man's mastery of himself and his environment, programed instruction directed specifically to this purpose should be maximized. The units of discrimination, or the bases for decision, can be made larger, and more data can be processed in the decisions. Although Skinnerian programing does not preclude this larger step, programers tend, for the sake of convenience, to narrow the concepts of programing to minutia.

Cybernetic control and programing are ways to free the human organism from much of its susceptibility to disruption and defeat and to make possible higher levels of performance, by instituting control devices that will enlarge man's capacity to deal effectively with his environment. This can come about by erecting models which exhibit more generality and expansiveness and which emphasize the organism as a growing, expanding entity forever in a mutual relationship with its environment, never immobilized for long, and never looking back to past concepts of achievement.

Programing Psychotherapy

Why not, then, program psychotherapy or behavior change? Is this not the next logical step? It can be done through written or oral exchanges with the patient, through experimental situations that need minimal or no verbal exchange, and through many other means (McKee, 1963).

All methods of programing therapy, however, would involve these assumptions:

1. The behavior problems to be overcome exist because the patient has not used or found an effective way to overcome them. Alternatives to ineffective behavior are not difficult to find and to specify.

2. Not only must the alternative, desired behavior be specified, but the individual must move to the desired behavior through successive steps that can be specified.

3. Self-defeating behavior can be replaced by effective behavior through a sequence of steps designed to produce the change. Through these steps the individual can move toward the desired behavior and toward solving his problems.

4. The above-stated measures are to be repeated whenever and wherever needed. Learning to overcome one kind of behavior will apply generally to other behavior, although the patient may need reevaluation to determine whether the plans should be extended.

5. Personality factors are less important than the specifics of the experimental or clinical situation; that is, after the relevant learning variables are identified, personality and motivation have only secondary importance. The important variables are in a well-arranged programed learning situation.

Some programing involves reading, following directions, and otherwise cooperating in the learning situation. If the individual is willing, these procedures if made attractive, can be effective in teaching him. If he is not willing to follow these procedures, the conversational process of teaching is also likely to fail.

In programing using little verbal or oral instruction, little if any interpersonal cooperation or internal impulsion seems necessary. Behavioral change such as that described in relation to smoking might be conducted without verbal interaction between subject (patient) and experimenter or teacher (therapist).

The major problem in using written programed instructional methods lies in ensuring that their results will apply outside the programed instructional situation—the major problem in any psychotherapy.

How would one proceed, then, to write programs involving behavior change or psychotherapy?

In ordinary therapy, usually the beginning point is determined by the patient's ability to name and locate problems. Or perhaps the therapist assists him by pointing up test results or posing the problem which precipitated the referral (for example, "You've been absent from work a lot lately—is that right?"). But how does programed instruction begin, since the beginning is to be a standard situation and one that presumably is common to many patients?

One way to begin would be to have a library of problem statements.

Sources could be items common to personality inventories, items most often rated as "like me," problem behavior from a Q Sort list, or statements taken from protocols of therapy hours (Phillips, 1951; Sheerer, 1949). A collection of complaints commonly presented could thus be a suitable starting point for programing instruction.

Given this collection of items, one could write frames for a book or machine to lead the person through some knowledge areas and behaviors to more successful living. One item might be, "I tend to lose my temper too often." A series of frames discussing this problem and leading the individual to different ways of considering the problem, and various steps toward its solution, might follow in this way:

Loss of temper is better described as "loss of self-control." One may notice this tendency when tired, ill, or highly irritated by another person's behavior. Whatever the reason, one has to develop ways of showing better s——— c———.

self control

People experience "loss of temper or self-control" in more than one type of situation. I tend to lose self-control of temper most commonly in the following ways: (Write in replies)

Given knowledge of a situation in which loss of self-control is common, one can then attempt to foresee such situations and develop means to counteract this tendency. One does not need an "explanation" of the temper loss, only ways and means of ——— the temper.

controlling
counteracting

To prepare in advance for a troublesome situation is the best way to offset a tendency to lose one's temper. One can use humor or delay his external action to someone when he is provoked. If one thinks ahead about his probable reaction, he can often ——— a tendency to react with anger or temper loss.

change

These and similar frames should, of course, be tested empirically for usefulness, and a great variety of changes in them could be made. As with any program writing, much care is needed in writing the frames, developing the sequences, and determining the proper amount of repetition. Concepts, behavioral acts, and prescriptions, not factual knowledge, could be taught in the same way that facts would be taught in the programed teaching of history, science, or a foreign language.

Information desirable to produce behavior change could also be programed, beginning with topics derived from any suitable list of symptoms or problems. Programs of this type are currently being tried in such diverse areas as study habits, marriage counseling, and social behavior skills.

If a library of topics for which programs existed were available, the prospective patient could be introduced to the library, asked to select those topics which were his major concerns, and begin to learn from these programs. He would thus select his own therapy, beginning with his strongest concerns, and proceed from there.

The orientation of such a library would differ according to the population served. Thus the library in a school setting would be slanted differently from the one in an outpatient mental health center or a child-guidance clinic. There might be considerable overlap in the range of topics, however.

In a broader context, programing might also be directed toward the treatment of general mental health, rather than toward specific complaints or problems. For example, mental health information could be provided through programed frames in much the same way that instruction is often given in regard to physical hygiene measures, for preventive purposes. Here, it would be assumed that the individual patient's life lacks structure in specific ways, and instruction would be designed to help him firm up effective habits of living. Such instruction could act therapeutically by teaching him better habits of behavior, regardless of his specific complaints; the results could be objectively evaluated; and programs could be modified to be made as effective as possible.

A few frames of a program for teaching good living habits (empirically determined) might read as follows:

An emotional problem or a problem in handling a situation arises because the person lacks the desired behavior at a particular time. To handle a situation better, one must determine what is needed and act in the d_____ w_____ in that situation.   desired way

---

Emotionally disturbed people do not appear to regulate small daily matters very efficiently, or as they would like. For example, they may not do what they want to do about jobs, daily reponsibilities, or meeting deadlines or appointments. This failure to r_____ one's daily life leads to confusion, piling up of one's commitments, and personal dissatisfaction and emotional problems.

regulate

A very simple way of regulating your daily life is to make an hour-by-hour schedule of specific activities that are most important and can be done. This kind of r_____ makes you decide what is most important to get done and makes you see how much you can reasonably expect of yourself.

regulation

You should also keep a record of how well you have followed your daily schedule. This schedule may have to be adjusted to make it more realistic, particularly if you tend to schedule too much or too little or if some important things are left out. This plan allows you to regulate your life better and to get the most important things done most efficiently. The use of a d_____ s_____ serves not only as a planning guide but also as a way of determining your progress and success.

daily schedule

After a few days' or a few weeks' experience with a d_____ s_____, you can usually judge with considerable accuracy your strengths and weaknesses and decide where more p_____ and r_____ are needed.

planning
regulation

A "branching" technique may be useful in getting the patient to write out his schedule and, further, set down the extent to which he has kept to it.

One criticism of this "answer blank" type of program is that it is overly simplified and may not pertain to the bigger problems of daily life. The single-response answer form is by no means essential—it merely illustrates how programing therapy may be initially attempted. More complex forms of programing will suggest themselves to therapists taking an interest in this activity.

Techniques other than single answers may include a "comparison" method, in which the respondent (patient) compares his written answers to the programed answers in a variety of relevant problem situations, or a "branching" technique, in which the patient selects the best answer, from among several alternatives, to a problem which he has already identified as his own. He could in this way gain instruction on the value of his choice compared with other choices.

After a patient has worked with a program, he may have an opportunity to see a therapist in person. Such a meeting would be valuable because the patient's progress up to a given point could be reinforced, and there could be some give and take between therapist and patient on factors or problems not programed.

The content of many interpersonal therapy hours might well prove to follow roughly a kind of branching procedure, where first one and then another alternative is set up and examined in regard to a given problem and a particular person. The fact that this procedure can be more systematically explored through written programs is an intriguing prospect.

The content of these programs illustrates the theme of this book concerning development of effective behavior-change methods. This material emphasizes the importance of order and control applied in daily living. Scheduling is important in communicating to the patient the relevance of control in simple, daily matters. In a sense, this is not actually dealing with "pathology" but with teaching the individual how to discriminate between acting impulsively and setting out to achieve goals. Thus, he learns from his own "cumulative record" about the specific effectiveness and deficiencies of his daily acts.

Still another way to apply a programed method to accomplish behavior change is through oral instruction or persuasion.

In the method of oral instruction, the sequence of items to be conveyed to the patient could be recorded on tape. The previously described written programs might be taped and played to the patient, who would then write his answer. His answer could trip the machine and move the tape to the next frame, and so on through dozens or hundreds of frames, or his answers could be recorded on a parallel band on the same tape that recorded the correct answers. A master recording could score the results or could feed back alternative (better) answers to the patient.

To adapt the approach of Philpott and Boyer (1964), the patient would hear, through earphones, a "message" on a given problem. The message could be either prepared in the manner previously described or specifically based on an interview with the patient and tailored to apply to the particular patient's problems. The value of a repetitive program presented orally through earphones would be that the message would have no auditory competition for the subject's attention and would profit from the summation of stimuli. Of course, if the patient did not have to respond orally or write down a response, the method would not be fully programed. However, it would be possible and perhaps desirable to have the patient reply during "blank spaces" in the tape, following the format suggested for various written instructional methods applicable to psychotherapy.

A number of programed or programable methods might prove suitable in getting the person to respond in a way different from his undesired behavior. The behavior change effort could be kept very simple, or it could be wired up in a sophisticated intercommunication system to obtain, record, and reply to the responses of a group of people. Two-way or multiple-channel communication systems are already in use for classes in modern language instruction.

Criticisms of programed methods arise, it would appear, largely from the confusion between means and goals. However, the means are essentially identical to those of any efficient teaching methods, and the most effective human teacher and the most effective mechanical program should use the same procedures. Even the warmth and humanity needed to encourage students and clients can be programed. Whether the physical presence of another human being is a vital part of an effective teaching process in producing desired behavior change efficiently may be a moot issue, but what evidence there is does not substantiate the theory that there are significant advantages in having another person present. The burden of proof would seem to fall at this point on the side of demonstrating the desirability of the teacher's or therapist's presence—considering that scarcity and costliness often make such presence impossible in conventional ways if social needs are to be met. At the very least, the advantages of the teacher's presence should be better pinpointed and then efficiently implemented.

The problem of "pathology" can be redefined in terms of the person who, in given, definable situations, behaves in ways that block achievement of his most desired goals. It is usually irrelevant to determine how unwanted and undesirable behavior came to be. Such behavior is maintained because no effective counteractive measures have been put into effect. If relevant counteractive measures can be applied through verbal or nonverbal media, behavior can be changed and problems overcome. In principle, it seems possible to program most of what is now included under the rubric of "psychotherapy," and far more of behavior change than is reached by present psychotherapeutic efforts. Further aspects of programed therapy through verbal or printed means will be discussed in Chapter 9 on "Writing Therapy."

7 Recent Systematic Follow-up Studies

In the preceding chapters some short-term efforts have been described which have yielded very promising, though not definitive, results. Many programs in short-term therapy still lack a purposeful selection of variables in advance of the therapy. Even fewer have measured behavior before and after treatment, and most have omitted control (or contrasting therapy) groups.

In this chapter, four short-term therapy and behavior-change studies will be reported that were carefully designed specifically to explore the effectiveness of brief treatment. Pre- and post-therapy measurements have been used, as well as control cases or contrasting therapies. Despite deficiencies, these studies are outstanding in the literature.[1]

Study 1: A Comparison of Structured and Unstructured Therapies

The Batrawi (1964) study began when high school-age students applying for psychological help were divided into two groups. The first group received therapy which approximated the Rogerian position, a relatively permissive, reflective type of therapy, with no reference to assessment or to the development of a specific plan for correcting any problems that might have been identified.

[1] If study 4 has not yet been published, it will be shortly.

From a theoretical vantage point, this permissive or unstructured group was treated in terms of O variables (see the discussion of O in previous chapters); that is, internal, covert, cognitive variables were held to be the vital ones for any change. Any overt behavioral change was regarded as a fortunate, but unsolicited, by-product.

The treatment of the contrasting group derived from a behaviorally oriented theory and emphasized the R, or response, variables. That is, the conduct of the therapy hour stressed plans and daily schedules related to personal and social problems and to studying. Each student kept a log of daily experiences, in order to define and describe daily problems and to provide examples of progress.

At each step in therapy the therapist used three highly specific and pointed procedures: first, for *defining the problems* (such as where, when, how, and under what general circumstances each problem was found to occur); second, for *acting on problems* (such as what the patient did or did not do, how he might have acted differently, and what others did or said); and third, for *evaluating the outcomes from action* (such as how the patient handled present situations differently from the way he handled past ones, whether he acted in ways suitable to problem solving, and whether further analysis was needed of the conditions under which the problem or distress was encountered).

Batrawi (1964, p. 11) states the problem for research as follows:

> It is felt that the problems of the high school adolescent are, in essence, those resulting from his inability to handle or to deal with environmental conditions (home, school, etc.). This inability or inefficiency to make proper responses (R) to environmental conditions (S) is not necessarily a function of an internal disorder (O). An adolescent may display inability to concentrate on his school work not because of guilt feelings or anxiety, but simply because he has not learned how to concentrate. In other words, disorders in (R) may not have central representation (cognitive or affective).

A total of 52 cases were studied; of the total, 26 were randomly assigned to the permissive (or O-centered) procedure, and 26 to the R-centered procedure. Twenty in each group were males, and six were females. The age range was from 16 to 19 years, and all were high school juniors or seniors. All cases were selected on the basis of emotional, social, and academic problems, labeled by the clients themselves, by the parents, and by school authorities. The study excluded any students with known organic or brain damage, physical deficiencies or abnormalities, or mental retardation.

A battery of pre- and post-therapy tests was administered. Although other tests were administered, major attention was given to the Otis Self-Administering Intelligence Test, the Iowa Tests of Educational Development, the Edwards Personal Preference Schedule, and the Minnesota Counseling Inventory, plus grade changes. Tests of homogeneity applied to the Otis intelligence test before therapy showed no difference in the mean IQ or in the dispersion of scores between the groups, nor did the groups differ according to the Iowa Tests of Educational Development pre-therapy means and standard deviations, the grade-average Quality Point Index (QPI), or the average correlation between self and ideal Q Sort on the Bulter-Haigh 80-Item Q-Sort.

Each group had a total of 10 interviews, limited by the length of the semester and the termination of the academic year (a condition known and accepted in advance by the patients); the length of the interviews ranged from 45 to 60 minutes.

To measure the extent to which each type of therapy was faithful to its purpose, excerpts from both the "permissive" and the "structured" interviews were recorded at random and later given to judges. Thus, in Batrawi's study, validating steps were taken to ensure that the study dealt with contrasting therapy procedures, a feature missing in most studies of contrasting therapies.

At the end of the study, the Iowa Tests of Educational Development showed a significant increase in the highly structured, or response-centered, therapy group over the O-centered group. The after-therapy differences reached the level of $p = .01$, in favor of the R-centered group. Grades for the response-centered group also showed a reliable gain at the .05 probability level. Before therapy both groups earned QPI means of about 1.35 (a C— average); after therapy, the QIP of the response-centered group rose to between a C+ and a B level (QPI mean of 2.90), while that of the O-centered group rose only to a C level (2.1 QPI mean). In both groups the variability about these means remained similar (.23 QPI points).

Seven of the fifteen variables on the Edwards P. P. S. showed significant differences. The p values for differences in Achievement, Order, and Endurance were at the .02 level or better, in favor of the response-centered group. As expected, movement in scores favoring the O-centered group appeared on the scales dealing with Affiliation and Intraception, with differences in favor of the O-centered therapy group significant at the .10 and .01 levels, respectively.

Thus, the method of handling the cases in each population receiving therapy had its effects: the response-centered population moved reliably further in the direction of more orderly and achievement-centered behavior, and the O-centered group changed toward greater introspection and affiliation.

This finding may be significant for all therapeutic persuasions. All therapists perhaps teach their patients through what they (the therapists) *do* in the very process of therapy, not just through their stated goals. Although therapist A may teach A values well, therapist B may perform as well for B values, and so on; each may leave large gaps in the spectrum of personality and behavior change. If so, the therapist must begin not only to specify more objective goals for therapy but also to seek *rapprochement* among the limited goals or achievements of different therapists—or at least to state and offer the patient the choice among them.

In determining what changes occur in therapy, personality tests like the Edwards P.P.S. may not measure behavior out of therapy but only subjective effects of the therapeutic process. Students' grades and standardized measures of educational achievement provide objective measures which could be studied for relationship to subjective changes.

Also pertinent to this problem are the results of the Butler-Haigh 80-Item Q-Sort, which measured changes in views of self compared with the ideal, as suggested in the Shlien, Mosak, and, Dreikurs study (1962). These results were essentially negative in the Q Sort portion of the Batrawi study. For the O-centered group, there was only slightly greater congruence between self and ideal sorts after therapy, compared with results for the response-centered cases (r was .52 for the response-centered case and .63 for the permissively handled cases, or a difference significant at the .10 to .15 level). For each therapy population, no other self and ideal correlations showed any reliable movement toward congruence after therapy, as indicated in Table 1.

Table 1   Self and Ideal* Correlations before and after Therapy, for High School Student-Patients, in Two Different Psychotherapy Regimens (Batrawi, 1964, p. 67)

Constructs Correlated	Psychotherapy Approaches		
	R-oriented	O-oriented	Differences
S_1–I_1	.51	.49	NS
S_1–I_2	.42	.47	NS
S_2–I_2	.49	.46	NS
I_1–I_2	.61	.59	NS
S_2–I_2	.52	.63	.10–.15
S_2–I_1	.41	.45	NS

* S_1 denotes self before therapy; S_2 denotes self after therapy; I_1 denotes ideal before therapy; I_2 denotes ideal after therapy.

The Batrawi Q Sort results differed from those reported by Shlien et al. (1962) and by Rogers and Dymond (1954), although they did corroborate the findings of Phillips, Test, and Adams (1964), which showed no consistent self-ideal congruence movement in a comparison of before- and after-therapy measures. Batrawi (1964, p. 69) concluded: "The differential effects of the two therapy techniques on the response aspects of behavior were highly convincing that the response-oriented technique was more effective [than the O-centered technique]. . . ."

Batrawi also suggests that the Intraceptive change for the O-centered therapy group on the Edwards P.P.S. connotes that this group had "practiced" introspection probably as a result of the therapy influences and that the affiliation need appeared to have increased as a function of the posture of "unconditional positive regard and acceptance" by the therapist. Thus the permissive, reflective therapy approach may very well unwittingly have involved "manipulation" of the patient's verbal behavior, at least.

This impact of nondirective therapy upon the client's verbal behavior has also been observed by Eysenck (1961), if only or primarily on a semantic level, perhaps in the absence of more active behavior change. In Batrawi's study, there was only a very slight overt change in the permissively treated group. However, even the expected cognitive changes measured by the Q Sorts were not at a significant level, so that the very type of change most anticipated from the permissive approach did not develop here.

On the other hand, the therapy regimen that sought specific ends through specific means did yield substantial results. For the R-centered group, not only did the manner of perception change, in direct relation to specific goals in therapy (considering the questionnaire as a self-report), but there also were overt changes, in the form of grades and standardized achievement.

In the highly structured R-centered therapy, wherever there was a problem indicated, the therapists worked on specific changes, whether the locus was schoolwork, hurt feelings, lack of social skills, self-abnegation, or whatever.

The actual interview was conducted in what Batrawi called "discussion units." These discussions avoided predominantly emotional topics; searched for behavioral referents, that is, specific things to be communicated; and set up planned steps or sequences for solving problems. These discussions were not centered on the report of feelings or other symbolic (verbal) representations, but on the referents available to describe the unwanted or disturbed behavior.

In the O-centered therapy, the discussion units permitted free discussion of feelings, allowed the patient to elaborate upon his complaints as much as he desired (reflections by the therapist and suggestions of possible origins and meanings), showed no special interest in specific action to overcome any stated problems, and provided an atmosphere of permissive acceptance.

The manipulation of R variables was simple: the behavioral referents were sought, detailed reporting of problems and problem-solving efforts was encouraged, and plans were continually made, altered, and refined to help the patient respond more adequately.

Although Batrawi's data were not developed in a laboratory-type conditioning arrangement, they show fairly prompt and significant changes through verbal therapy. This similarity between the highly structured verbal-oral therapy and conditioning or laboratory methods has its origin in the definition of variables for change and in the methods of encouraging change. Structured oral-verbal therapy seeks to simulate the precision of a conditioning experiment as closely as possible and to produce definite directly observable changes in behavior. Permissive therapy tends to yield more nebulous changes, not so easily measured; it does not clearly identify its variables or manipulate them in specific goal-centered ways even when they are available.

If manipulation of some sort is present in any therapy, which it seems to be, and if it is needed to produce concrete behavior change, why should the therapist hesitate to structure for specified change which the client wishes? In Batrawi's words (1964, p. 73): ". . . if manipulation is a necessity (or if it is more evident in producing change), then why not introduce it openly and define the aspects of behavior which it can economically and more efficiently change?"

This question arises again in the following study reported by Phillips et al. (1964) and by Test (1964).

Study 2: A Comparison of Different Approaches to Structured Short-term Therapy

This study of the effects of structured short-term therapy, which was reported by Test (1964) and by Phillips et al. (1964), is a portion of a longer and continuing study at the George Washington University. The latter will be reported upon further as additional findings become available.

The first study, by Test, involved 39 university students who were referred for help primarily with emotional problems, but with scholastic and social problems also evident. These 39 cases included 22 men and 17 women, between the ages of 18 and 26, who were given a standard battery of tests before and after therapy. The most relevant tests for this report were the Minnesota Multiphasic Personality Inventory (MMPI), the Edwards Personal Preference Schedule, the Butler-Haigh 80-Item Q-Sort, the Otis Self-Administering Intelligence Test, and a personal data sheet. Grades before and after therapy were also studied in a 6-month follow-up.

These patients were assigned to three therapy regimens on a random basis. Patients in a fourth group were offered therapy, but, after their test findings were reviewed with them, they declined the help. Although they were not considered a control group, they are discussed here for general description and comparison of what happens with patients who decline proffered therapy.

The three formal groups included a group therapy population ($N = 11$), an individual therapy population ($N = 8$), and a "writing therapy" population ($N = 12$), or a total of 39, including the eight cases followed up after declining therapy. The importance of including a no-formal-therapy group is suggested by Bergin (1963), who notes that a patient already receives some degree of informal help when he makes a statement or takes any action that suggests his candidacy for therapy.

Each of the three therapy groups had 10 sessions. The 39 cases came from a pool of 53 cases; the greatest attrition was attributable to the no-formal-therapy group (8 of 16 cases were lost to the follow-up evaluation). In the three formal therapy populations, there was an attrition of only six; this was a 16 per cent loss, as compared with attrition as high as 75 per cent reported in the literature (Haddock & Mensh, 1957). Any attrition, however, weakens a study.

The group therapy procedures yielded no reliable changes on the MMPI. For this group, the Edwards P.P.S. showed decreased Deference, the post-therapy score yielding a lower mean, significant at the .05 level; increased Affiliation ($p = .10$); decreased Endurance ($p = .10$); and decreased Aggression ($p = .01$).

Nonparametric statistics (Siegel, 1956) were also used to examine Edwards P.P.S. score changes. Mean score changes were studied, and also any evidence that a large percentage of patients changed in a similar direction, even though the change was not reliable quantitatively. If a change in direction could be found, the therapy could try to increase it to the point where a linear change would be reflected in mean scores. The nonparametric changes on the Edwards P.P.S. were not encouraging; there was downward movement on Intraceptiveness ($p - .11$) and an increase in Heterosexual Need ($p = .11$).

On the group therapy procedure, there was also an increase in grade average (from C— to B—), significant at the .01 level. No changes appeared on the Butler-Haigh 80-Item Q-Sort.

The marked improvement in grades for the group therapy population after 10 group sessions may have stemmed from the fact that grades are prone to be discussed. Moreover, members of the group were often seen continuing the discussion after the formal hour was over, and this probably increased the therapeutic impact. Students seemed more ready and able to help one another during the discussion hour with such problems as grades and study techniques than with social and personal problems.

The eight cases receiving individual therapy also showed improvement. Significant changes on the MMPI were as follows: lower mean scores on the Schizophrenia, Psychasthenia, and Depression scales, significant at the .10, .06, and .05 probability levels, respectively. Nonparametric findings revealed no other movement on the MMPI.

On the Edwards P.P.S., the following changes were recorded for the individual therapy population: Less Aggression ($p = .10$), more Endurance ($p = .15$), less Abasement ($p = .15$), more Dominance ($p = .001$), less Succorance ($p = .15$), and less Autonomy ($p = .10$). These findings, while showing some inconsistencies, suggest that movement took place somewhat in the direction of more cooperative behavior, more persistence in pursuit of goals, and less dependence on others.

No grade changes were associated with the individual therapy procedures, despite the fact that information on study habits was provided.

The largest number of changes, and the most significant ones, were in the third formal therapy group—those involved in writing therapy. In brief, in this method of therapy, the patient kept written accounts of his problems in a notebook bearing his name, which was stored in a locked file between writing sessions. The student came in for his writing session just as he would for an oral interview, but he was not seen by anyone except when he obtained his notebook. After writing for about 45 to 60 minutes, the patient turned in his notebook; he received an answer from the therapist before his next appearance, usually a week later. This method, too, was subject to a 10-session limit; some wrote weekly and some biweekly, according to their respective work schedules.

The MMPI changes for the writing therapy population of 12 cases were: lower mean scores on the Depression, Psychasthenia, Psychopathic Deviate, Schizophrenia, and Social Introversion scales, at p values of .05 or better. In addition, Hypochondriasis and Hypomania mean scores declined somewhat (p .15 and .10, respectively).

The significant changes on the Edwards P.P.S. for this group were a rise on the Heterosexual score ($p = .10$) and a decrease on Abasement ($p = .01$). Although grades did not improve in terms of mean QPI results, there was a shift upward in grades, resulting in a nonparametric p value of .07. Q Sorts changed in the direction of more congruence, as Rogers would describe it, and represented a significant shift in self-ideal r ($p = .04$).

What can be said of the results generally? Each method produced some personality and behavior changes. The results seem sufficiently hopeful to warrant the further systematic study of such short-term therapy methods. It would seem desirable to stretch the capacity for innovation by planning for the use of as many different types of short-term therapy methods as possible, to explore various potential avenues of short-term therapy change that are possible. It may be that any method of short-term treatment that sets out in quest of some specific goal will produce some desired results. If further studies of various short-term methods substantiate this tentative conclusion, not only therapeutic efficiency would be improved, but also the understanding of therapy as a *process.*

But the no-formal-therapy population improved also. Even though there was a 50 per cent attrition in the original group, the eight cases on whom complete data could be collected during subsequent follow-up testing changed in the following respects: MMPI follow-up results for Psychasthenia, Schizophrenia, and Social Introversion showed lowered mean scores at p values of .01, .02, and .02, respectively. In addition, a nonparametric test of the Hysteria scale showed a tendency toward downward movement ($p = .02$).

The Edwards P.P.S. changes for the no-formal-therapy group were higher Orderly scores ($p = 0.5$), higher Autonomy scores ($p = .13$), higher Aggressive scores ($p = .10$), and lower Affiliative scores ($p = .15$). There was no change in grades.

This study again points up the importance of having two sets of control data. The first set should include the attrition cases between the starting and finishing of therapy. Sometimes this group is so large, and the follow-up is therefore based upon so selective a sample of the original group, that any outcomes are suspect. The second set of data should include cases who were available for follow-up but who were not formally treated.

Some comparison between the Batrawi and the Test studies may prove useful. In the Batrawi study, all cases were seen individually; in the Test study, only a small group was seen individually, and the rest received group therapy or writing therapy. This fact may account for the relatively greater gains in grades in the Batrawi study. Changes in the two populations, as far as test scores were concerned, were not the same. The psychometric instruments seem to operate as a broad net, screening out one kind of change and passing another, somewhat haphazardly from the standpoint of the theory and goals of the therapy operation itself. In short, the test and the therapy are not intended to serve each other's purposes since they have different frames of reference. For scientific purposes, they require independence of each other—but not irrelevance.

All the subjects in the Test study considered that the therapy had been beneficial. In the Batrawi study, about 60 per cent of the structured group thought they had received a good deal of help, compared with slightly over half of the permissively handled cases. These figures can be misleading, however. What really needs to be determined is the type of change achieved through a given therapeutic procedure with a specified population. Moving toward this goal, as these two studies do, a closer relationship becomes apparent not only between a response-oriented therapy and effective results but also between the kinds of change to be expected in different therapies.

Another important lesson to be learned from these studies is that more relevant criteria are needed for evaluating behavior outside of therapy. Within therapy, verbal, semantic, and attitude changes reported must be viewed skeptically. Therapies centering on cognitive and emotive changes can perhaps go no further than these internal changes.

In the Batrawi and Test studies, it appears that in the structured therapy groups, changes in attitudes have been paralleled by overt behavioral change outside of therapy, for example, changes in grades and results on standardized achievement tests. And much more demonstrable relationships need to be established between attitude changes in therapy (whether psychometric, Q Sort, verbal content, or therapist rating) and extratherapeutic behavioral changes. Since the patient comes to therapy principally because of his behavior problems or reactions in external situations, such reactions and behavior should be evaluated in the therapeutic results.

Perhaps the ideal change circumstance would require both the presenting problems and the needed change process to be identified in terms of specific variables that could be manipulated according to clear theoretical principles. Also remaining to be demonstrated on a broad scale is whether experimentally induced clinical changes can be sustained and applied to out-of-laboratory situations. This problem will be discussed further in Chapter 10.

To the extent that the behavior changer is seeking specific ends through specific means, the oral (or written) therapeutic exchange seeks to simulate the laboratory. It is useful to check the verbal therapy change model against a laboratory model and to attempt to define the variables and the expected avenues of behavior change in the way envisaged in interaction between laboratory and clinical settings. There are problems in the clinic which at this time may not yield to laboratory-type procedures; this may be due to inadequacies in formulating the problems, in controlling the relevant variables, or in other technological problems. But as verbal change methods in the clinic are fashioned toward closer approximation of laboratory methods, better results may be anticipated through verbal means.

Study 3: Comparison of Short-term and Long-term Therapy

A comparison of short-term, time-limited, and long-term therapy in a college population, over a period of about 5 years, has been recently reported by Muench (1964). One hundred and five patients were involved, 35 in each therapy group. Pretesting and posttesting were done on the Rotter Sentence Completion Test and the Maslow Security-Insecurity Inventory. The tests were scored by clinicians who were not aware of whether the patient's questionnaire responses were pre- or post-therapy.

Short-term therapy was defined as three to seven interviews and not terminated arbitrarily; time-limited therapy had a termination date prearranged by the therapist and lasted from 8 to 19 interviews; and long-term therapy was defined as 20 or more sessions, not terminated arbitrarily. The choice of these particular limits on the number of interviews stemmed from research which suggested the existence of a kind of "failure zone" between the twelfth and twenty-first interviews. Consequently, there was hope that shortening or limiting therapy by the means specified would preclude the development of this precarious period.

On both the Rotter and the Maslow inventories there were significant changes for the short-term and time-limited therapy, but not for the long-term therapy. The two methods of reducing the therapy time resulted in changes at the .001 and .05 levels, respectively, for short-term and time-limited therapy, on the Maslow Security-Insecurity Inventory, and at the .02 and .01 levels, respectively, on the Rotter Sentence Completion Test.

Muench considered the possible effects of the therapist's skill and of greater patient disturbance in the long-term patients. He concluded that these effects were minimal: the distribution of short-term, time-limited, and long-term therapy cases was about equal among the 12 therapists, according to adjudged success of therapy, nor did the pre-therapy status of patients in the three groups differ significantly on the instruments used.

Another provocative finding was that the therapists' judgment of therapeutic change, as measured by a movement scale, showed little congruence with test results as measures of change. Thus, again therapists' judgments do not coincide with independent change measures, just as independent patient and therapist measures of judgments of change showed little correspondence. This finding again raises the question of the therapist's perception of his activities, and his ability (or bias) in judging the patient. The evidence is accumulating to challenge the therapist's capacity to judge movement or assess outcome, in comparison to patients, or to more objective measures—even when objective measures are themselves peripheral to some objectively stated and measurable goals. At least, much more objective and relevant measures of therapeutic outcome need to be developed.

Study 4: A Comparison of Time-limited and Time-unlimited Psychotherapy

In this study, Lorr, Young, Roth, Rhudick, and Goldstein[2] compared the therapeutic effects of time-limited (TL) and time-unlimited (TU) individual psychotherapy. The study involved 60 patients from 16 mental hygiene clinics in 18 weeks of individual psychotherapy. To be accepted for the study each patient was required to be male, less then 50 years old, diagnosed neurotic, without brain injury, and not receiving tranquilizer treatment; none was to have received psychotherapy in the past 6 months. The typical patient was 40 years old, married, employed, and a high school graduate. The patients were randomly assigned to TL or TU treatment.

It was hypothesized that, after 18 weeks of treatment, the time-limited patients would report greater overall improvement than the time-unlimited patients, as well as less severe somatic distress, greater self-acceptance, less anxiety, and a greater reduction of hostility.

It was also hypothesized that the therapists would report the time-limited patients as more improved than the time-unlimited patients, as well as less anxious and hostile, more sociable, more accepting of others, and less severely ill.

All patients were examined three times. The first examination occurred within 10 days of the first treatment interview; the second, within 7 days after the eighteenth week of treatment; and the last, 40 weeks after the first interview. Therapists were to rate their patients after the third session and after the 18th interview. The comparison of pretreatment and posttreatment self-reports showed that TL patients improved

[2] Lorr, senior collaborator on this study, has kindly provided in personal communication this advance review of findings. The study is included here, even though in somewhat tentative form, since it is the most relevant to this chapter of a series of excellently designed and conducted investigations of various aspects of psychotherapy, in which Lorr has been a vital mover.

significantly with respect to Somatic Distress, Tension, Depression, Bewilderment, and Fatigue, but that the TU cases made no improvement on these measures over the 18-week period. Moreover, according to the first results on the 40-week follow-up, the TL patients did not lose these gains.

Patient measures used included a 70-item Adjective Rating Scale, a Somatic Distress Scale, and a Change Inventory. Predictor measures included an Expected Somatic Distress Scale, a Word Fluency Test, and a test of Patient Perception of the Therapist. Data were also collected on the patient's age, marital status, education, employment status, and occupational level.

The therapist measures included a set of Interview Behavior Scales, a Change Inventory, and measures of Problem Severity, Degree of Treatment Success, and Global Improvement.

Preliminary results using analyses of covariance with control on initial or other related measures showed no significant differences between TU and TL cases. Therapists, likewise, saw little difference between the initial and 18-week status of either type of case.

Although the therapists reported slight differences in the two approaches, the patients saw much greater differences in favor of the time-limited approach. There is a question as to whether the therapists' attitude toward time-limited therapy, which tended to be negative, may actually have colored their evaluation of its effectiveness, in spite of the patients' favorable reaction to it.

Although these findings are still tentative, this study again underscores the enormous difficulties in initiating new approaches to psychotherapy. Obviously, the patient rarely has the same commitment to a conventional method of therapy that the therapist has. Consequently, the patient may be better able to judge the effectiveness of a new approach without the risk of being influenced by theoretical considerations that do not concern his problems. Should not the therapist, then, try to be as sensitive as possible to the patient's working environment and to focus his efforts maximally on helping the patient to change his self-defeating interactions with his world as directly and efficiently as possible?

8 Protocols in Time-lapse Form

The Time-lapse Form

Although a full, verbatim protocol of an interview is valuable in illustrating a therapeutic procedure, it tends to be boring and unclear to a nonparticipant; moreover, it does not accurately reproduce the highly personalized setting in which the therapeutic interaction takes place.

Consequently, in order to illustrate more clearly the approach to psychotherapy recommended in this book and to distinguish between it and other forms of therapy that are most popular today, this chapter will present an edited form of interviews which may be termed "time-lapse protocols." These are named and modeled after the time-lapse technique in science photography, which is used to record phenomena that occur very gradually (for example, a flower budding, blossoming, and dying), in separate frames at set intervals (such as every 5 minutes, 5 hours, or 5 days) that can be later presented in a swift, unbroken sequence.

So that the therapeutic process being described in this book can be readily contrasted with alternative forms of therapy, time-lapse protocols from four separate approaches to psychotherapy have been arranged to highlight significant differences. The more routine verbal exchanges in these approaches have been omitted.

Contrasting Approaches: Accuracy of Representation

The authors have both been closely associated with strongly committed exponents of two of the therapeutic approaches presented here—the psychoanalytic and the nondirective. And although the following interpretations will inevitably be considered unrepresentative by some such therapists, they are presented in the belief that they are reasonably accurate interpretations of these approaches. The authors not only have had some training and practice in these forms of treatment but also respect colleagues in these areas who practice as indicated and have spent many hours in discussion with them. However, these colleagues appear to produce their often best results when they depart from such practices, even if only temporarily.

There is no homogeneous body of literature that actually represents the eclectic approach today, since the range in this approach is enormous. Generally, it is a loosely organized approach, offering no consistent set of principles by which to guide the patient in integrating his life and handling his personal problems. The eclectic approach is usually characterized by the absence of consistent, discriminating, step-by-step suggestions to aid the client directly in solving his particular problems. Since it lacks a consistent theoretical bent, its success appears to depend largely on the temperament of the therapist and his own empirical skill with select problems he has encountered before.

A problem which has arisen in reporting protocol material here and which needs special amplification is that the progress of therapy as it will be presented may seem roughly equal in all four approaches. Obviously we do not believe that all are equally effective. Attrition occurs in each method at each stage presented, but especially in the depth and nondirective approaches. Moreover, it should be apparent here how the three alternative approaches tend to progress less efficiently than the structured therapy, for each is diverted into bypaths following each of the patient's statements.

Successful treatment needs to end up at roughly the point toward which it will be portrayed, in this chapter, as heading, whatever the therapeutic approach. But the casualties are great, considering premature terminators and those who are discouraged even from applying by the very nature of most therapy. And there is a prodigious waste in digressions that fail to take clear and direct aim on the problems at hand and their solutions, utilizing the available resources of the patient and his environment.

Of course, there are as many different therapist responses as there are therapists, regardless of "schools." Alternative paragraphs can be inserted by the reader as he guesses at what the patient would be most likely to say next, following each of the therapist's responses. But the therapist in training can and does seem to learn characteristic patterns of talk from his teacher. For example, a depth therapist is generally committed to questioning and interpreting (unpublished study by Wiener). The nondirective therapist attempts chiefly to understand, reflect, clarify, and draw out—indirectly and with constant emphasis on the client's expressions.

The cutting edge of therapy can be much sharper, however, and the approach of the structuring behavior-change therapist portrayed here is consistent with what has already been described in this book and is actually practiced.

Although the style of the therapist may vary, the essence of a therapeutic approach can be fairly accurately portrayed. In fact, each therapist who reads another therapist's protocol is likely to find certain wordings, interpretations, or timing with which he disagrees strongly. Even if the therapist is of his own "school" or is a respected colleague, he is likely to say to himself, with varying intensity, "That's not what—or how—or when—I would have spoken." Because of this distraction of style, and believing that the reader is more interested in content, we have concentrated only on preserving the essence of each approach.

The Choice of Therapies

Why have only depth and nondirective therapists been chosen as representatives of other theories? Basically, because they and the eclectics appear to represent the mainstreams of therapeutic practice today, together with the still narrow stream of structured behavior-change therapy, as described in this book.

The depth approach has many variations and versions. Schisms among the nondirectivists seem to widen also, as Rogers continues to modify his views; some of his students have remained orthodox, while others have changed idiosyncratically. But the theoretical mainstreams still appear to consist of commitments to depth interpretation, to self-cognitive elements within the patient, or to structured, direct problem-solving action.

Which Is the Real Therapist?

The reader who wishes to discover which of the alternative methods described have actually been used with the cases cited and which have been interpolated may wish to know that the cases presented here involve real people, who have presented the problems in the structured therapy as described. Each person also has had previous therapy in one of these alternative processes. Their real names and identifying details have been changed, but their problems and personal situations are taken from clinical files.

Going on Stage

The reader may wonder, in reviewing this protocol material, why therapy should not really proceed as efficiently and with as much impact and interaction as portrayed here. The answer would seem to be that structured behavior-change therapy actually does try to proceed in a manner that closely approximates this presentation. The protocols of structured therapy are crowded with relevant interaction between the therapist and the patient, with relatively few digressions or silences. Effective action by the client in his environment is a natural and inevitable result.

The presentation of protocols orally or in writing may give the therapist the feeling that he is "going on stage" and is being challenged to do his best before an alert and critical audience. He may decline to present his work in critical detail, saying that he was inactive while trying to gauge his client's capacity to accept interpretations or fearful of discouraging or frightening the client. He may also be reluctant to display his mistakes and weaknesses, or he may excuse long digressive periods by saying that problems are so deep and chronic that a sense of timelessness is imperative. Such caution and delay in treatment are defended also with such statements as, "Well, it took him years to develop into what he is, and he can't get over it quickly," and "We can't go too fast; he isn't ready for the next step yet."

In structured behavior-change therapy, the therapist can act more freely. Respecting the client's ability to judge and use the therapist critically, he trains the client, in fact, to do just this; moreover, in using observable behavioral material, the therapist is in little danger unwittingly of spinning a web in which the patient becomes frightened of unknown forces that seem to envelop him and which only a highly skilful therapist, in whom he has great faith, can get him out of.

Moreover, structured therapy allows the therapist to use all his intellectual and informational resources directly and openly in his sessions with his client. If the client disagrees or does not understand, no harm is likely to result. An ideal of give and take is encouraged between teacher and student; they work together, hard in pursuit of solutions that are acceptable and useful to the client.

The prediction is made that the structured therapist will be more willing to "go on stage" than other therapists and will be able to demonstrate more accurately the essence of his process and objective results at any point in the therapeutic procedure.

In short, many therapists operate with extreme conservatism and anxiety. Many feel their way along slowly, worrying about making harmful mistakes. Of course, no therapist should behave recklessly and plunge thoughtlessly into the treatment of any patient's problems. However, the efficient therapist can nearly always offer a definite reasonable plan—or comment—to his client, which can contribute encouragement and evaluation to the patient's progress. In the end, the therapist's efficiency will most likely stem fundamentally from structure and consistency at theoretical and clinical levels.

Case-history Material

Since case histories, test results, and data collecting are not inherent in structured behavior-change therapy, no attempt is made here to represent the varying attitudes of therapists toward history taking, except in situations where such information has a specific and obvious value.

If the therapist suspects brain damage, intellectual deficiency, intellectual brilliance, or job maladroitness, he should, sensibly, test the client on these characteristics. The patient's marital status, family background, and job history also can be useful facts, as previously discussed. But these are peripheral matters in the progression of the therapy as portrayed here; what is needed for change seems to develop naturally during the therapeutic process as described. The depth therapist is likely to spend a considerable amount of time, however, in gathering a case history for interpretation; so is the eclectic therapist, particularly in the clinic where time is a secondary consideration.

Obviously, these protocols omit the prefatory remarks of the therapist about matters like appointments and charges, as well as any statements about his therapeutic approach, what the client should expect, or what is expected of the client. These are vital to the therapist's subsequent interactions with the client, and are discussed elsewhere in this book.

Protocol 1

GENE AND HIS HOMOSEXUAL PROBLEM

Gene
(*Statement A*):

I've got this problem, you see, being homosexual and all that. I'm afraid about it. I go to church and I feel guilty and I can't confess. And I'm nervous all the time. Can you help me get over this nervousness? I'm afraid I'll lose my job and all.

Therapist
(*Depth*):

Tell me about your home and family. What were they like? How did you feel toward your father? And mother? What dreams have you had lately? Do you see how this fear of getting too close to your mother, with her seductive ways, can make you fear women? And fear what your father would do if you loved your mother too much?

Therapist
(*Nondirective*):

You feel very nervous about your homosexuality and don't know what to do about it. I wonder whether this feeling can be clarified. If I catch it correctly, you seem to be saying that you're worried more about being caught, and about your guilt, than of the sex act itself.

Therapist
(*Eclectic*):

Don't worry about homosexual thoughts. Everyone has them some time. And almost everyone has at least one homosexual experience. But try to control it or forget it. You should go out with girls. Keep busy, And try going to church, where you can get a grasp of good principles of living. If you feel too nervous to control the impulse, you can take a tranquilizer I'll give you a prescription for.

Therapist
(*Structured*):

Can we decide, even tentatively, what your problem is and what you want to do about it? As a beginning, do you want to get over being a homosexual, or do you want only to get over your nervousness connected with it? You have this choice, and you must make it sooner or later if you want to get over your nervousness. You may not like the consequences of being homosexual, but you have to accept and suffer the consequences in terms of social dangers and penalties, if you practice it.

Gene
(*Statement B*):

I think I understand myself better, and how I got into the fix I'm in. But I'm still all mixed up and confused. And I can't seem to resist going home with these men I meet at the bar, and then I feel bad about it. What do I do now?

Therapist
(*Depth*):

Perhaps we've not gone deeply enough into this. What have been your recent dreams? What are your associations with your mother? Have you considered what it might be like to pick up a woman? After all, not all women are like your mother, and you aren't punished for having sexual relations with them.

Therapist
(*Nondirective*):

Apparently you had hoped that once you understood yourself better, you would feel better. But now you still go ahead and have homosexual contacts anyhow and feel bad afterward. Perhaps you'll have to consider other ways of acting if you're not to feel bad—or consider why you still feel bad.

Therapist
(*Eclectic*):

Why don't you try harder to go out with girls. And consider talking with your minister about the problem. Meanwhile there's nothing so bad about the homosexuality; at least if you can relax, you need not suffer so much from it. And let's try this new medication for awhile. Or perhaps you should take a vacation or a short rest in the hospital.

Therapist
(*Structured*):

Understanding your problem this way probably only means that you are stating it accurately. But to get over your nervousness, you need to substitute some other kind of action for the kind that gets you into trouble with yourself. You have sexual desires you can satisfy with men or women. We'll work now on how you can meet and get along with women. It's the reasonable thing to do, before you decide against them—or decide that only men appeal to you sexually.

Gene
(*Statement C*):

Well, I've tried to go with women and can't seem to get anywhere. They just don't appeal to me sexually. I never get an erection with them like I do with men. I can be friends with them all right. But there's no good company like at the gay bar.

Therapist
(*Depth*):

That homosexual experience when you were nine, combined with your fear of your sexual feelings toward your mother and of punishment or jealousy by your father, still has a marked effect on you. It's as if you stopped developing before you reached the stage of sex with women. You must learn that these fears belong to the past and that there is nothing wrong with enjoying women today. You need feel no guilt about this; it is all right.

Therapist
(*Nondirective*):

You feel that you've made efforts to go with women but they don't excite you the way men do. And you must wonder whether this is just the way you are, whether somehow you're meant to have sex with men instead of women; yet this does not solve your problem. The question is, where do you go from here?

Therapist
(*Eclectic*):

Not being able to have an erection at times is a very common problem. If you relax and approach it more easily, you can probably help yourself. Sometimes it also helps to have a drink or two beforehand to get over the tension. But you've got to keep trying. Sooner or later you'll probably run across the right girl for you.

Therapist
(*Structured*):

You continue to go to the gay bar for company, and also when you have sexual desires, so of course you continue to get involved and suffer the consequences. And of course it will be hard to get sexual pleasure with women since you never have before, and since you associate sex with men. If you had a sexual past with women, then they would probably be your habit today instead of men. The problem now is to get enough actual experience socially and sexually with women so that you can make a fair comparison and choice. Now, let's consider some places where you can meet girls, and just how to approach them. . . .

Gene
(*Statement D*):

I finally took out this girl that I met at the office party, and when we parked, I made myself put my arm around her and kissed her. I wasn't very good at it. I felt like a jerk. And I took her right home afterward and walked her to the door and said goodnight. Whew! I don't want to go through that again.

Therapist
(*Depth*):

Tell me any dreams you've had since then. Did you feel guilty or anxious about the experience? There again you may be thinking about your mother, or about losing your manhood if you get involved with women. You may be dominated by them or tied down to them. Exactly what were your desires toward her, what did you want to do? And why would you consider it bad?

Therapist
(*Nondirective*):

You did finally get up the courage to take a girl out and make a play for her, and then you got scared and got rid of her soon as you could because you felt awkward and embarrassed about it. And you feel it would be a relief simply to give up now, not to struggle with it anymore. So where do you go from here?

Therapist
(*Eclectic*):

Well, that was a good start. And of course you might not be very good at first. But you've got to keep trying. Of course, she might not be the kind of girl you should kiss. Maybe you'll have to find a different type. Or maybe you should talk about it with her first.

Therapist
(*Structured*):

Well, you put yourself into a situation where you could find a girl and begin to approach her sexually. And it was rough for you, as a first time often is. Now if you will see this through, you can get to the payoff from your efforts, and the pleasure. If you quit prematurely, at this point, you'll be right where you started. You have to keep in mind and continue to work along toward your longer-term goal before making your decision. Your next step will be to practice the kissing, and then go on to the next step.

Authors' Note on Protocol 1

In this time-lapse sequence, from four points of view, it should be clear that, while there may be accuracy, competence, and empathy in each therapist's responses, there is a considerable indirectness and inefficiency for behavior change involved in the depth and nondirective approaches, especially if by contrast the structured approach can move ahead by direct steps. The eclectic approach, like a shotgun blast, may hit its target, but in such an imprecise, inefficient way that it is almost impossible to refine, describe, and improve upon the modes of its effectiveness.

It may be argued by those of other theoretical persuasions that a firmer or more direct approach than theirs would defeat or delay effective therapy, that theirs is the best strategy, and that they operate most effectively by eliciting or developing confidence, insight, empathy, transference, and sense of purpose, first and primarily. But these would be gains centered around activity within the therapy sessions. Instead, the structured behavior-change approach would determine gains by what the patient does to solve his problems outside the therapy interviews.

Thus Gene, at each step in the above progression of his statements, moves toward increasingly effective action taking him toward his goal. This seems much less likely to happen at all, or as directly, in conventional therapies as in structural short-term treatment. The depth therapist's responses insistently beat the drum of interpretation and understanding, as if they were the most important parts of the change process and as if proper action would follow naturally and with a minimum of further therapist intervention and direction. But what of the man who has never learned where and how to pick up women, who has misinformation leading him to believe that homosexuality is constitutional and fixed, or who has never verbalized the dangers of homosexual behavior or the self-defeating nature of much short-term gratification? He *may* arrive at corrected perceptions through depth therapy, but at best haphazardly.

Similarly, the nondirective therapist beats the drum of empathy, implicitly if not explicitly, believing that it will lead to problem solving. Gene would, in this view, naturally choose women once he saw his problem clearly (or perhaps get over his nervousness about continuing with men). But why should the therapist not try directly to teach Gene what the therapist knows about problems and their solution? Presumably the nondirectivist believes in education; at the very least, he tries to teach students the fundamentals of psychology and how to do nondirective therapy. Why should he not also try to teach Gene some facts about how to find women, about homosexuality, and about the formation of habits and ways to achieve long-term goals?

The eclectic therapist, if he is flexible, tries almost anything. His advice, suggestions, and interpretations are not shaped and kept consistent by an underlying viewpoint, however. He seems likely to be neither as successful nor as unsuccessful as the other therapists portrayed. But in any case, he contributes little or nothing to science or to the progress of therapeutic technique. He will always, by definition, be characterized by his borrowings from contemporary theories and their practitioners.

It was tempting to make the structured behavior-change therapist's responses much longer than they are in this protocol. He probably does talk a lot more during therapy than most other therapists, as well as being more active in seeking out and utilizing all available variables for change. He does not hesitate to try to teach. He has a lot to try to teach Gene, and he is interested in Gene's responses primarily as statements of problems—and as indicators of the success of, and desirable directions for, his teaching. He moves as directly as possible toward goals, repeating and hesitating only when necessary because of Gene's activity or inactivity outside of therapy.

Protocol 2

MRS. LARSEN AND HER MARITAL PROBLEM

Mrs. Larsen
(*Statement A*):

Dr. Hartford said I should talk to you while I'm off today from the hospital. He said you'd be able to help me with my condition. He says there's nothing the matter with me physically. But I just can't get going. I feel terrible all the time. I've got these terrible headaches and stomachaches and I'm nervous. What's going to happen to me? (*Cries*) Can you help me?

Therapist (*Depth*):	I hope I can. I will be able to best if you can have confidence in me and cooperate completely with this treatment. I will need to know all about you and especially when you get your headaches and stomachaches. They often stand for things, you know. They say things to us like, "You give me a pain." For the time being you'd better keep on taking the medicines Dr. Hartford has given you, but we'll ask him to cut down gradually. Now, tell me just how you feel, all your thoughts, don't hold anything back.
Therapist (*Nondirective*):	Your're feeling terrible, and discouraged, and wonder whether there's any help for you at all. Still, you hope. And we will try to work things out here together. But the effort and solutions must come from you, and I can only help you to find them within yourself. Perhaps you have some ideas about how and when these terrible feelings come on?
Therapist (*Eclectic*):	You know, nerves often produce physical symptoms, when there's really nothing the matter with you. But nothing much happens to you. You can't die of them, you know. But tell me about your family. And when you get these symptoms. Meanwhile try to sit back in the chair and relax.
Therapist (*Structured*):	Dr. Hartford can find nothing wrong with you physically. We therefore believe that your symptoms, real as they are to you, come from problems in your life that you haven't been able to solve or control. I think you can best learn to handle these problems by figuring them out in your day-to-day life, so I'm suggesting to Dr. Hartford that he discharge you and reduce or eliminate your medicine. Then we'll try to find out what your problems are and what you can do about them as quickly as possible. Now, can we run through a typical day in your life which shows how your problems come up?

Mrs. Larsen (*Statement B*):	I can't stand it when my husband orders me around. He never really hits me or anything like that, but he's just terrible the way he raves and rants. And I can't ever please him. Nothing does, by me or the kids. I just can't do anything about it. It makes me feel terrible all the time.
Therapist (*Depth*):	Apparently there's a great deal of hostility between you and your husband, and you can't stand it, so you develop symptoms and get sick. Now, why shouldn't you get angry when he treats you badly? Why shouldn't you even hate him at times? But tell me also, is this the way you felt toward your father?
Therapist (*Nondirective*):	You can't stand to be ordered around. And you feel pushed around and unappreciated no matter what you do. So you end up feeling bad, and getting sick, is that it?
Therapist (*Eclectic*):	Your husband probably doesn't mean anything by it. He's good to you otherwise, isn't he? Maybe he really loves you, but doesn't know how to show it. You'll have to try to pull yourself together. Have you tried this new drug yet?
Therapist (*Structured*):	Your husband orders you around and acts unreasonable, and you feel terrible because of the way he is. But if that's the way he is, and he's not about to act differently just because you want him to, then you have to look to yourself to change, to learn what you can do differently so that you don't end up feeling so terrible. Can you sometimes handle him in a way that brings him around?
Mrs. Larsen (*Statement C*):	Well, things are better with my husband now. At least he doesn't raise such a fuss, and I go about my business. But it's just as bad as ever with the kids. I just don't seem to be able to get over worrying about them when they're out of my sight. With the

weather nice now they go outside, and I worry all the time about what's happening to them. Terrible things, like falling down stairs or out of trees, or getting hit by a car. . . . I've got to go out looking for them every 15 minutes, and I worry all the time in between.

Therapist
(*Depth*):

You must have very mixed feelings about your children. Tell me about them, everything, positive and negative. How did you feel about having them in the first place? And now? Do you have dreams about them? And how do you suppose you'd feel if something really did happen to them, if they really got hurt? Love and hate can exist at the same time, you know.

Therapist
(*Nondirective*):

Well, now that you've learned how to get along better with your husband, you are paying more attention to your relationship with your kids. And you find you worry about them too much when they're out of your sight. So you keep checking on them, as if that would stop the worry, but it doesn't for very long. So apparently you need to find some other way to handle your worrying.

Therapist
(*Eclectic*):

Nothing ever happens to your kids, does it? So what's the use of worrying? You know, lots of parents worry about their kids this way and it never does a bit of good. You've got to get yourself in hand and make yourself quit running after them all the time.

Therapist
(*Structured*):

Well, you've apparently learned how to live with your husband without feeling terrible or letting him interfere with doing what you want or need to do. Now we've got to figure out how you can handle this excessive worrying about your kids, since it interferes with your work, probably annoys them, and is useless. You do need to assure yourself that they're not exposed to unusual danger.

Beyond that, you're trying to control more than you can or is your responsibility, you're not concentrating on your job in the house, and you go through wasteful motions, namely, checking on them every 15 minutes. You can begin to solve this problem by extending the period of your follow-up to every hour, but requiring them to stay within hearing distance. Tell them exactly how far they can go, and then concentrate on what you're supposed to be doing.

Authors' Note on Protocol 2

Mrs. Larsen's major problem sooner or later would probably have centered on her relationship with her husband and her sense of control and direction—regardless of the therapeutic approach used. But learning just how to handle her husband might never occur without some specific suggestions from the therapist. Thinking up such specific suggestions and transmitting them to the client effectively probably occur best only when both adopt a theoretical stance and a specific purpose that encourage such processes through practice.

Practice, after all, is vital to the effective use of any therapeutic approach. Experience does seem to affect the therapist's competence in achieving results, and it can be assumed that analyzing and interpreting to Mrs. Larsen—or reflecting and empathizing, or structuring and suggesting—all improve with practice, provided that the therapist is practicing something which can be designated and delimited.

Protocol 3

MRS. PLANER AND HER DAUGHTER

Mrs. Planer
(*Statement A*):

I can't do a thing with Ann. She's wild, she won't eat, she hardly sleeps. She bites her nails all the time. She can't get along with the neighbor children. She has nightmares and talks in her sleep. And I lose my temper and yell at her. She drives me wild and I can't do my work. Then I worry that I'm treating her like I was treated, and that she'll end up like me, divorced and a mess.

Therapist (*Depth*):	Your daughter sounds seriously disturbed, and someone should probably see her two or three times a week. I can recommend someone if you like. But now let's talk about you, and why she drives you wild, and why you worry about her turning out like you. You don't like yourself very much, it sounds like. Tell me about your early life.
Therapist (*Nondirective*):	You're feeling very frustrated about not being able to do anything with your daughter. Then it makes you angry, and then guilty. You just don't see a way out.
Therapist (*Eclectic*):	Your daughter needs help, and perhaps I can see the two of you, or I could see her alone or recommend a child psychiatrist or psychologist for her. Then I could see you occasionally and give you some encouragement. Children this age often give you trouble. And you've got a tough problem anyway, trying to work and raise a daughter alone.
Therapist (*Structured*):	It sounds as if you and your daughter both lead a pretty disorganized life and as if your main reason for being upset is not knowing what to do. Now, I think that we can develop a plan of specific action that will help you to reach your goals both for your daughter and for yourself, first by outlining what you want to accomplish, being as realistic as possible, and then by making up a day-to-day program for yourself.
Mrs. Planer (*Statement B*):	Well, Ann seems to be behaving a little better now. She's a little more relaxed, and she gets along better with the other children. And I don't yell at her so much. But I still don't seem to be able to get going on my life. It's such a mess!
Therapist (*Depth*):	And how do you feel about your daughter getting better? It may bother you because she may seem stronger than you, and show you up as worse. Or you may be afraid of

her becoming more independent and not needing you as much. Tell me more about your feelings of inadequacy and any thoughts you have about her becoming better.

Therapist (Nondirective): It seems that Ann is doing better, but that you're not doing so well. I wonder if there could be a connection here, and if so, what it might be. You feel that there's progress in the one area but not the other.

Therapist (Eclectic): I'm glad that your daughter is improving. That should make you feel better. You're certainly getting better control over yourself. But you've got a way to go yet. Your life can't really be so bad as all that. But you have got some neurotic problems, all right.

Therapist (Structured): Now we have a pretty good idea of how you were able to help Ann. You set definite hours for eating and going to bed and doing household tasks, and so on. And you gave her rewards when she did show good habits, and reduced her opportunities to use the bad habits, and withheld the rewards when she didn't behave properly. Now we have to work somewhat in the same way with you. Of course we don't have anyone with as much control over your life as you have over your daughter's. But you can use a schedule better, you can defer some of the things you like to do until you have done what you must, and you can remind yourself what following though will get you in the long run that's so much better than the temporary relief you get by postponing things.

Mrs. Planer (Statement C): Well, I've been trying to think along the lines we talked about last time, and it just doesn't make sense to me. I admit that you've done me some good, but my life still seems like such a mess and so hopeless that I can't see any use in going on with these interviews. So I've decided that this will be my last session.

Therapist (Depth):	You seem to have reached a point where you're anxious about going on. I wonder why this is, what it is that's too threatening for you to face. And you have some positive feelings toward me, but also apparently some negative ones, and you have some resistance about going on with me. But wouldn't it be better to analyze these feelings? You don't have to be afraid of them. You can talk freely to me about them.
Therapist (Nondirective):	You've been trying to follow through on what we've been talking about, but you just can't figure it out. And you feel so hopeless that you've decided to give up at this point, and quit, is that right?
Therapist (Eclectic):	You're feeling pretty depressed, aren't you! Many patients have periods like this. But why quit now, when you've begun to get out of the woods? Of course, you could quit for awhile and see how it goes. Maybe your life isn't really such a mess as it seems right now. Perhaps you could go off on a vacation for awhile, and then come back and reconsider.
Therapist (Structured):	You're having trouble moving ahead along the lines we've been setting up, and you want to fall back on your old habits. But isn't that what got you into trouble in the first place and made you decide to see me? It is hard work to change long-time habits, of course. And you will always have periods of being discouraged. But if we go over your program again, and perhaps try to improve on it, you can get back to work on it. Then if you can continue to succeed with it as you began to do—instead of falling back on the old ways—you know that in a week or a month you'll be much more likely to feel good about yourself than if you follow your impulse of this moment.

Authors' Note on Protocol 3

Mrs. Planer's problem raises questions of initial approach that have been resolved here by keeping her in individual treatment alone with the therapist, rather than having him see the daughter individually also or the mother and daughter together.

Sound theoretical bases for choosing any one of these approaches over the others are lacking except in the case of the structured approach. In this latter approach, the mother would be seen alone unless exceptional conditions arose such as a significant diagnostic question, a confused picture of interaction, or the need to demonstrate what to do. She would be seen alone because it appears that she can be the most effective and efficient change agent for the child and also because she needs help herself.

The problem of quitting which is portrayed is one of the more crucial points of divergence among the different approaches to psychotherapy. Trying to analyze "resistance" and "transference;" or permissively going along with the feeling; or minimizing and reassuring; or explicitly structuring modes of failure and success—these different ways of handling Mrs. Planer's expressed desire to quit touch upon vital differences among the four kinds of therapists. They also point the way to the nature of the subsequent sessions if she remains in therapy.

9 Writing Therapy: A New Approach to Treatment and Training

The development of training procedures and aids in psychotherapy has begun to sprout into a gangling adolescence. The use of recording machines, sound movies, television, one-way-vision screens, and observational posts is becoming much more common in communicating the student's behavior to the expert practitioner. Frequently these methods are also used in reverse, with the expert demonstrating for students—or peers. In another approach, the supervisor "broadcasts" suggestions during the interview to the tyro therapist, who wears earphones. These mechanical devices are rapidly enlarging understanding of the interpersonal verbal exchange in therapy. In experimental adaptations of therapeutic situations, specifically designed to produce a behavior change in some limited aspect of behavior, one can now hear and see what is happening, which makes an experimental approach more amenable to measurement.

What is still sorely lacking in training for and in observing psychotherapy is a way to *control* the process during training or research, as well as a method of introducing the novice therapist to patient behavior under limited conditions. Such a controlled process would be of great value in that the student therapist could learn, step by step, some of the many ways of reacting to and affecting patient behavior. The possibility of developing such a method is especially intriguing, since it gives the therapist greater opportunity to introduce structure into the therapy—as well as into the patient's life.

A procedure called "writing therapy" has been used in the Psychological Clinic at the George Washington University for several years. Precipitated by pressures from a waiting list, it was established out of theoretical considerations that had already minimized interpersonal effects in therapy.

In Chapter 7, on follow-up studies, some research is described which supports the use of writing therapy. So far this method has been used only with college students; the results cannot yet be generalized to other populations, except in an experimental way. The discussion here points out some implications of writing therapy not only for treatment but also as a method of training students in structured behavior-change therapy.

Rationale for Therapy through Writing

Writing has apparently seldom been used as the modality for psychotherapy; references are few and thin. In his discussion of therapy at a distance, Meiers (1957) notes that much of what could be called therapy has probably occurred transiently and in an unplanned manner in many lives, with some benefit. His therapy at a distance is mainly the treatment of an individual through another (nonprofessional) person, an idea similar to that of the change agent's role in bringing about behavior modification. Shor (1955) even had clients listen to themselves, with no therapist present at all, after making a tape recording.

Ellis (1955a) proposed several therapeutic methods that involved the use of writing: checking significant conflict from a printed list of possible conflict areas; having the patient write out a dialogue or story, which is later given to the therapist; conducting the actual interviews in writing, instead of talking, especially if the therapist or patient is hard of hearing; having the therapist accumulate notes during the therapy hour to be reacted to later and written about by the patient; having the patient keep a diary; and having the patient and therapist write letters when they are removed by space. Bibliotherapy is suggested as an adjunct.

Lowinger and Huston (1955) have written of a study of transference techniques when the patient and therapist are in different rooms but conversational interaction is still possible. Saul (1951a) wrote of conducting therapy over the telephone. In suggesting that legitimate, full-fledged analytic work was possible through the use of the telephone, he noted one special merit: anxiety, which often interferes with the flow of material in an interpersonal setting, is apparently reduced in telephone conversations.

Several writers have commended the use of the autobiography in therapy (Danielson & Rothney, 1954; Ricco, 1958; Shaffer, 1954). Not only may an autobiography convey much about a client that may be of therapeutic value, but in some cases it may become the instigating agent for therapy and later provide some useful leads to significant subjects for discussion during the therapy hour. Compared with spoken historical material in interviews, the written material can be more quickly and economically reviewed for significant leads.

The impersonal nature of the therapeutic exchange through writing allows some patients to communicate better than they would in face-to-face situations (Widroe & Davidson, 1961). Written daily accounts of experiences and problems also can aid the patient to get started talking when he comes to the oral session of therapy.

Favorable clinical results have been noted from the writing that is almost ubiquitous among prisoners, and frequently among others far from familiar settings—such as isolates in hospitals (Landsman, 1951).

Messinger (1952) has used what he calls "auto elaboration" in psychoanalytic therapy. In this procedure, the patient makes copies of the therapist's notes from a therapy session and keeps one copy to elaborate for his own benefit and for future discussions with his therapist. The patient may add related thoughts and emotional reactions to these notes to enlarge his self-understanding.

Another report on written communications in therapy dealt with a situation in which the therapist was deaf (Farber, 1953). The patient wrote or typed his statements of problems, and the therapist replied orally. Farber observed that it seemed to make little difference in therapeutic progress whether the patient wrote or spoke.

Stone and Simos (1948) reported research in which 214 unemployed cases receiving vocational counseling in person were compared with 201 unemployed counseled-by-mail cases. The follow-up questionnaire revealed that sending the information by mail apparently assisted in getting jobs, increasing self-confidence, and sustaining good employment records. The differences between the responses of the two groups were not statistically significant, although there were some differences in favor of those who had been counseled in person. Although the data did not concern what are ordinarily considered psychotherapeutic topics, any factors that affect self-confidence and the ability to act on knowledge are of significance in psychotherapy.

Clark (1953) described correspondence between a married girl and her physician in regard to marriage and sex problems. Alston (1957), in a report on psychoanalytic therapy by correspondence, cites Freud's correspondence with Fliess and with the father of a 5-year-old boy about the child's phobia.

To sum up, writing therapy has been used in several forms as an adjunct to, or a replacement for more formal, oral therapy, especially where the latter was not possible or practicable. Like much of the reporting on short-term therapy, the existing literature on writing therapy consists mostly of clinical impressions, however.

Procedures and Advantages

If the patient is reasonably articulate and can write with a degree of clarity, and if he is willing to accept writing as a therapeutic tool, it is relatively easy to find out what his problems are. Many patients prefer this to a face-to-face interview and can write more directly and openly about themselves than they can talk. In general, however, the comparative advantages and disadvantages of writing and of direct oral communication are not the focus here; this chapter is intended only to point out the efficiency and effectiveness of this relatively new approach as another way of helping to solve some of the client's specific problems.

Patients often report that setting down their problems in writing enables them to communicate more effectively with others outside the therapy hour. Whether this is true and, if so, whether it occurs in other modalities equally is of course an open question.

In this procedure, the patient is not simply given a notebook and told to write about himself, but is given guiding instructions. He has a regular weekly appointment which is scheduled at a given hour, just as if he were appearing for a personal interview. Inside the cover of the notebook assigned to him is a one-page description of what is expected of each patient. These instructions are as follows:

To the Student Engaging in Writing Therapy

1. This procedure—called "Writing Therapy"—is intended to help you in regard to personal, social, and academic problems.
2. You are to keep your appointments as precisely and conscientiously as if you were appearing for an interview with a staff member.
3. Your writing is kept confidential; your notebook is kept under lock and key.
4. Please be frank, complete, and cooperative with us, and we shall be the same toward you.
5. Some specific suggestions regarding the procedure, intended to help you get along, are the following:
   A) Write out as completely as you desire, your ideas about yourself, your observations, etc., spelling out your problems or concerns as clearly as you can.
   B) These problems or concerns may include study habits, concentration, worry about exams; they may include difficulties

with other students, with instructors; they may include difficulties with yourself, or with family members.

C) Think of ways in which you have tried to cope with these problems, either with or without success.

D) No problem is either too minor or too gross to report. Only with your candid cooperation can we be of the greatest help to you.

6. At the close of this series of writing therapy sessions, you will be asked to retake some of the initial assessment procedures, in order for us to help evaluate, along with you, the value of these sessions.

This reevaluation may come at the end of the semester, or at the end of the academic year; or at any time agreed upon by yourself and us.

The accompanying "Letter of Agreement" is to be signed by you now and turned in at the end of the first writing session. This shows us your good faith in the writing therapy enterprise, helps us meet university obligations showing the value of this (and other) procedures to students, and allows us here in the clinic to place full confidence in our mutual enterprise: Helping you in important ways.

This method can be especially effective in the training of novice therapists, for student therapists are often at a loss to know how to react to patient data (Group for the Advancement of Psychiatry, 1954; Ruesch & Bateson, 1951). When they are listening to patient data, novices (and even experienced therapists) frequently tend to behave nondirectively or, alternatively, to ask for more information. Frequently they are uncertain of how to reply to the patient without uttering banalities and yet keep the interview moving ahead constructively. Perhaps this is why they tend to ask more questions or to fall back on nondirective silences or reflections or why they make interpretations which become crystallized as therapeutic techniques that do not serve optimally to advance therapy.

Questioning or nondirective replies can be planned to advance therapy at a given point, but they should not occur merely because the therapist can think of nothing else to say. The point is that in writing therapy, the novice therapist has time to reflect, consult, and sharpen his therapeutic wits before he has to reply to what the patient has "said." As this skill develops, especially if he is guided by a specific theoretical viewpoint of therapy and behavior change and by an evolving set of empirically derived specific rules, his replies can become increasingly effective in modifying patient behavior.

Since he is thus allowed considerable time to prepare an answer to the patient's statements, his answers may be more cogent and selective. He may ask the patient for more discussion of a given problem; he may make a suggestion or give the patient some useful information; or he may point up facets of the patient's situation which the patient has overlooked or which are inconsistent. The statements of the patient do not come so fast as to be kaleidoscopic, as they often do in oral therapy. In short, he has a better opportunity to program the behavior-change situation, to prepare a plan for reaching change.

The same advantage which is afforded by this extra time to mull over responses also accrues to the patient. He may consider different ways of explaining his problems, or he may want to clear up an issue between himself and his therapist. The greater advantage, however, seems to lie in the fact that the patient, having set down his concerns, is then able to look upon them with a clearer perspective and greater objectivity, and this enables him to gain more leverage on his problems.

In interview therapy, much of the therapist-patient exchange (or the exchange between patient and patient, in group therapy) in discussing problems and their solutions is wasteful. In terms of communications theory, there is much "noise" in the system. Often there is so much noise that the patient cannot tell another person what actually transpired in the therapy hour, what he was supposed to have learned, or any other crystallization of its content.

Many traditional therapists, however, will defend this occurrence as a virtue. The "free flow" of monologue, or conversation in a relatively free-association sense, will presumably reveal important material, so that ruminations and random verbalizations should not be discouraged. There is growing evidence, however, that this random activity is essentially distracting to the clear definition of problems and efficient methods of solving them. Not all communications can be zeroed in directly on therapeutic objectives, of course, but it is important to think theoretically in these terms and to work constantly to approximate the ideal degree of effectiveness.

In therapist-patient written communication, "noise" is reduced by brevity. When transcribed, the average 45- to 50-minute oral therapy hour produces about 20 to 30 double-spaced pages, taking about 4 hours to type. In contrast, writing therapy usually produces from three to five handwritten pages; transcribed, this makes about two to three pages of double-spaced typescript. The therapist's reply adds another page or two of typescript. Generally, the therapist can read the patient's report and prepare the written response in 20 to 30 minutes, or in even less time when he becomes experienced. The ratio of time spent by everyone involved—patient, therapist, and transcriber—is generally about 4 or 5 to

1 in favor of written over oral communication, in the standard procedure. While such a comparison of time spent has no direct bearing on therapeutic effectiveness, it does have implications for results in terms of time spent and the impact of increased structuring of communication.

Written therapy has another advantage in that the protocol is always available for such purposes as immediate rereading, research, and checking up on past views, directly and without further, special intervention. The continuity of therapy is easy for both the patient and the therapist to follow. Each has access to all the previous writing at any time. Consequently, when there are differences in interpretation they can be checked, and the data are present from which a solution may be fashioned.

But what of the warmth and acceptance presumably so important and so exclusive to the interpersonal therapeutic situation? Their importance in therapy can be questioned. There are ways of indicating regard, warmth, and acceptance other than through personal, face-to-face interviews. Writing therapy may even be more likely to stimulate the subtle capacity of the therapist to instigate relevant and discriminatory action than oral therapy is. It has not yet been demonstrated that unconditional, indiscriminate warmth and acceptance and understanding are fundamental, or even essential, to therapeutic change—in fact, under certain conditions such as dependency they may delay therapeutic change. Salutary results have been achieved in many conditioning methods that involved little or no interpersonal relationships.

Although writing therapy is primarily experimental at this time, it represents a pragmatic attempt to shorten therapy without sacrificing the essence of the therapeutic exchange, and to make this exchange more explicit and objective. Only longer experience and more data will furnish a better answer as to whether the personal oral exchange is vital to the sought-after behavior change.

Written materials from several cases are presented here, exactly as they were treated in a special project on writing therapy (see also Phillips & Batrawi, 1964; Phillips, Test, & Adams, 1964). Following these specific cases, a list of tentative "rules" will be presented in an attempt to conceptualize the writing therapy procedure. These rules are not final statements, of course, but can best be described as programmatic or procedural, to be crystallized later into a more precise mold based upon further research and clinical experience.

Certain words or phrases in the protocols that are presented here have been underlined (in italics here) by the therapist to draw the patient's attention to the remarks the therapist considered most important. Generally, they were matters which the patient had emphasized or which were of topical significance. If these were numerous, they were usually numbered by the therapist, so that the patient could more easily determine the sequence of the therapist's replies.

Imperfections in the instructions of the therapist are obvious and gross as compared with printed programed learning material, which they so closely resemble. Since they are tailored to the individual client and session, however, developing better instructions on such an individualized basis would take so long that it would defeat the attempt to shorten therapy. The process must be judged in the light of the results.

Two other points need emphasis. First, this method is obviously limited to patients who can write fairly well, probably coming mainly from college and professional populations, although the *theoretical* implications of the approach are of much broader scope. For example, tape recordings used in a similar way would be applicable to almost universal populations.

Second, the style and precise methods of the therapist in the writing therapy protocols presented are not as congenial to the authors as the previous time-lapse protocols were. Phrases, variables selected, timing and pacing, and speech mannerisms would even be criticized or changed by the authors, but, withal, the method shows through clearly, and others who may apply the method will inevitably display other idiosyncrasies.

THE CASE OF E. W.

This young married male undergraduate came to the psychological clinic for help with many problems. After a test battery, he was given the opportunity to engage in writing therapy. He was next on the list to be offered writing therapy, and he did not turn it down; if he had refused it, he would not have been referred to a therapist.

His test battery showed high scores (T of 70 plus) on the following scales of the Minnesota Multiphasic Personality Inventory: Schizophrenia, Hypomania, Psychopathic Deviate, and Masculinity-Femininity. There were moderate elevations (T of 60 plus) on Paranoia, Psychasthenia, and Social Introversion. He showed strong Dominance tendencies on the Edwards Personal Preference Schedule, with the rest of his scores in the middle range. He described himself on the data sheet as lacking self-confidence and motivation for schoolwork (although he "wanted an education") and as confused about planning for his future and facing numerous problems with his family.

Patient's Protocol

My two greatest problems in school ever since I can remember have been my *study habits* and my *handwriting*. Perhaps compared with study habits, handwriting seems minor, yet for me to write a careful and legible hand is difficult. It not only requires extra concentration and fatigues my arm and hand very quickly, but also slows me down immensely. My arm is already a little tired from writing these few lines. When I have to take notes in class or write rapidly on exams, *my writing becomes atrocious.*

The handwriting problem involves more along the lines of taking notes. To me, the organization of my notes in class is pretty poor. I have been particularly trying to improve this during the last few months, with no recognizable success.

Lack of organization enters into my studies as well. While I have really been able to keep up with my work this semester, I haven't been able to do enough reviewing necessary to make the grades I should. This may cause my average to drop, but I certainly hope it won't. The funny thing is that my high grades are not in my major, Political Science. I have A's in Psychology . . . and in . . . Geography, a B in Politics . . . and C's in two other related subjects. I need to do well on exams and make those C's into B's. There have been other problems this semester as well. My family has never been happy about my marriage, and only since the death of my father . . . have we begun to draw together again. The necessity for taking care of arrangements for him, and the birth of my son the evening of his (my father's) funeral kept me very busy. My mother has remained with her parents and this has necessitated visiting, etc. Then, too, there have been problems with my wife's family. After a battle royal with her mother this summer, things have improved. Her mother is very helpful, and even does our laundry for us. Her problem is being lonely without her daughter, and the constant harassment for the last seven years by her husband who is trying to get a divorce. They have been separated since my wife was 13. We haven't seen her father in four months. He had been trying to cause trouble between my wife and myself and she told him she did not care to see him again until he was willing to accept me as a son-in-law.

So you can see that I have had a *great deal on my mind, and concentration on my studies has been difficult.*

The sad thing is that this has always been true. Ever since I was in prep school these problems have been present: inability to concentrate, poor organization, and poor penmanship. The only thing is that in spite of them I have been able to do fairly well, graduating with honors, from prep school and maintaining over a 3.00 Q.P.I. here at the University. My two years at —— College are a different story. This problem of concentration has shown up in courses requiring the greatest amount of it, for instance here my only work below B so far has been two semesters of . . . for which I received D's both semesters. At ——— College, I failed Geology and received low grades in Calculus, both failed and received low grades in French, all indications of poor concentration as far as I can tell.

My saving grace has been a love of reading, which has caused me to read very extensively since I was very young. Thus I have a great deal of background material, as well as doing well in most of the Social Sciences.

Therapist's Written Reply

Your appraisal of your academic difficulties seems realistic and your diagnosis of your two primary problems seem clear. We will list some specific techniques to help in these two areas; however, before doing so it would perhaps be helpful to take an overview of your entire situation so that these academic difficulties may be given proper but not undue emphasis. In doing so, we may clear the air a little so that your energies can be used more fully and more specifically to deal with academic problems.

Your troubled relationships with both sets of in-laws have surely created tension and, as you say, made it even more difficult to study. This is quite understandable and perhaps you are not giving yourself enough credit for having maintained a good effort while coping with a serious and emotionally loaded situation. This is not to say that you should feel sorry for yourself; each of us has problems of one kind or another and the measure of our maturity is to deal with them without our daily life being greatly disrupted. However, you sound as if you have had a double dose and when these troubled family situations are added to the natural trials of a young man who is working *and* going to school and meeting the natural pressures and responsibilities of a young family, one may see that perhaps an inordinate amount of energy may be going into these situations rather than into daily tasks. In sum, if you could stand back from these situations a little and see that you are weathering them, although at a cost, perhaps academic work and intensive study will seem somewhat less of a burden.

There is no record of the hours you work per week, but you are carrying a full academic load. Some adjustment here might be helpful if your financial situation allows it. Perhaps a shorter work week or fewer courses per semester will ease some of the pressures.

Specifically, the following suggestions may be helpful:

1. Handwriting—This lack of skill in handwriting is a common problem among school age boys who tend to be large and who prefer big muscle activity. Eye hand coordination somehow may not proceed at the same rate as with normal sized children and this may have been some part of the original problem. Since you mention your father's career was in the Armed Forces, presumably you had more changes of school than is usual. However, no one insists that a grown man write anything other than a relatively legible script—and yours *is* legible. If when you hurry (as in taking notes) and the handwriting is "atrocious," as long as you can read it, what does it matter? Have you considered the typewriter for all other kinds of correspondence, such as letters, term papers, etc.? Your handwriting does not seem so bad to us but if it is really an effort for you, perhaps you should consider becoming an adequate typist. Shorthand is another technique that might prove valuable. This specific solution for a problem is the kind of technique we would like you to try in all troublesome situations. One may be aware of the genesis of a problem and be facing the problem squarely, but another step is helpful—that of a specific technique or perhaps techniques as possible solutions.

2. Study Habits—Your test results show that you have good ability, but perhaps you are like a sluggish motor in that you are not using your ability efficiently. The causes for this may be numerous and could include poor attitude, emotional problems, distractions. We do not think it is necessary to cope with all these problems, but rather, we should center attention on *specific items*. If you try out our suggestions, the various causes of poor study habits can fall under your control and you can likely improve your situation.

Whatever the causes of your poor study habits and relatively poor achievement, *correction is needed*. Let us give you a brief but usually effective set of procedures. Try these *daily—faithfully—specifically—consistently*.

A. Study same time, place and under same conditions each day insofar as possible.

B. Read assignments over lightly first, getting topics, major subdivisions, sequences, etc. in mind.

C. If your assignment has a *summary*, read it first.

D. A second time through the material take notes on 3 x 5 (or 4 x 8) cards. This we call the *Card System*, and will be referred to frequently. Use these cards for lists, definitions, causes, reasons, dates, persons, theories, facts—adapted to the specific subject matter at hand, of course. When in doubt about what you know, use cards; as you read or study, convert subject matter to cards; study for short periods of time (as short as 15–20 minutes), then gradually increase up to 45–50 minutes or so; take a "break" of five or so minutes between these study times (even the short ones); "breaks" should be designed to refresh, not distract you. Using the cards will help in several ways: To read more carefully, to abstract better, to select relevant items. Shuffle the cards so you can see the same facts, relationships, etc. in different contexts. Cards will help you to *avoid cues* from the printed page (or your notes) which you probably rely on more than you realize; cards will also help you repeat or rehearse the items frequently, thus aiding *overlearning*, and you will really know what you need to know.

E. Begin studying with easy or short assignments first. This may differ from day to day. This allows for a feeling of satisfaction and aids accomplishment, thereby motivating you more. (If you study the difficult or long assignments first, you may not only fail to finish them, but preclude doing the shorter and simpler assignments.) *Don't immediately reject* the details of the Card System as wasteful—they take longer at first, but save time in the long run, promote better and more accurate learning, force you to be specific.

Next time you write, please let us know how these suggestions are working out. Also, please list specific courses and the amount of time you spend on each daily. You may want to explore further your relationships with your relatives in your next writing session; perhaps, too, your wife's views on these problems might be explained. We think it would be helpful for you to think in specific terms about what you can and cannot do about these problems and report to us any conclusions you have reached.

Evaluation

The immediate focus is on study habits. This usually produces specific items of success and is, in a conceptual sense, like the specific behaviors called for in conditioning studies. Something positive which the patient can accomplish should be started.

The therapist in this case referred, in one or two sentences, to background items that could actually have been left out. *But there was no postponement of the action needed to correct the problems and to get the patient mobilized and self-directing immediately.*

This patient came in for seven writing sessions. In the last session (about 3 months after his first one), he reported that his course work was progressing well, as part of a detailed statement about his grades, his experience in taking notes, his greater efficiency in studying, and other improvements. He also decided that he should reduce his outside work load to 20 hours per week (from 30 or more hours per week) and that while he still needed to perfect his study habits and manage his schedule even better, he felt he now "knew the ropes" and would move ahead. His problems with his family had begun to diminish, according to his report, and he began to distinguish between the problems he could change and those he had to accept. He was less concerned over changing people and more realistic about what to expect from himself, and he had learned how to use his own energy more effectively.

His MMPI profile changes are shown in Figure 1, which corroborate his self-reports. He was informed that he might return to therapy later if he felt it was needed.

THE CASE OF I. N.

I. N. is a 24-year-old college senior, concerned about marriage and career and their interrelationship. She terminated her writing efforts at the eighth session, saying that she was not progressing as much as she thought she would. However, at the time of her 6-month follow-up she wrote that the writing sessions had been of value and that she was now realizing the validity of the efforts of the therapist. Her retest MMPI results also showed substantial change. Her first writing session produced the following.

Patient's Protocol

I somehow feel caught in a revolving circle as far as my problems (both academic and personal—for I consider them closely intertwined) are concerned. And with another school year starting, the spin becomes faster, I become dizzy—and although I know I don't dare let go, sometimes I wonder just how long I can hold on.

And so . . . where to start—study habits? I know the rules of good studying, but can't follow them. My mind wanders—sometimes thinking about people, often about life, and always, always, ad infinitum, asking myself Why (don't ask Why, ask What? The answer is not Why anything). Inevitably these philosophical ram-

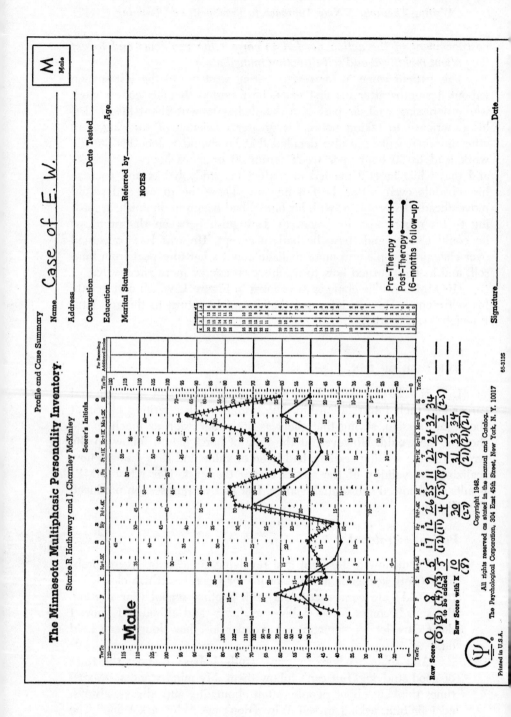

The Minnesota Multiphasic Personality Inventory.

Starke R. Hathaway and J. Charnley McKinley

Profile and Case Summary

Name Case of E.W.

Address

Occupation _____ Date Tested _____

Education _____ Age _____

Marital Status _____ Referred by _____

NOTES

Scorer's Initials

Male

Pre-Therapy •++++++
Post-Therapy •———•
(6-months follow-up)

Copyright 1948.
All rights reserved as stated in the manual and Catalog.
The Psychological Corporation, 304 East 45th Street, New York, N. Y. 10017

Printed in U.S.A.

65-313S

Raw Score   O   1   8   9   5   17 12 26 35 11 22 24 32 34
             (0) (9) (4)(13)(5) (12)(11) 4 (25)(7) 2 9   2   0

K to be added

Raw Score with K 10   30   31 33 34
                  (9)   (17)   (21)(21)(21)

blings (call it daydreaming if you insist) cut into my study time. I still make good grades (although there was one year at another school where my rambling took over completely—and I was dismissed for poor academic performance—hence my fear that history will repeat itself). But I have to study inordinate amounts of time to do so. In fact, I study all the time—I just can't let go. I'm afraid that if I consciously relax for awhile, I will lose the grip I have on myself and won't be able to regain it.

I know I'm not stupid, but at the same time I have absolutely no confidence in my ability to do well—especially academically. Even with a year here behind me, and a good record and some recognition of my intelligence, I can't help remembering that I am capable of sinking, too.

Before S—— (the other school), I was of the persuasion that grades aren't really that much of a measure of a person. I breezed through school doing generally well and was accepted by all the colleges I applied to. I chose S—— because they offered me a nice, fat scholarship. There followed nine indescribable months—by now, two years later, I have been suitably impressed with the value of one's "record" and with the necessity to make good grades—and so that's what I do. My grades are better now than they have been in my entire academic life before. And still I don't believe it. I sweat a lot and die a little with each exam I take. I rarely can tell how well I did—and when I receive the grades, I accept them but I don't really believe them. (I wonder if there's been a mistake, or if the prof. was just being kind—which I'd hate worse than an F—or something of that sort.)

And so I go on with the semesters stretching ahead of me—but I don't really see them because my nose is always in a book. I'm not trying to imply that I dislike studying—I love it; I couldn't live without it. I'd just like to be able to say that the time I put in studying was actually devoted to just that. And I also don't want to imply that I'm against meditation—for study without reflection is a waste. But, please, one thing at a time, and weed out the daydreaming.

Therapist's Written Reply

It was good that you wrote so candidly. To reverse the usual order of things, we shall consider your last remark first. You say, 'Let's weed out the daydreaming.' This seems to us to be a good over-all picture of what you present—that is, you are quite unaccepting about failure to meet your preconceived ideas of what your life should be and how you ought to act and feel.

There is nothing wrong with "philosophical ramblings" or daydreaming or meditation as long as these things do not interfere seriously with your performance. We will define your performance as your work here at school. Your grades are excellent—at first glance, how are these factors interfering with your performance?

You say you study an inordinate amount of time. Compared to whom? Studying is highly individualized—some can study for 30 minutes and need a break, some can last five hours. You study but you break it up with "ramblings" and still do a very fine job with your school work. We fail to see that this is bad, or any reflection on you or your abilities. The troubling thing about it seems to be how *you* are viewing it.

You seem to be making yourself more uncomfortable, more "caught in a revolving circle" by setting up certain standards of behavior, failing to meet them, and somehow turning all this on yourself. If you could ease up on your expectations, but keep your performance unchanged, your feelings and evaluations about yourself might change a great deal.

One suggestion is that you allow yourself to be a "daydreaming" young woman for a while. After all, at your age, life presents many unanswered questions. You have artistic and creative interests on your tests; you may have to perform less efficiently than you desire if you are to have time for thought and questioning. Anyhow, no evidence exists that these tendencies really injure your performance or productivity.

Some other specific suggestions may help:

1) Put aside if you can (and tell us the success of this effort) the failure you had at S____; that was a learning experience, profit from it, but don't carry it around as a burden.
2) Give more information about how your studying is taking time away from other pursuits. How about your sleeping? Do you allow time for recreational activities? Do you eat on-the-run? Develop more the context in which you study, in terms of a daily schedule.

We hope to be able to make more specific, rather than general, recommendations to you. Next time, we'll make more specific study habits suggestions; right now, try seeing some of your regular activities in a different light. Letting go some may sound dangerous to you, but you should try it—when away from the studying, pitch in to whatever you are doing, and try to sweep away the study concerns. Also, when you find your mind wandering from your study (at the time of intended study), get up and leave the study area (desk, room, library, whatever). Take a "break." At this time, put the studying behind you. Then when you feel more like studying, return to it without guilt for having taken a break if it produces better results. See if you can do this, and let us know your reactions and results.

In writing next, please try to answer #2 comment above, and give your reactions to all we've said.

Patient Reaction

The following protocols did not seem to clear up the issues at hand as much as had been hoped. It was difficult to get important specifics from this patient. She became somewhat discouraged and wrote the following for her eighth, and last, writing session:

If I knew what was bothing me, I wouldn't be here now. I didn't come to the Center to have my problems solved—I came to find out what they are. Toward this end—as you say—I don't feel I have made much progress. When I started writing in this notebook I included things that I felt were indicative of superficially manifestations of a deeper seated problem. I didn't know how to tie them together and bring it out—I had hoped that you would.

Despite these apparent signs of failure, this patient made progress as suggested by her own later report and by a retest on the MMPI. The results for the pre- and post-therapy testing on the MMPI are shown in Figure 2.

This patient indicated at the time of the 6-month follow-up interview that she had needed to "balance her life better" and to give less urgency to her academic work. She felt that she had accomplished this "on her own" after the termination of therapy, and without any ill effects on her scholastic marks. Her actual grades confirmed this, and she stayed at about a B+ average. She had, in her own way and in her own words—and perhaps in her own time, too—confirmed what had been said to her in the writing sessions. She had been looking and hoping for an "explanation" in some "deep" terms for her plight, rather than trying to change her immediate behavior in specific ways.

It appears that she needed an explanation in causal terms before the behavior-change effort would have met her expectations of it. She may have been too concerned with a theory of therapy and the stereotypes of "depth" therapy to get directly to work on her problems and possible solutions as quickly as her therapist wanted to.

A more forceful and specific set of replies, or a somewhat more leisurely, indirect approach, to this patient might have changed her atti-

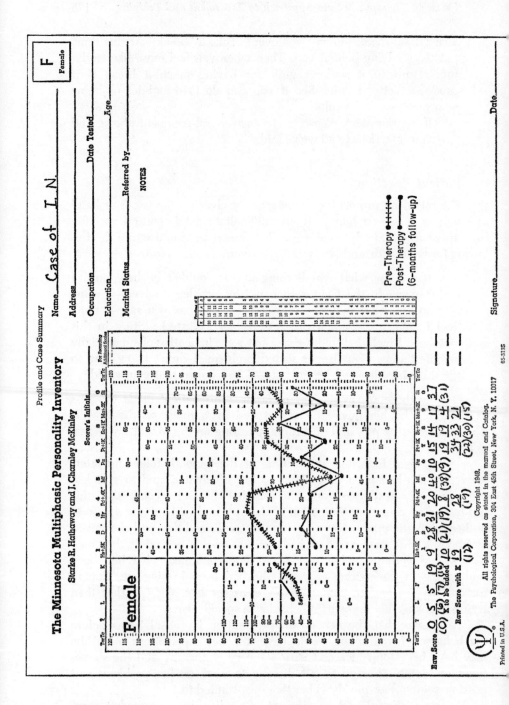

tudes during therapy. In any case, she did not stay with it long enough to find out. There is no implied criticism of the student therapist in this case, for this patient's perspective on emotional problems is a common one, and failures are common because of initial (false) expectations of (any type of) therapy. The task of the therapist who is behaviorally oriented should be to discuss and resolve such false expectations, with the result that the client either understands and wants to work with the therapist's methods or chooses to work with a different therapist and method.

This patient also made progress as measured by test-retest on the Q Sort. Her first, pre-therapy Q Sort yielded an *r* of +.03 between self and ideal. After therapy, the *r* became +.69, despite her disappointment and premature termination.

THE CASE OF G. A.

This patient was an extremely volatile young man. He was 29 years old and single, and he had been indulgently reared. He was a whirlwind of activity in the interview following his testing, and he eagerly grasped the opportunity to get some help.

Patient's Protocol

Let us start with two week-ends ago and see if I can make everything past, present, and future flow from there.

It was Friday afternoon; thus school week was over, and I didn't feel quite so guilty for awhile. Naturally with all the week-end in front of me I had lots of time for my schoolwork. I cut my German class. Anyway, my thoughts went to my 17 year-old girl friend in ———. After balancing the pros and cons of things back and forth for an hour or so, I decided how much I'd like to marry her, but then I've been doing that off and on for months. You'd be amazed how rationally I approach the subject of marriage thinking to myself or talking to her. It kills me that she can't see anything but the destruction of love by being rational about marriage—love and marriage being two different and overlapping things to me. She actually isn't necessarily as naive as I make her out to be, but I'll get back to that later. All excited over my love and well rationalized marriage concept, I decided to call her up in ——— for an inspiring conversation. Then about ten at night, I called and right from the beginning her voice sounded strange. She didn't seem to care that I was asking her. I have no fear I'm losing her love, but nevertheless, I felt at the time that she should have been more excited. She had written me that her parents wouldn't be home that weekend, but I had forgotten. It came out in the phone conversation. I asked her (quite unawares) if one of her girl friends was there. The answer was "No." I asked her who was there. The answer J——. He said something from the background and I hung up. In fact, I slammed the phone down. To say the least I was angry—yet it was not exactly that way. The word "angry" is too ambiguous. In the conversation preceding this little "trauma" she had told me about a B+ she had received and the driver's license she had finally gotten. Both of these things had made me very happy, so I was well set up for the blow. But again, the word "happy" is too ambiguous. Let us assume that I am in love with the girl I am talking about, but I assure you that there are lots of things concerning the word "love" I would like to subjectively discuss.

[There follows the lengthy description of an episode between his girl and another man and of his reconciliation with his girl.]

Q—— spent the night with the other girl and I spent the night with S——. It was innocent for all of us really. Q—— passed out in bed fully dressed, and his girl joined him and they probably didn't stir until morning. S—— and I spent the night in another bed somewhat less innocently, but just the same nothing very immoral happened. I enjoyed sleeping with her but I felt guilty in other respects. Neither Q—— nor I should have been in the house with the girls. My real feelings were that S—— had again been irresponsible for ever letting us in, though I knew I was partially to blame. We all were, but she was the sole one with responsibility. I don't think anyone else was bothered by breaching honesty. The next day, Sunday, I wished that S——'s parents would come home and catch us all there, but that probably would not have bothered the other kids much either. Why didn't they feel the injury to self respect that I did? Because they were younger? Because they weren't brought up as well? Because they are stupid? Or does everyone sneak and cheat and completely dishonor their self respect and *social pride?*

This is the way it is with everything for me. The way I see it, we have lots of social standards that we can and probably should live by. I am not narrow minded, so most social standards look pretty foolish to me, but nevertheless I don't see why I should be forced to break them just because people around me do. I am fairly well versed in social rights and wrongs and whether I value them personally or not does not seem important to me. They exist, so why should I go against them in an unintelligent immature way. Yet everyone around me seems to be too weak to follow social rules. I feel that other people corrupt my own standards. That sounds like I'm displacing the blame, but I don't think I am. I would rather battle social dogma with a logical essay than creep around my girl's house when her parents aren't home. It seems that everyone around me is sick and weak "willed."

I shall use an example. I know that there is no earthly reason why I shouldn't copulate with my girl. That is, no reason in any sort of ultimate reality. I also know that it would not be hard to talk her into it, but I will not do it because there is a social sub-reality factor to be considered. In this sub-reality, the act would be "wrong." Even though ethical standards may be way short of reality I am willing to accept them. I'll be darned if anyone else seems to be willing to. No one wants to be responsible—drunk on Saturday night, sleeping with this girl and that girl, divorces at all ages, striving for nothing but money, etc.

It sounds like I am preoccupied with sex, but that is not the case at all. Everything is the same in school, too, or at least has been for years in the past. Nobody seems to study because they're interested in what they're doing. I would say that I have sought education for its own sake for about four years. Before I was 15 I did the same thing, but not directly applied to school. I built a chemistry lab at age 13 and enjoyed experimenting though I must admit it wasn't very intellectual—bombs and rockets, etc. In school I rapidly discovered that little boys were too ill-equipped to work with explosives. That, of course, didn't make much sense to me, for I managed to reinforce myself with successful bombs and rockets. Naturally my mother was scared that I'd hurt someone or myself—I have not a scar on my body (perhaps that's luck) from chemistry. If I wanted to draw something, I drew it. If I wanted to go fishing, I did.

Very few creative things seem to get any reward except from myself. Then again, maybe I'm not very creative. It seems that everything I did or said during grammar school has had to have been entertained in my thoughts until college before receiving any kind of reinforcement. This comes only occasionally from lectures of a few professors. Some graduate students are also interesting because a few of them are working for something be it money or status or grades. This makes up a very small group of people that are interesting in any kind of approximation of reality. Even professors can be pretty narrow-minded. . . .

I would like to get married and send children through college.

You say, how can you become a teacher? That poses a problem. My girl is accustomed to a fairly wealthy background and so am I. This is where everything breaks down. Where does the money come from? The people who seem to make money don't seem to stack up to my ethical standards. By God, I may rationalize myself out of any kind of work—so I'm lazy—now what do I do?

1. I try to do too many things at once:

   a) None of them get done well.

   b) Then I see that none of them get done well.

   c) Once seeing that none of them are being done well, I get sort of depressed.

   d) When I get depressed very little gets done at all.

   e) Then I see that nothing is getting done at all.

   f) When I see that nothing is getting done at all I start worrying and questioning values.

   g) When I question my values and other people's, I start to rationalize.

   h) I know I am rationalizing when I am rationalizing yet my answers seem quite valid anyway.

   i) Then I start hit or miss studying to correct my rationalization.

   j) I feel guilty if work isn't done for each class and I start cutting classes to avoid embarrassment.

   k) I know that cutting classes makes things worse, but it reduces the immediate anxiety.

   l) I look forward to the weekend to get things caught up.

   m) I usually study or sit around all weekend long while other people are fooling around.

   n) I convince myself that getting out and fooling around is an irresponsible waste of time if my work isn't done.

   o) My work is never done or caught up so I never relax.

   p) Even during summer vacation I think about all the studying and learning I have botched in the past.

   q) I usually waste my whole summer vacation, too.

   r) I know relaxing is good but I don't seem able to do it with guilt of wasting time hanging on my shoulders. When I start to go to a movie or something (even out of my room) I feel like I should not waste my time that way. Recently I've learned to relax by reading ahead in my Psych. book.

   s) When I read outside literature then I feel like my courses are pretty weak, etc.

2. It seems that someone who knows a whole lot about something doesn't want to be bothered by telling you about it. Especially if you don't know much about it.

3. I don't mind telling someone who knows less about something than I do what I know, but that gets sort of boring after a while.

Therapist's Written Reply

You did well to write so candidly about your experiences and concerns. We will now comment upon some aspects of your writing which seem especially useful to give attention to.

You report a great discrepancy between your own judgments and beliefs and values, on the one hand, and those of other people, on the other hand. You appear both confused and concerned because this is true.

Yet you probably realize, if you think about it, that such discrepancies are common, and sometimes they are very great. It need not in the future surprise you to see this difference; and it is a problem for us to try to reduce this surprise and unhappiness with the discrepancies—or to reduce *them*—as you choose.

You have to learn to live by your own values, and not constantly defer to those of others which after all are not necessarily of your choosing. This does not mean insensitivity to others, or a bland dismissal of them, but simply full knowledge of the difference, an acceptance of its existence, and an appropriate adjustment to these facts.

We do not imply that this is an easy set of attitudes and decisions to come to. You may see the world as full of injustice, and emotional and unreasonable differences between people. Being confused or feeling "let down" by all this does not change the situation; it only reduces your effectiveness. It is a difficult job for a young person to learn to live by his own emerging ideas and ideals, properly tuned to the real world. It is one of the most useful lessons one can learn, and one needs to keep re-learning it over and over throughout his life.

You indicate that your preoccupations are not only in the area of sex, but in all areas of life. We see this difference between your way of living and your values, compared with those of others, as your central problem, and as the main problem we face in these writing sessions.

We may be able to help you handle and reduce these great discrepancies as you report them by several additional comments. First, it is useful and worthwhile to be original, and to work things out for yourself; but if it is this originality that makes you feel bad, we question whether you are confident enough in your own right, and whether you are expecting too much approval from others, and we suggest that you need to become more comfortable with yourself despite these differences. You wear your differences with too much uneasiness; which is to say, they may not be as firm as you now think.

You will always find people who differ with you, and others perhaps who agree. Most people probably experience this if they are thoughtful of their values and come to strong personal ones. You can learn to appreciate more those "few professors" and "some graduate students" with whom you share values.

Other problems concerning your present life, according to your writing, are the relationships with your girl, and your inability consistently to buckle down to your scholastic pursuits.

Your troubles with your girl friend are common for young men, with the opposite sex. You are confronted with strong sexual urges, in conflict with certain strong cultural and social values; the latter seem to oppose you as an individual. We suggest that you write more about your outlook on the "social rules" and your feeling that it is immature to go against them. And write more about any further developments along these lines, especially if you are troubled by them.

You also indicate that you do not meet your own standards for studying and achievement. This appears to press greatly on you. We will pose a few questions for you to consider.

First, how rigid or perfectionistic do you think your standards are in regard to studying? What academic performance do you expect of yourself in various courses? Are these feelings of laziness, worthlessness, and guilt related to this problem of aspiration? We think they may be, but solicit your thoughts on the subject.

Second, in our emphasis on the specifics of your behavior and action, we strongly suggest you keep a record of time spent studying each day in the week. A model chart is enclosed for your consideration. You seem to lose much time in fretting over what you have not previously done, thereby wasting more time. Perhaps a tight schedule would remedy both the realistic problem of actual time lost, and help you to be successful. Time well spent and jobs accomplished will usually bring rewards that you want, and reduce tension and guilt—also, you will be charting a realistic course for your studying in this way.

There is no way for you to accomplish these small but meaningful objectives except for you to settle into working on them. Make a small beginning by the time of your next writing.

Another implication follows: When you have done your scheduled studying, take time out for recreation. You will find you can do this without guilt, if you have already met your realistic standards reasonably, and it can refresh you and make you more efficient.

Please bring in a copy of your study schedule as well as your reactions to these comments next time. And feel free to bring up additional problems that may occur to you.

Evaluation

The test-retest MMPI results on this patient were hopeful. Whereas before his writing therapy he had three scales above T score of 70 (Mf, Sc, and Ma), after therapy none were elevated. The K scale did move upward, which may represent an increase in this patient's desire and ability to control his psychological appearance. His profile changes on the MMPI are shown in Figure 3.

This patient has been seen informally several times during the academic year since his formal 6-month follow-up. He continues to show academic improvement, and his grades have increased about one letter grade on the average (from C to B). Interestingly enough, the strong emphasis on behavior change with this young man brought about a Q Sort change from −.08 (self-ideal before therapy) to +.85 (self-ideal after therapy), a figure equal to the one reported by Rogers and Dymond (1954) in his single case. It would appear that behavioral emphasis cannot bring only overt changes but also the type of cognitive changes stressed by Rogers and Dymond as representing successful O-centered therapy. Thus, as previously discussed, changes in the individual's response capacity in therapy do not appear to depend on changes in the cognitive structure, but such a cognitive change may actually represent a shift in self-references brought about by successful overt, behavioral changes.

Suggestions for Writing Therapy

Several guidelines can be suggested for the therapist who is interested in trying out writing therapy:

1. Establish a set time for the writing session, just as for an oral therapy session.

2. Allow the patient to write as he wishes, but suggest topics that might get him started if he is blocked.

3. Have the writings go on for about 1 hour or for some other regular period of time practical for the patient and the therapist. Such struc-

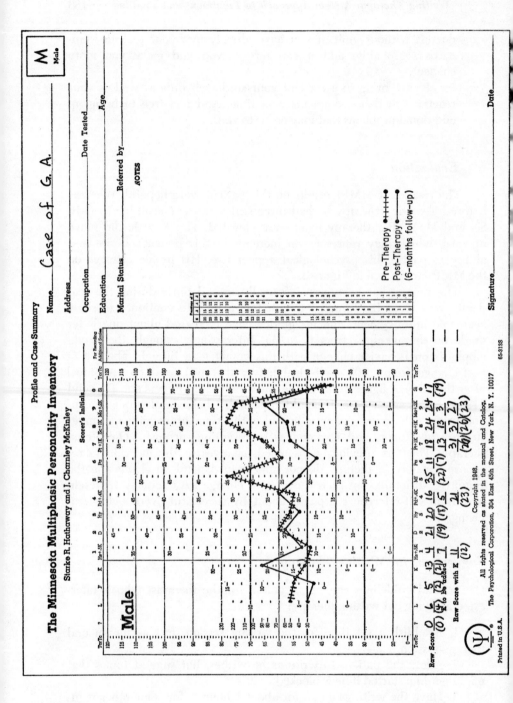

turing of procedural details is just as important here as it is for personal interviews.

4. Ask the patient to write down as specific a description of his problems as possible. If these are not described adequately in the first writing session, ask him to describe them again and give an illustration or two to guide him.

5. Underline the words or phrases that seem to represent the essence of the patient's problems (or write in the margin) and use these as the basis for your reply. Accept the patient's statement of the problem and proceed from there toward solutions, additions, and revisions.

6. Stress the importance of action at all times. Emotional problems are conceived of as reflecting the fact that appropriate behavior has not occurred at the right time or to the right extent. The emphasis on behavior is uppermost.

7. Clarify rewards if there is any evidence that the patient is moving toward solving his problems. The patient's hesitant and perplexed state of mind in meeting the requirements of daily living makes it imperative that any small amount of progress be clearly registered and reinforced. (Generally, the environment will, if properly perceived, provide inherent rewards. The therapist's reinforcement comes primarily from his labeling progress and his tying together of bits of new behavior with desired goals.)

8. Encourage the patient to set even more specific goals. This in turn helps to refine his present goals and to move the therapy along, with the patient and therapist working together.

9. If the patient's reports seem inaccurate, ask him to cite the evidence for his statements. People who are disturbed frequently misperceive and misinterpret events; situations must be described as specifically as possible.

10. Feel free to differ with the patient, but state your reasons, cite evidence to support your position, and be prepared to admit and learn from errors. Differences will inevitably exist, almost to the extent that the therapist and patient adopt the experimental behavior modification view and are active.

11. While writing therapy by itself can succeed as a therapeutic technique, the door should always be left open for the patient to request a personal interview or to switch to oral interviews. More research is needed on writing therapy with other populations. For purposes of research, however, writing therapy can apparently be used effectively without introducing any additional modes of therapy.

10 From Microcosm to Macrocosm: Structure in Society

The assumption has often been made that social forces are entirely different from individual or personal forces. This may not be true, and acting as if it were true may dampen originality and experimentation in the most significant sphere of action for any behavior-change science. Social change can be considered in the light of individual change, and the chief differences viewed as quantitative. In the social macrocosm, one is dealing with more *systems in operation* than is true with individuals, but the systematic nature of both can be described. The merit of such a position should be determined by its empirical products.

Social change involves principles of feedback, already discussed, and the emphasis on behavior or response changes, so important in the clinic, is also important in the social realm. Similarly, there are processes at the social level which can be described as deviation-amplifying and deviation-counteracting.

However, the conceptual aid offered by such notions as those just mentioned requires deliberate and careful specification at the macrocosmic level. It is more difficult to delineate and apply these concepts at social levels, and to attach specific consequences to social actions, than it is at the clinical level. One major problem involves the amount of control needed and available to the change agent. Another involves obtaining the informed and selective co-operation of the change objects within the democratic process.

It is also important to make social change for the sake of its directly observable and verifiable *consequences*. Judged by ideo-

187

logical conviction alone, its processes become as vague and confused as those of psychotherapy which are judged solely in the light of theory. It is the criteria of ideology which seem to have sent men into such inhumane directions as religious intolerance, ethnic discrimination, and authoritarian control. It is often hard, of course, to discriminate the selfish reformer from the idealistic one; the demagogue often uses the language of "total" reform, as well as ideological stereotypes, and makes an effective emotional appeal, although the behavior he seeks is nowhere clearly stated (Hoffer, 1951). The goals *and* methods, if not clearly and specifically stated, cannot properly be judged and democratically assented to.

Starting with the statement of problems, in ways that permit development of specific action and measurement of success in achieving concrete goals, social change can be accomplished through the same methods by which change is achieved with the individual.

Conceptually speaking, there are several ways of stating the problem of how to get from the microcosm to the macrocosm to produce behavior change. One way is to look upon the effort as a "game" in the modern sense of the notion of "game theory." Wiener (1964, pp. 25–28) writes that a line of human effort can be included in the notion of a game if some objective and discernible *criterion of merit* can be specified.

Another way of looking at the problem of getting from the microcosm to the macrocosm is to develop an objective account of the *constraints* or the *conditions* characterizing the narrower effort and seek to apply the same notions at the broader level (Goldiamond, 1964).

Special Problems

Despite the available conceptual and empirical help, bringing about social or individual behavior change is often difficult. Experimentally and clinically induced changes can be achieved under limited circumstances, but when these changes are tested in different or broader circumstances, the original amount of change may not hold. There may be a kind of "regression to the mean," in statistically describable ways—a widely observed phenomenon. The composite set of variables operative at a time when measurement of, or change in, some characteristic is initially achieved may not obtain fully when the same effort is cross-validated or exported in some way. Some variables cannot be completely controlled in the new situation. Even in well-controlled experimental situations, error occurs. Failure to recognize the full extent of limits and exceptions may induce further error.

Nor will the effort by the experimenter or clinician—or social changer—be steady. Attempts to modify neurotic behavior, to teach improved study habits, and to develop more effective social skills—all changes which may be genuine and reliable in a limited context—inevitably shrink, sometimes greatly, as the original "push" on the part of patient and therapist alike is not sustained. When control of the feedback is shifted from the therapist or behavior changer over to the patient, some of the important elements may be lost, perhaps because of some failure or change in the reinforcement pattern or a change in the factors in the loop involved.

In some other ways the system "loosens up" with use or over long periods of time or under somewhat different conditions from those originally observed.

Another source of difficulty in exporting change from one situation to another occurs because change does not necessarily generalize—it may have to be *applied differentially*. The learning problem involved is differentiation, not generalization. Realizing and acting on this fact seem vital; behavioral changes do not automatically generalize and remain useful. The differential application of change in behavior to new situations implies continuing analysis and a constant recognition that new contingencies may have to be handled in new ways. A new situation is, in fact, a new set of variables, which carry with them new response possibilities.

Extrapolation from this observation in clinic or laboratory to society at large presents enormous problems. Not only does society contain variables that are empirically more varied, but there is greater flux in the macrocosmic milieu, which compounds the difficulties in defining conditions for change.

The so-called demonstration study illustrates some of these problems. Such studies attempt to develop methods or variables applicable to some practical situation whereby a degree of change may be brought about or maintained. Demonstration studies may portray methods of handling disturbed children, various family problems, special educational techniques, and other social problems. It is often assumed that for the population involved, the methods used are marketable as a total package and that wherever a similar population or situation is found, the package can be appropriately applied. In a recent communication, Lagey (1964) reports that of over one hundred demonstration studies in the area of remedial efforts with delinquent and social offenders and with family problems, only three or four such centers have survived, in the sense or providing continuing guidance to a community on how to solve or work on some relevant problem.

Lagey (1960) indicated that of 136 efforts in as many cities to devise a consistent system for making budgetary allocations for community services (such as to crippled children, mental hygiene clinics, dependent mothers, and cancer victims), none has survived the conflict and competition over money, and priorities for service.

In another report, Lagey (1962) found that of 143 programs purporting to erect models suitable for community initiation and incorporation in the area of treating "multiproblem families," only three or four have been converted into day-to-day working arrangements by existing community agencies. It is as if these programs were window dressing, nice to look at and to exploit temporarily, but soon removed when hard results had to be measured to justify local financing and priority consideration.

If specific demonstration or model projects in various areas of social welfare (actually, behavior-change efforts) cannot be incorporated into the fabric of agency activity in the community, to an extent greater than that represented by these attritional figures, then surely something is amiss. Projects are now under way, according to Lagey (1964), to determine why such demonstration projects were not taken up by the community, why the changes they suggest were ignored by existing agencies, and what more viable demonstration models or projects might be needed to accomplish desired aims. The rate at which miniature or micro projects are translated to the macrocosm seems extremely low at this time, even while an urgency about attacking social problems intensifies.

Several reasons might exist for the failure of such demonstration projects. One might be that the variables in the model are, themselves, not ready for application in other settings because they are too poorly defined. One might watch another person drive a car, cook, or act, but such a demonstration is itself far from an effective specification of the variables needed to teach the novice to perform each of these skills.

Another reason might be that the variables, even if specified and defined, are not properly incorporated into the habit structure of the (new) agency. Older approaches may utilize competing skills, and thus all that is demonstrated is a conflict between skills, not a demonstration of how to employ new skills.

Still another reason might be that the specification of the new behavior needed is too weak to provide a clear prescription of how it can be incorporated into ongoing practices, even if there is a willingness to assume the new skills and no significant conflict with old ones. The person who breathes incorrectly, for purposes of singing or swimming, may try hard to acquire the necessary new method of breathing but be unable to do so until an exact analysis of the nonadaptive practices in made and corrections and new methods are instituted.

It may be that all methods intending to export a behavior-modification complex will have to be pared down to clearer basic elements. The following clinical applications will concern us first, followed by some general societal applications.

Some Specifics of Application: Clinical Observations

As has been indicated in this book, one step associated with short-term therapy is that of setting clear, concrete goals. This effort helps to define one or more means to these ends. Many resourceful means have been invented and used by behavior therapists.

One might think first of attempting to bring elements from the macrocosm to the clinic or laboratory. The behavior change sought in the smaller situation, once it reached an acceptable or workable level in the clinic (or laboratory), could be "complicated" by the introduction of typical elements from the environment outside. It would be important to select very specific elements from the macrocosm, an example of which might be that of teaching non-self-conscious behavior to patients. One might want to begin with simpler behavior, such as appropriate study habits, and then move on to more socially defined behavior.

Self-conscious, self-defeating, or socially inadequate behavior would be defined by the patient as part of his presenting complaints—as specifically as possible. The patient might be taught actual routines useful for meeting people under novel circumstances, meeting new people, and introducing people. In a behavioral approach, once these topics were introduced in the clinic, not only would the therapist and patient discuss them, but the patient would be led through steps in the clinic intended to better his skills in these problem areas. After an acceptable level of performance had been reached, satisfactory to both patient and therapist, the "outside" world could be brought into the clinical situation via the introduction of individuals or groups whose presence was intended to test out the patient's improved behavior. Time and place would be allowed for prompting the patient, and even a kind of practice session—resembling the practice session of an individual musician in an orchestra, when he goes over his own difficult part before it is combined with the whole musical group—might be used as an oasis within the larger social context, to be quickly applied in social settings outside the office as soon as possible. The similarities to role playing and group therapy are apparent, but here the emphasis is less on words and descriptions than on actual deeds. The method of successive approximations would be used to help move the patient to more viable and complex social performances.

Another way to study the exportation of change from the microcosm to the macrocosm would be for the therapist to follow the patient around, getting to know his environment and the characteristic ways in which he reacts to important situations. At first, this may operate as simply a descriptive enterprise—getting to know the patient in his natural habitat. Later, the therapist could either introduce change efforts at the time they were needed in the social context or perhaps refer to them later in a therapeutic session to propose useful, specific actions.

When parents or teachers report on disturbed children to clinicians and seek help, there is a matrix of social descriptions applicable to the therapeutic exchange between the adult and the therapist and an expectation that this interaction will have external effects, in terms of improving the child's behavior.

One advantage associated with the therapist's opportunity to observe the patient in vivo is that the therapist does not have to rely on secondhand data: he sees the patient as he really behaves. Words and distortions do not get in the way of objective descriptions of behavior or means to overcome problems.

Still a third way to study the exportation of behavior change from a clinic situation to life at large would be through the setting up of a model in the form of another person whose behavior the patient can usefully emulate. This model might be constructed from a commonsense definition of how to meet a circumstance, or it might be modeled after the patient's own desires (unrealistic as they might be at first).

One value of this method would be that it would largely preclude the patient's preoccupation with his feeling states and would center more on the usefulness of the model for the patient's problem. This method is practiced daily by teachers in helping students to say their lines well in a play, to tackle an opponent on a ball field, or to write effectively.

It would be possible through firsthand observation of both the model and the novice (or patient) to improve the behavior of both through successive, corrective efforts.

In the cybernetic terms discussed in Chapter 5, the methods of exporting change described above would be based heavily on early and precise feedback of information, upon controlling the effects or consequences of behavior change, and upon extending the loops from the smaller situation via precise steps to the larger situation. One might say that first the small loop is taught and then is expanded to include more variable conditions, thereby being translated or exported into the larger situation. There would be an implied matching of junctures of the loop between the smaller situation and the larger one. Thus the words spoken to a "stranger" in the clinical situation would be like those spoken to a real stranger in the larger situation, the elements of which would be similar yet not identical. As feedback from the smaller situation allowed for the patient to control the effects (get the results he desired), he would establish a basis for more confidence (reinforcement) and be ready to expand his behavior in new directions.

Some Parallels with Society

Not only can the individual's change in behavior be directed from the clinic (or laboratory) to the world beyond, but also the same models can be utilized to change the social situation itself or to change part of the social context in order to accommodate larger aims. And the same methodological problems discussed with regard to individual psychotherapy are involved in social settings: diagnosis; static versus change variables; the importance of circumstances or contingencies; how change can be created and directed, rather than waiting for it to occur "spontaneously"; the importance of blocking off unwanted or disturbed behavior; and how elements may be "installed" in, or "retracted" from, the system as a whole without prejudicing the operation of the system.

Divert Emphasis from Social "Diagnosis" toward Social Change

This statement follows from experience with individual behavior change in the clinic or in experimental situations where individuals or small numbers of people are introduced to some change effort. Society has been "diagnosed" thousand of times—seldom with practical usefulness. Diagnosis at any level is barren unless specific action can be derived from it or, better, the specification of some variables that can be operated on in specific ways under given conditions.

What are some of the specific actions needed and possible at the social level? The list is probably inexhaustible. As solutions are found for existing problems, new ones will appear, and solutions at one level make possible solutions at higher as well as lower levels of generality and accuracy. New "devices" applied with social problem solving in turn become part of complex stimuli for new responses, and the spiraling can go on and on. Such spiraling needs control, to be sure, but the solutions to problems are never static, and the interaction between solutions and new problems and further solutions is ever in flux. Furthermore, success tends to beget success, and once a technology of solving problems is developed, increased flexibility in innovating often follows (Ellul, 1964).

In the United States, the Bill of Rights and similar statements of personal freedom and integrity can be the framework within which social change efforts are developed. The elimination of prejudiced hiring and voting practices can then be the object of the change efforts.

Social action, analogously to individual action, should be intended and adjusted as a remedy for a given problem. It is not efficient to wait for change to take place in some obscure way when everything is "ready" for change. It is putting the cart before the horse to suppose that everyone must want equal voting rights or any other kind of social change before the change can be effective. Just as change in the individual can be induced or "legislated" as a consequence of changing the "system" by which he operates, so can social change be produced by system changes in society at large under many circumstances.

Cybernetic principles cited previously can operate as a theoretical guide to much social change. Thus, in hiring members of minority races, the emphasis can more efficiently be put on changing the behavior of the individuals (or organizations) doing the hiring, at the time and place of hiring, rather than at a more remote juncture in time, such as at school or church meetings (as desirable for other reasons as these might be). The government can give tax advantages to organizations doing systematic nonprejudicial or corrective hiring or assisting in desired democratically agreed-upon social change in other ways. Money can thus be used as a powerful "reinforcer" to achieve predetermined goals. The Federal government has begun to do so in programs such as those concerning highway beautification, aid to education, and military contracts.

Shift Emphasis from Static Variables toward the Social Capacity to Change and Solve Problems

Resistance to change is a basic fact which must be handled. Speed of change, reasons for change, and circumstances under which change is inaugurated and maintained are all sensitive points providing grounds to thwart change. In her recent book, Mead (1964) has suggested the importance of "clusters" of individuals and the concatenation of influences of groups which are able to foment and crystallize change efforts which effect "controlled evolution" and social progress. It is important to single out individuals or groups capable of joining new ventures and giving direction to large segments of social action and change. Mead attaches great importance to creative individuals who can muster support and initiate new and more favorable climates and directions for change. Skinner, with his operant-behavioral position, can be viewed as a source of such power. Publicly, the influence of a Skinner may seem minuscule, but over a decade the singular importance of the apparently limited phenomenon of programed instruction as a vehicle for improved mass education is enormous.

The manner in which President Kennedy was able to crystallize and encourage change—with a momentum continuing long after his death—was quickly and widely recognized. The vast social changes precipitated by the few men responsible for the atomic bomb and its scientific underpinnings are still being felt and will be for generations.

Sometimes social change can be carefully planned for and directed, such as the social security system. Sometimes change is thrust upon society, as with the atomic bomb and its awesome implications, in which case there is a scramble for quick means of control. However, a society that is already used to measures of control that foster effective community change minimizes the problem of unexpected change. There are bound to be unexpected atomic "bombs" as technology advances, and any general preparation, as far as the physical and behavioral health of the individual is concerned, will facilitate effective change when the necessity arises.

Mead's book is instructive at the social level, although there are many implications for the individual as well. Potential for systematic change is evident among the many social groups making up mankind, and it can be a goal of society to identify and develop this potential so as to preclude drifting and to increase the certainty of desirable directions of change.

Following a cyberneticlike formulation, one would change small elements of social behavior first; also, one would change first those elements most amenable to change and would direct the change effort at those junctures where the goals for change are most obvious and acceptable.

The major attention is thus given to getting a foot in the door to change, in some small way first, just as the therapist needs to do at the clinical level. The change effort begins where it is easiest and most likely to succeed, in the knowledge that small amounts of change will feed back a "success" report, thus acting as reinforcers; a facilitating change orbit will follow. Change efforts should be directed first at the point closest to the criterion of change, so that the number of elements needed for control is reduced and the payoff is clearly and quickly known. If change is sought too far back in the history of the system or otherwise afield from the immediate problem, the necessary tools are blunted.

Emphasize Human Ability, Not "Circumstances" Alone

Historians still debate the "great man" theory of social change. It is impossible to decide, as the question is stated, whether the man makes the times, or vice versa. What does need restating and developing is the problem of discovering, cultivating, and utilizing the talent of individuals, promoted by large-scale social actions.

To discover and develop human talent is a difficult task. Wolfle (1954) has indicated that society now loses the trainable abilities of about 75 per cent of the potentially gifted students at a point below the college degree. Isaacs (1962) reports that only about 10 per cent of the gifted children of school age receive special training. Society does not now act as if it needed to use the full talents of its members.

There is a tendency also for society to repudiate or ignore the gifted, the innovator, and the creator, probably because of discomfort with change and the challenge from those who propose it. Change is often unnecessarily coupled with destructiveness, which is loosely viewed as including any personal inconvenience brought on by change.

The mechanics of identifying, developing, and using human abilities can be built into the social system so as to reward the individual as a change agent. The innovator or creator can be considered and used as an architect of change. Society is both the change agent—when it begins to absorb and elaborate on small beginnings—and the change object. The search for talent is a search for the potential change agents and architects of change, particularly the latter, who envisage change on the widest theoretical bases.

In order to find the needed talent, large-scale screening devices—an "educational radar"—are necessary. Recent talent searches are a small step in this direction. Schools could search for and reward intellectual and creative prowess as diligently as they do athletic prowess. If schools could be compensated in some concrete and meaningful way for developing the individually talented (or, where appropriate, talented groups such as musical, theatrical, scientific, or other aggregations) through monetary or other prestigeful (and socially reinforcing) rewards, vast human resources could be usefully tapped.

Cybernetically speaking, the talented individual, with his change-agency potential, can act as an element in a new loop of widening scope and possibility. The more elements are involved, the more inclusive and expansive the potential of the loop. New response possibilities are in this way created for the rest of society, and new stimuli impinge upon almost everyone.

Create Change Instead of Waiting for It to Occur

At all junctures in social life, there is a tendency to wait for conditions for change to ripen. There is some vague assumption that change will come forth by itself at the propitious time.

At worst, the idea of spontaneous change retards maximum efforts to produce change; at best, it provides no guidance as to what conditions help produce the desired change and how to profit from such knowledge. Readiness to change can most usefully be viewed not in terms of some static condition of maturity but in terms of a cybernetic type of analysis of social elements. Which factors lie closest to the point of desired change and which factors carry a high coefficient of effectiveness in producing change are vital questions (DeLatil, 1957). The discovery and encouragement of talent are examples of factors which can contribute to change.

To illustrate, suppose that a busy intersection is jammed with cars because of failure of the signal system. Cars pile into the intersection from four directions, and with each added car, the congestion becomes worse. There is no ready way to solve this problem in terms of individuals, whether by appealing to them, threatening them, or making any kind of psychological analysis of the situation. Individuals, as such, are essentially helpless here. One can talk at length about the depravity of man, how the traffic situation allows for the working off of aggression, and how the personalities of the drivers determine their driving behavior—and get endlessly involved with useless diagnoses, regardless of their correctness. What is needed in the congested traffic situation is some overriding form of control. Repair the lights and direct an unsnarling process, under orderly control, and the problem will be efficiently solved.

There is, in cybernetic terms, no coefficient of effectiveness in trying to diagnose or analyze each individual's motivation or psychological makeup in such a situation, nor would such an approach hold any greater promise in solving minority group problems. Analyzing traits and distant origins provides no efficiently viable solutions. Change through systematic control is far more hopeful.

Emphasize Social "Needs" in Terms of Human Variables, as Well as Nonhuman Materials

To keep an economy prosperous, there is constant analysis and indirect if not direct control of prices, interest rates, taxes, and other vital variables. No economist or political thinker can today ignore these facets of social living. Large-scale computers are now at work on many segments of the economy, plotting trends and interactions and assessing and predicting as necessary for effective controls to be instituted.

The concept of an economy of "scarcity," with its implications of permanent poverty, uncontrollable economic forces, and unmotivated workers and dependents, is being seriously challenged. As in the case of the traffic jam, the problems of the economy seem increasingly to be amenable to effective controls to achieve predetermined goals.

Economic thinking which enthrones a balanced budget (like the static goal of "adjustment" for the individual) tacitly appears to accept human waste and poverty as inevitable or as lower priority problems. Social problems, like clinical problems, can be defined in static, trait-centered, motive-centered ways, which fail to take advantage of manipulatable variables. A politician, for example, recently stated that the War on Poverty program was a farce because the Bible says that the poor shall be with us always.

Society can develop and utilize effective and democratic ways of controlling itself far more than it has. Society can direct its own changes to a far greater extent and can become freer from obscure or unanalyzed forces called "natural" or "inevitable," which impede progress to its goals.

In the emphasis on economics, the psychology of human change is often neglected. The two sets of considerations—people and commodities—must be integrated and not treated as separate and independent entities. The war on poverty cannot be assumed to solve the problem of school dropouts and delinquency. Emphasis on more effective social cultivation and education of individuals is at least an essential part of a solution.

Suppress Pathology to Facilitate Problem Solving

In the clinical treatment of symptoms, the unwanted behavior is identified and the change operations conducted as necessary to seal off or preclude the undesired behavior, while at the same time fostering alternative, desired behavior.

A similar process can be described for social problems. Is a curfew relevant to the suppression of disorderly adolescent behavior in urban areas? Many say "yes"; others believe that disorderly, even mildly destructive youthful behavior is necessary to growing up and that adults should not dampen it. However, extreme actions may produce a consensus for strong restraints. Surely driving cars is properly of great concern in our society as well as being a serious problem to families with very young or very old drivers. More stringent age and other driving-condition limits are continually being adopted by states, and the goal of these limitations is to lower the number of traffic accidents' and driving infractions. Some suppressive control, as well as improved education and better road and car construction, seems likely to be necessary to solve the problem.

In a society that stresses individual choice and freedom, there is always the risk that the democratic social process will be abused by a minority, to the harm of all. The deviation-amplifying potential of license in any group, such as in the case of an irresponsible youth who is permitted unlimited use of automobiles and whose forms of recreation are unrestricted, or the case of psychopathic imposters who gull people charmingly, can transcend the limits of harmless or useful individual freedom and endanger the freedom and vital rights of everyone else.

News reports on the rioting in nine Northern cities during the summer of 1964 (the *New York Times,* 1964) bear on this issue. Many commentators thought that the rioting in New York, Rochester, several New Jersey cities, and elsewhere was fomented by racial tensions and agitators. But the *New York Times* (Sunday, September 27) further reported that study of the rioting by the Federal Bureau of Investigation indicated no ulterior motives on the part of racial or other groups. The *Times* stated: "Each of the seven major city riots, with one exception, was an escalation from a minor incident, normal in character. Similar incidents, usually routine arrests for disorderly conduct, had happened hundreds of times in most communities involved and in other cities throughout the country" (p. 84).

This report is cited for two reasons: (1) to underscore the need to detect and redirect unwanted behavior at the social level (as at the individual), with a channeling of energies into more constructive directions, and (2) to indicate that a kind of deviation-amplifying phenomenon operates socially as well as individually ("escalation" in the *Times* report). Many social phenomena of this type—riots, panics, gang fights—can develop through escalation, or a rapidly developing deviation-amplifying process, without necessitating explanation in terms of remote or ulterior cause. Useful solutions begin with suppression of the variables contributing to disorder—as an immediate alternative to license—and proceed from there toward institution of positive alternatives.

Many of society's problems are beyond changing through individual choice and responsibility. However, social correction also must reach the individual. Many social problems can be considered "educational" in nature. Through societal control exercised by way of education, individuals can be directed, usually by their choice, toward behavior which is not inimical to the welfare of all. This is a matter for empirical social planning—sometimes down to small details.

Whether one begins by suppressing unwanted behavior or uses other methods, it is likely that control will be decried by some. Suppression has been considered "unhealthy" by some clinicians, social scientists, and philosophers, who do not want to institute concerted societal control. The notion that unwanted behavior will somehow spend itself if left alone, or that desirable behavior will automatically develop in a free atmosphere, has already been discussed. There seems to be no substantial empirical support, much less cogent theory, for these notions. The alternative to a laissez-faire policy is some kind of control at some point or points. If the occurrence of unwanted behavior can be controlled, the opportunity is greater for alternative problem-solving behavior to take its place. This is a proposition that fits as well, despite more complications, at the social as at the clinical level.

Install or Retract Elements in the System Rather than Alter the Entire System

As discussed in the previous chapters, the method of much behavior change can be described in terms of ways and means to remove unwanted behavior from the system and to install wanted behavior. In-stalling social skills among adolescent patients; eliminating obnoxious be-havior among children; inserting in a given loop behavior which is new to the loop in question but not necessarily new in the behavioral reper-toire of the person—this is the approach to individual change advocated in this book.

The same approach can be applied to the larger social fabric. Exam-ples include controls on the use of city streets or public accommodations, regulation of behavior in the public school system in order to cope better with school dropouts, and the suppression of spurious charity drives.

This viewpoint at the clinical level or at the macrocosmic level consists of developing new attitudes on controls that promote change without the necessity of "major surgery."

Much in the way of change can be activated by surprisingly simple means at times. The potentialities for mundane (although significant) change should not be overlooked simply because the change does not entail overhauling the system as a whole.

Altering the entire system implies the imposition of a set of outside standards which dismisses the value of the whole system. This is an entirely different problem from setting out to help make the system work as effectively as possible to solve existing problems, which this book takes up as its main task.

The Unchanging and Change

Despite this stress on changes in societal processes to achieve goals more effectively, there are aspects of a system which must remain fairly stable to permit the installation of effective change agents. The cyber-netic view of systems in operation takes note of the fact that there are facets of the system—conceptual properties as well as concrete aspects—that need to change relatively little to permit the achievement of goals. If all aspects of a system change at once, chaos is likely to result—or at least inefficiency stemming from a disruption greater than the minimum necessary to achieve a stated purpose.

The purpose in the clinical setting is to bring about selective (most efficient) change, centering on unwanted or self-defeating behavior, not change in all facets of the system. One crucial way to define unwanted behavior is that it is a condition that precludes useful alternatives. The goal here is to develop a system which changes and can accommodate change continuously without being destroyed, without prejudicing its ability to function effectively, and without precluding (or seriously limit-ing) its capacity to observe and direct change.

There are some aspects of society, then, considered as a system that should not change, once achieved. Included are:

1. The ability to absorb continuing change
2. The opportunity for any (social) elements to alter their hierarchical status within the system as a totality
3. The rejection of change that would damage the resilience of the system (society) as a whole
4. The assurance that change is the property of the system as a whole and is not dominated by part-systems consideration alone (that is, in a way that would injure the stability and flexibility of the total system)

Translated into concrete social terms, these generalization yield the following notions.

Assuming that change is inevitable, it should be planned so that it is not disruptive, damaging, irrelevant, or retrogressive to humane or social problem-solving efforts when it occurs. Open hostilities between various social groups may occur when social change has not been planned for in ways commensurate with the "needs" of the system and within the system's capabilities of known strengths and weaknesses.

Change should not be precluded indiscriminately. The status of, say, religion or of particular aspects of morality or ethics, or even the regard for more objective features of our society, during the next 5 to 10 decades is uncertain. Organized religion, and many moral and ethical elements in our present society, are considerably different from what they were 5 to 10 decades ago, and further changes will occur even though their form cannot be foreseen. "Hardening" or insulating the role of any social element such as moral or ethical views against change is at best an irrelevance and at worst an invitation to unnecessary future trouble. State blue laws would appear to be an example of statutory hardening of moral views which unnecessarily creates friction, even turmoil, for future generations and which often is not necessary to accomplish even a temporary purpose.

Selectivity in promoting and absorbing change appears to be the most efficient approach. Change that would destroy the system as a whole should generally be eschewed, such as may occur from the use of the atomic bomb; complete economic blockade; the total destruction of major insect groups or other natural forms of life, which would prejudice the "balance" of nature; or lifetime incarceration or execution of troublesome people.

Near total (but never complete) destruction in the system in individual therapy is probably best exemplified in lobectomy, in which a portion of the brain is excised; and in radical electroshock therapy, which reduces a man to a purely vegetative level of existence temporarily on the grounds that there is no other hope of interrupting a chronically convulsive or psychotic condition.

Insofar as possible, change should be geared to the properties of the system as a whole. Knowledge of society, or of the individual, however, is probably never going to be complete enough to permit system control to proceed wholly by logic (that is, by hypothetico-deductive chains of reasoning). There must be continuous experimentation, observation, guessing from testing, risk taking, and checking everything with data empirically derived (Mendelson, 1964; Todd, 1964). The system as a whole is always in the process of definition—or, better, redefinition. The system is always changing; it is never definitionally complete in the empirical sense.

Even though change is planned, it is likely to fall short of idealized versions. This is the way in science. One hypothesizes about what will be the case under a given set of conditions, but forces which are not yet controllable or predictable contribute to the answer and to changes in the answer from time to time and under various circumstances.

Experimentation, then, must be built into all social systems. Franklin Roosevelt conspicuously experimented with economic reforms and with other facets of the social order; these efforts proved useful in many ways, and every President since then has done so, in varying degrees. If, however, instead of this experimentation, only previous states of the system had been utilized and only deductive principles based on the previous state of the system had been applied, effective changes (or ineffective changes which led to effective ones) might never have been instituted. More drastic actions might therefore eventually have taken place because of pressure or apparent necessity.

Currently, tax reforms are being experimented with as a measure for injecting the economy with new vitality, and the efforts appear to be successful. Such changes are being inaugurated with at least some view toward the total system's enhancement.

Values, and Society as Change Agent

In the case of the individual and his neurotic or antisocial problems, clinicians have traditionally tended to speak of changing his views and values and then have expected more or less automatic change in his behavior. In this book the route of more direct behavior change has been outlined, instead, and applied to the macrocosm as well as to the microcosm.

Value changes eventually do appear when behavioral change is dictated by law, as, for example, in minority group relations. With greater opportunity (behavior change, new response potential) for a minority group, value changes develop in the ways in which minority group members are viewed by others. Values held appear to have no priority over, and no independence from, other behavior. Value statements are, in essence, simply summary statements about the behavioral preferences or statements about preferred ways to maintain control over behavior (or over people—oneself or others) in given types of situations. The values of individuals and societies show themselves reliably only in observable behavior.

In the clinical setting the traditional therapist is usually uncertain about value changes in patients. Clinicians may infer value changes but seldom document them. This problem of values and their behavioral significance can be clarified if values are viewed as derived or inferred from the behavior observed in specific situations, rather than assuming that their significance transcends their behavioral expression or that their verbal representations are of major importance.

The unwanted behavior observed in individuals and in society represents by-products of a coalition of variables in which the system is not operating well. The unwanted behavioral products can be altered by manipulating relevant variables to produce change of a desired type. Thus the emphasis is on finding effective manipulable variables, and the setting—whether individual or social—would seem to be a secondary problem.

Society thus acts both as a massive change agent and as the change object. This means that one facet of society (government) takes hold of large or small elements in order to induce change. There are countless instances where individual change is too insignificant to solve large problems, where only concerted social action will meet the demands of a situation. And there are cases where individual change, even if accomplished, can be washed out by overwhelming social pressures against it. This fact can be as well documented on the clinical as on the social level. However, other individuals, and society, can throw weight behind individual change; this is what Mead (1964) seems to be writing about and is an important way of encouraging and maintaining individual change.

How social change implements or bolsters individual change effort cannot yet be precisely detailed. One of the large-scale scientific and social enterprises of the rest of the twentieth century in the area now loosely designated as the social sciences might well be the formulation of procedural details on how small-scale changes can be amplified at broader social levels with accuracy and relevance.

11 Controversial Issues

The therapeutic methods that have been presented in this book may be controversial, as indeed any type of psychotherapy seems sure to be today. Moreover, there are certain details in therapeutic method upon which even the authors do not fully agree. However, these are in no sense basic differences about theory, practice, or ultimate goals, for example, about the superior effectiveness of therapeutic methods that favor direct, specific intervention with current problems; the importance of applying all current knowledge of how learning and behavior change occur and of trying in every reasonable way to make psychotherapy more efficient and effective; and the fact that through such methods, the current state of psychotherapy can be rapidly improved and extended to begin to meet the social needs of today and tomorrow.

Nevertheless, the reader may wonder whether the "pro" statements do not support views contrary to the basic themes of this book. These statements should instead be interpreted as an attempt to focus on the merits of conventional views and methods (particularly the depth and nondirective approaches); they are not recommended as ways to achieve the most effective and efficient behavior change through psychotherapy, but rather as methods of interviewing and analyzing human behavior that are not closely associated with efficient behavior change. These methods have different results, which are peripheral—or even irrelevant—to behavior change and psychotherapy; they will be discussed this way here. The reader should understand, then, that the pro view does *not* represent a belief that the view is effective for behavior-change purposes, but states *the most favorable view of alternative methods considered possible within the theoretical framework of this book.*

The "con" statements, on the other hand, indicate a stronger concern with the ways in which the therapist has been diverted and confused by conventional views and methods in trying to change human behavior. Except for extremely small and inefficient contributions to psychotherapeutic change, these methods are viewed as having little merit. Since behavior change is ostensibly their purpose, they should be judged only in that context.

The very concept of this chapter has already struck preliminary readers as novel and controversial. It may even appear foolhardy; critics are seldom so readily provided with ammunition. But to gloss over or otherwise obscure differences of opinion for strategic purposes is better intended for success in the marketplace than in the search for truth called "science." As in court, differences are aired in the hope that the truth will be more likely to out this way than when unity is imposed for strategic purposes.

We have tried to present both views of controversial issues as effectively as possible, and while our sympathies obviously lie in one direction, perhaps our intellects can acknowledge others fairly.

The Value of Anamnesis

PRO

Recalling early memories, verbally "reliving" traumatic experiences, and tracing the development of attitudes vital to the uncovering process appear to have been greatly exaggerated as therapeutic tools. However, when current problems seem particularly intractable to change, a review of past history in therapy sessions (occasionally even at great length) can be useful. Sometimes it appears to be easier to persuade a patient to define and speak usefully of past problems than to induce him to discuss present embarrassments or troubles. In this way the past may serve as an effective entry to the present and provide the therapist with clues to current problems.

As a process, anamnesis can also provide the patient and therapist with a sense of the underlying consistency of the patient's behavior and of his roots and identification with man and society; it can give the patient a feeling of oneness with his environment and of understanding, as opposed to an attitude of mysticism, about how his problems develop. The almost universal client complaints of isolation and uniqueness bespeak the feeling of mystery about how problems develop, which the patient can profit from dispelling in preparing to solve them. By coming to see himself in the perspective of his personal history, the patient can acquire a sense of the naturalism in the development of problems; this in turn can make it easier to show him the way to solve them by concentrating on living habits designed to undo this behavior and substitute other, more effective behavior.

Whether this process of reviewing the past results in therapeutic inefficiency may depend on how the therapist handles this review. Anamnesis is not the most direct, efficient way to handle problems; it is a second, alternative way of trying to help the client when more direct methods falter. It would seem undesirable to start with it since it will usually prove unnecessary.

When it might be useful, the therapist should make this review as brief as possible and use it only for patients who seem to need a different vantage point from which to view their problems. It should be utilized only when it is necessary to reach current problems that are the primary focus and criteria of the review. Certainly it should last no longer than necessary to achieve the specified ends of therapy, which are always kept in the forefront.

The uncovering process should not be an end in itself unless the client comes to the therapist for the specific purpose of discovering and uncovering his past. If he wishes to do just this instead of, or as a supplement to, therapy, it would seem unnecessarily rigid to refuse him, if the therapist is interested and time and money are readily available. In such a case, however, the goal would not be efficient therapy, and this should be clearly stated by the therapist from the start. Rather, it would be the study of a personal history presumably for the purpose of helping one to understand himself better, in the same way that one might study the history of his ancestors, community, or national origins.

Such a purpose would be a rare one, for most clients who ask for the uncovering, analytic process are looking for more achievement, control of troublesome emotions, and enjoyment of life. The therapist matches such expectations with his faith in the uncovering process, although often on a more modest scale than his client. The therapist who enters the process with doubts, and who states them, may change the outcome, as when the efficacy of pills or hypnosis is questioned, by dispelling an irrational belief in the efficacy of the approach. The therapist might be able to preserve the placebo effects of therapy by keeping his doubts to himself. Any psychotherapeutic advantages that inhere in learning about one's psychological roots have yet to be proved, but the search for truths about himself and his world will probably always be valued by Promethean man.

The accuracy of the self-reports of historical material is of course open to serious question, and most therapists assume distortion even though they use such reports loosely as if they were accurate or inaccurate according to the way they fit the therapist's theoretical mold. But a fair degree of accuracy seems possible in documenting a person's life history, even when he is the primary source of information, if the therapist follows scientific rules of interviewing to provide objectivity and cross-validation whenever possible. Such a search can use other sources—relatives, friends, schools, records—that the interested client can learn to consult objectively. The rules for making objective observations are the same as in any scientific endeavor.

CON

Even though the examination of past history has been overemphasized in psychotherapy, an anamnesis review may occasionally be beneficial, when the discussion of current problems is unproductive or at an impasse. But the current situation is really the productive one. This view must be kept firmly in mind always. For the patient's recourse to the past may be only a further attempt to escape from his problems. The anamnestic review has little merit for the following reasons.

First, therapists often discover, as did Ellis (1955b; 1957; 1958) and Stevenson (1961), that when they abandon the long-term exploratory, depth approach, their therapy is as effective, or more so. Phillips and Johnston (1954) also found, within a specific setting, that an ahistorical approach to parent-child problems produced better results than a more probing, historical approach.

Second, many patients are likely to be poor self-reporters. Some people do not resonate well to verbal therapy or utilize self-reporting opportunities. Passing over the current setting often acts to make these unresponsive patients even more unresponsive or dependent instead of enabling them to understand their plight and control their behavior more adequately. The very change of emphasis from the "self" to very objective and matter-of-fact elements in a patient's life is more helpful than the search for historical material.

Third, the resourcefulness of the therapist is not challenged by a review of patient history as it is when he must make his counsel specific to the present and project it beyond the consulting room; yet such specification and projection are necessary to effect change in behavior, particularly with those who are least amenable to verbal, consulting-room therapy (for instance, children and adolescents, very anxious and hostile adults, many psychopathic adults, and most psychotics). Therapy for such patients cannot depend upon the verbal exchange in the consulting room, for this would be hopelessly limiting. In such cases the recourse should not be to even more untenable and unreliable methods that require still more searching and valid self-reporting; rather, there should be an attempt to project the therapeutic arena out into the patient's life beyond the consulting room.

Some *change agent* must be identified. The presumptive theoretical reason for the ineffectiveness of psychotherapy springs from the lack of a change agent which acts on or in the change object. This should be clearly recognized, and if the patient is not his own change agent another change agent should be sought. The kind of case cited in the "pro" discussion is not being encouraged to function as well as he could, as his own change agent. He is relying more than necessary on the therapist to find a cure partly through exploration of the past. The hope that anamnesis can help to overcome this problem is a departure from learning-centered or cybernetic approach to behavior change. It would also be uneconomical if any other shorter-term methods could be instituted.

Not only is the personal review of one's life not as valuable as a historical review of one's community or nation, but also the information is much less reliable when the individual reports on himself in his quest for self-understanding. Outside checks for validity of data on the individual are not readily available. In fact, to carry the individual's historical survey to its logical conclusion—analogizing between the individual and the community—would require seeking outside reference points and depending more upon the reliability of external data than subjective data.

How old does one have to be before he can report reliably upon himself and give perspective to his past? Probably adolescent at least, and even then most therapists would probably not be very confident of accuracy. Nor would one expect valid reporting from a person with psychotic or psychopathic tendencies. The therapist would therefore be able to work on such a historical review only with an individual who is *already* fairly objective, verbal, and self-critical. This paradox would violate the principle of making behavior-change theory and practice applicable to as many people as possible.

Using Transference in Psychotherapy

PRO

The patient's irrational love and hatred for the therapist have been endlessly embroidered and explicated, and the recognition of this phenomenon is probably one of Freud's greatest contributions to an understanding of difficulties in psychotherapy. The theory advanced in this book minimizes transference as much as possible, even to the point of recommending the use of programed mechanical therapy and proposing a model of the therapist functioning in this way. One cannot, however, pretend that just because the therapist's goal is scientific objectivity this will automatically become reality.

If the therapist is able to plan his procedures and relationship on a rational basis and function effectively in this way in his work with the patient, the psychoanalytic concept of transference, while it will surely crop up, will be minimal. The patient will receive the built-in rewards and reinforcements as he improves his behavior to reach his goals—for the therapist's approbation is not the emphasis, but rather the patient's own behavior and its consequences. The patient and therapist should hold, or come to hold as rapidly as possible, practically identical views of the desirability of certain patient behavior, and the patient should see and use the therapist rationally as a useful tool to achieve these ends.

But transference will occur. The patient will at times look upon the therapist as a savior or a devil, project past attitudes toward parents and others upon him, and attribute mystical powers to him or, for that matter, to the teaching machine, despite the fact that the therapist is trying to avoid such irrationality. One cannot ignore the patient's desperate hopes for succor, which lead him to endow the therapeutic machine with greater potentialities for good and evil than it possesses or claims to possess.

The therapist should try to minimize this transference process. His approach as outlined in this book should make transference much less important than in depth therapy, where it is often considered a desirable vehicle in the search for solutions, as a patient's blind faith in pills or hypnosis is believed to advance his cure. Even the silences and passivity in nondirective therapy seem likely to encourage fantasying about the therapeutic relationship. Making the goals of therapy and the specific functions of the therapist explicit to the patient contrasts sharply with the therapist's vague or ambiguous role in analytic or nondirective therapy, which may readily lead to the distortions of transference.

Yet, the patient's hopes and fears may range widely between the rational and the irrational. The fact that the patient projects hopes and fears onto the therapist is not necessarily unreasonable or useless, of course, for the hope may be the opposite of depression, and the fear may stem from a realistic appraisal of his prospects. But although neither depression nor hope may have much objectivity, they can represent the kind of mood that facilitates or retards the search for a therapeutic solution.

A theme of this book is that transference (that is, the projection onto the therapist of emotions properly belonging elsewhere or the blind hope or despair attending the therapeutic process) should be sharply curtailed, and often eliminated, in the best interests of desired behavior change. But it is a proper, even vital, subject for discussion within this therapeutic approach, as part of the attack or irrationality. The patient can learn to control and make his unreasonable interactions with other people rational.

The positive aspects of this approach can sustain therapy through bleak times when despair seems almost overwhelming. The major difference in this approach from that used by depth therapists lies in the attempt both to minimize it and to make it rational in the sense that the patient is helped to recognize it at all times, instead of the therapist's utilizing it without the patient's awareness, as if it were essential to therapeutic success, or analyzing it at length as if it was of highest priority.

CON

If by "transference" is meant any kind of regard, positive or negative, then the view is probably correct that "transference will occur," even if the therapist is a machine. If, on the other hand, one holds to a *formal* definition of transference, the matter is quite different. English and English (1958, p. 562) have defined transference as follows:

1. Displacement of affect from one object to another object to another.
2. Specif., the process whereby a patient shifts affect applicable to another person onto the psychoanalyst. E.g., the patient directs upon the analyst the hatred he feels toward his father.

In this sense, transference is not compatible with efficient therapy. It does not characteristically occur in most forms of psychotherapy; moreover, it should not occur if the most effective behavior change is to be promoted. Recent research is beginning to show that a variety of instruments can serve a therapeutic purpose. Such techniques as operant conditioning, reconditioning, desensitizing, and restructuring all rely on a set of variables different from those in a transference theory; in fact, they largely preclude transference.

To the extent that transference does occur in psychotherapy, therapy is vitiated. The emotional dredging, the state of dependency, and the casting of the relevant variables in the form of historical material, especially repressed historical material, all prolong therapy unnecessarily.

As transference develops in depth therapy, it has to be "resolved," which takes additional time, the entire process serving no purpose that is demonstrably salutary to eventual behavior change.

The Therapist as a Model

PRO

The patient may take the therapist as a model and seek to emulate him, despite the lack of encouragement. The patient may even develop habits from the teaching machine, that is, from its ways of "reasoning," as exemplified in its teaching methods, for some teaching machines try to utilize a model process of reasoning in arriving at right and wrong answers frame by frame. Some machines, of course, try only to reward correct responses rather than to stress the process by which the responses are reached.

However, the therapist must inevitably represent far more to the patient than the machines does (since he is at least more like the patient), so that the patient may well observe and imitate many facets of the therapist's behavior without the therapist's wish that this should occur outside the therapy sessions—or his knowledge that it does. For example, if the therapist is a machine. If, on the other hand, one holds to a *formal* plunges into or defers a discussion of sex, or acts or talks deliberately or impulsively, his client may adopt similar behavior. For the sake of efficiency, the therapist should focus upon the patient's problems and try to confine the patient's learning to the problems delineated during therapy, although, of course, the therapeutic process cannot always be tailored in this fashion. In fact, some experienced therapists claim they can tell which of their acquaintances have been in treatment with certain therapists because of certain distinctive new behavior that they exhibit.

This idiosyncratic influence can and should be minimized by concentrating on the patient's problems and attempting to exclude all that is irrelevant. The therapist should also be attentive to his presence as a therapist and to the meaning of his presence to the patient. Even though he attempts to minimize transference, he can expect it to occur and can be aware of it, and therefore he can constantly try to improve himself as a model of effectiveness for his own purposes as well as for the purposes of his role as a teaching machine—aside from the fact that, logically, he should be a model of what his theories produce.

How many times the patient comments with cynicism upon the behavior of leaders—religious, political, social, professional—who say or imply, "Don't do as I do, but as I say." True, this can easily become an excuse for the patient to continue self-defeating behavior and to cease working toward self-determined goals, but for the therapist's actions to be consistent with what he says is a form of good instruction.

Of course, the therapist may function simply as a behavior-change machine, and the theme of this book would direct him in this way. The best teaching machine today is likely to be a model of the rational methods of learning used by the best teachers. Unlike the old "educational" toys, in which chance determined the correct answer or which used hidden and seemingly occult circuitry, the best modern machine is intended to be a paragon of the scientific thinking and reasoning that the teacher hopes his students will learn to imitate—involving such behavior as reading carefully, evaluating knowledge, stating why one is right or wrong, and adding to and reusing prior learning.

If the therapist is not deliberative or rational or honest or perceptive, his client is not likely to learn to use these methods in solving his problems. For example, if the therapist attacks his own insomnia (or his anxiety about groups or his anger) by taking pills, it seems doubtful that he knows what or how to teach his client about solving such problems most effectively. Even if he knows a technique that might work for the patient but not with himself, it is not likely that he knows how to apply it effectively.

Of course the therapist is not the only model that can effect behavior change in the client. Many others can and do. But by the very process of coming to the therapist, the patient usually indicates his unusual regard for him or his role and so seems more likely to respond to the therapist's behavior.

CON

In "talking" therapy, the interpersonal influence is probably maximized, as observed above, with some patients especially. The statement that some therapists can tell when an acquaintance is undergoing therapy with a given therapist has its counterpart in child psychology in the statement that one can tell what kind of child the principal in a school (or a parent or a teacher) is going to refer for help by knowing what kind of person the principal is and what his attitude is toward children and their problems. The influence of people on people is of course extensive.

Such influences are mentioned only in an attempt to put in perspective the therapist's distinctive influence on the therapy and on the patient. The therapist probably should not try to efface himself, for his personal influence can and should be exercised for the patient's benefit. The crucial fact to remember is that this influence can, however, be harmful. Many patients may have been injured or their progress hindered by too strong reliance on the idiosyncratic thinking of a given therapist, thinking which is contrary to the views of other therapists and sometimes even of other therapists treating individuals from the same family. Transference is often considered necessary to the therapy, and the therapist is accepted as a model of a human being and as a healer, without criticism or limitations. The idea of the therapist as a model decision maker in such a case also sometimes looms spectacularly large. Some therapists are proud of the fact that their patients cannot or do not make even routine decisions without talking them over first in therapy.

The view of this book is that the therapist should be able to function for the patient as well outside his office as within it, through other environmental forces; that is, if cogent principles of change are utilized, it does not matter who carries out the change plan. This can be done as well, or perhaps better, by many nonprofessionals acting in adjunctive roles as by professional therapists. If the therapist has a realistic grasp of the behavioral and environmental conditions that give rise to the disturbed behavior, he can manipulate these variables from a distance or can instruct others on how to do this. If the therapist has to depend upon his own presence or voice in a personal sense, he is reducing his own effectiveness as a therapist and may even be reinforcing dependency.

Personal interviewing itself in psychotherapy may well have a vitiating, not enhancing, effect on efficient behavior change. The preliminary evidence on writing therapy (Chapter 9) suggests that it may produce better results than talking therapy. In the writing effort and product, apparently the patient identifies the variables relevant to his difficulty more rapidly, the patient and therapist have readier recourse to what has been said (written) in previous sessions, and there is a reduction of distractions.

It is pleasant to like people and be liked by them; this condition may be desirable or necessary in achieving certain goals, and few would want to exclude such a benignity from life. It may well be, however, that pleasant interpersonal interview relations, which utilize no specificity about the important variables for changing behavior, have little, or even a harmfully palliative, relationship to behavior-change circumstances. Much behavior does change without the benefit of specific interpersonal activity.

In the behavior-change process, the role of the therapist is to identify the relevant variables necessary to achieve specified goals and to identify and implement the means for the patient to act appropriately upon these variables. If an interpersonal relationship were *necessary* to point up the specific variables needed for behavior change or if the advantage of such a relationship in extending the therapeutic situation to life situations could be proved, interpersonal relations in therapy (or using the therapist as a model) would be as worthwhile as some theory now contends.

Just as an instructor in physical hygiene (or violin playing or grooming) can act as a model for his teachings, so the therapist can act as a model of effective habits. Many models in life are not only instructive but also invaluable; model behavior is not, however, inherent in any single person such as the therapist. It is a reference point that can be followed profitably by anyone. Aspects of behavior can be modeled by a variety of instructional media or by a wide assortment of people; the process is not limited to interpersonal communication between the learner and the teacher or between the therapist and the patient.

Is Rigidity the Price of Efficiency?

PRO

Oppenheimer has written of the necessity of narrowing one's behavior in order to reach goals: "Narrowness is not an accident . . . but a condition of knowledge . . . in all scientific things. . . . knowledge precludes other knowledge . . . by the very techniques, powers, and facts of its acquisition and by the way it organizes the chaos that is the world around us" (1960). This is a statement of the vital case for narrowing the aim in psychotherapy to the problems at hand and for avoiding the pursuit of much pleasing or even desired learning in therapy that is possible, but nevertheless incidental to the main task.

However, if the therapist, during the therapeutic process, were to abandon his concern with the broadening of interests, the fuller expression of emotional potentialities, the richer experience of talents, and the fuller understanding of man's life only in an effort to solve some relatively trivial problems that the patient may first bring to therapy, would he do justice to the gradient of goals within which he would hope man (including his client) would choose?

The nature of man's immediate problems may not readily reveal the breadth of his potential behavior. A parent may, for example, train his children to be capable students, or he may build a system of rewards and punishments into the family living which develops good habits of courtesy or effective social relations. But this parent may also be a heavy drinker who retires completely from affectional family relations, and he may impair his children's development in this way. But perhaps not. Perhaps the therapist cannot teach such a parent-client how to be effective as a parent without coming to grips with the parent's own problems, even though the parent may prefer not to. The child could suffer in important ways that therapy might not come to grips with if it were concentrated only on how to control the child's habits of courtesy or study.

Efficiency in living need not result in rigidity, unless the therapist fails to specify problems and areas of human development which impinge upon the patient's presenting complaints and the patient is unaware of or prefers not to discuss. The credo of the therapist probably should encompass the broadest possible human values that might become apparent during the therapeutic process. He may even need to assign a priority to problems and suggest a hierarchy of their importance.

Of course, solving even unimportant problems is worthwhile; to say otherwise would be saying that not solving problems could be better than solving them. How the therapist introduces the greatest breadth into defining them and into helping to determine their relative importance would seem to be the question.

This question does not concern how to get on with the process itself, for we have already discussed elements such as specificity, focusing, steps, substitutions, and interference. Nor does it suggest that the therapist be diverted from intense problem-solving efforts, to wonder during treatment whether it is worthwhile, what is life itself, or whether human beings are so continuously in flux that it is meaningless to define and solve problems.

The point is that one must choose during therapy what is to be worked on. This process involves a system of values, and someone must select the programs from the teaching-machine library, someone must even choose what to write for the library, and someone must steer the course of the interview.

Any success at problem solving is useful in moving the client ahead and facilitating his additional successes. Nor does the question about values challenge the therapist's role as a tough-minded scientist-teacher. The problem concerns solely what role he should play in emphasizing alternatives and priorities among problems available to work on.

Although narrowness and rigidity are not the price of efficiency in the type of psychotherapy advanced in this book, they can and do occur in all forms of treatment, among diverse therapists. To avoid them, the therapist should be alerted in developing his own sense of values.

CON

The depth therapist generally contends that a broad, speculative, inquiring therapy yields fruitful notions about behavior over and above solving problems, but to discuss therapy as anything but problem solving is to digress from the emphasis of this book.

Identifying daily problems and stating them as precisely as possible not only is necessary for efficient therapy but also helps to produce those broad social attitudes and by-products that the "pro" position above would tackle. Many children and adolescents are reported to be more loving, more responsive, more sensitive socially, and better able to relate consistently and well to others after a period of rigorous, response-centered, specific behavior therapy. In the study by Haring and Phillips (1962) of a highly structured classroom environment as a treatment setting for emotionally disturbed children, the children developed startlingly sensitive displays of spontaneous concern for others, as well as better motivation in schoolwork. Moreover, they were able to move out independently from minimal assignments to creative work and extra effort.

The therapeutic concern with the largest view of man, in the grandest sense, is like the search for happiness. Broad goals seem inevitably to appear as the by-products of mundane aspects of daily living; they are not ends pursuable directly. Of course such therapeutic goals may be used to rationalize any kind of therapy, since there is ultimately no objective way to evaluate success.

To paraphrase Oppenheimer, one might say that narrowness is not an accident, but a condition of psychotherapy. If the therapist cannot name, work on, and alter even the simplest ways in which daily life has gone awry so that it becomes more productive and satisfying, how then can he work effectively toward grander accomplishments?

The "Whys" of Therapeutic Failure

PRO

A rationale has been presented here for a new approach to psychotherapy. New systems come and go frequently enough so that wise laymen have good reason to challenge the permanence of any particular theory. The view here, however, offers more hope than a fad because it concentrates on problems which can be observed and formulated in their natural habitat and which can be solved empirically and validated scientifically. The derivations and reifications that have troubled therapists previously in the development of theories that eventually prove ineffective or inadequate in problem solving (though they might have other uses) hopefully have been eliminated.

However, since no method is successful with all patients, the rate of success and failure must be the ultimate test of all psychotherapy.

In explaining his failures, the therapist must say either that his theory applies only to a limited number of patients with specified personal characteristics or problems or that some patients are inaccessible to further psychotherapy because of the nature of their problems (such as organic, chemical, or physiological). Or he may conclude, as any therapist of any persuasion might, that he simply does not have enough knowledge yet to know how to modify or apply his theory to this subgroup.

The procedures outlined in this book call for exercising all possible therapeutic skill and knowledge toward making the patient function as a rational, effective man. This can be done far more often than many therapists appear to realize and has *not* ordinarily been well tried in the patient's past. However, even with this approach there are patients who drag on interminably or who stop coming before their problems are solved, and with whom a different approach therefore seems justified. Even in these cases, the change in method most likely to be successful, however, would seem to depend upon the choice of variables to be manipulated and processes to be obstructed or inserted rather than upon the very concept of the therapeutic approach—or whether change itself is possible. The variety of variables and agents and ways of manipulating them is almost infinite.

When a patient has not responded well, the ways of "backing up" are a crucial question. Somewhere between 3 and 9 months, perhaps, any approach should be modified when the client is not responsive. If he has not already done so, the therapist might suggest that the patient bring his spouse or join a group, perhaps in addition to his individual therapy; that he talk about his past more fully in the hope that this will shed light on his present problems; that he take or retake a personality test and have it interpreted; or that he try a different therapist. Eventually, however, the client will have to learn to structure, discipline himself, and plan well if he is to handle his life effectively. Developing these habits to achieve stated goals is vital to any satisfying life—and to successful therapy.

In a somewhat paradoxical sense, the problem could also be stated as one of training the patient in how to be a good patient—a rational and consistent man, accomplishing and integrating his activities and goals. Obviously, no patient who starts this way would need therapy in the first place.

However, when therapy appears to be failing for a period long enough to be a reasonable test, the alternative of a different therapeutic approach altogether should be considered for the same objective trial as alternative choices of variables, agents, and processes with behavior-modification theory. There is much to gain and little to lose, and an alternative approach may produce more successful results in a way that cannot be immediately explained. Occasionally this happens, even if the client only becomes more accessible to problem solving as a result.

There is, of course, always some danger that the willingness to use an alternative approach may determine one's ultimate success with this approach. For example, at the very point when one labels this kind of therapy a failure and is ready to resort to a less direct method (such as dream analysis), this may be the moment to search for another change agent, rather than decide prematurely to deny the patient the extra effort that might work (especially if the therapist is inexperienced, neutral, or has little confidence in this approach in the first place).

But somehow, through any approach, the therapist and client should be able to measure and label failure as well as success. Then they are properly prepared to experiment with an alternative approach, even as a temporary expedient, when the current method appears to be failing.

CON

In any therapy there are likely to be failures. The therapist should, of course, learn from his failures as well as from his successes. Establishing a theoretical rationale for a failure, however, may depend on whether the patient has a change agent. This makes it possible to distinguish among a patient who is not interested in change, a patient who is unwilling to make even a modest effort, and a patient who appears to try hard but makes little progress. It is a question of what variables are needed for behavior change.

Children usually cannot decide that they need help, and adolescents often resist help. In the case of children, the parents can act as change agents. In the case of adolescents, parents and teachers may sometimes be able to act as change agents to a degree, but usually not as much as with children. There is a greater handicap in therapy with adolescents than with children. The difference is that although both may fail to perceive, as do adults, the opportunity for change that therapy offers, the therapist is not deterred with children, but with adolescents, he often is.

There is the same distinction between willing and unwilling adults or between adults who are too upset to perceive their plights clearly and work on them and those who are upset but who still hope and try. Apparently, the difference lies in the therapist's ability to enlist the aid of the patient or his proxy. If the patient is his own change agent, well and good; but if he is not, what course is open to the therapist?

On the other hand, failure sometimes occurs when everyone concerned seems to have done his best. To what factors can failure be assigned in such a case? Effort and good intentions do not appear to be the crucial variables. Some methods are needed to get the patient to behave in ways that are relevant to the solution or amelioration of his problems. If the patient cannot be so impelled, there is little likelihood that he will change.

Failure can perhaps best be assigned to one or both of two general conditions. First, the circumstances for the desired behavior are potentially available, but the patient has not been properly guided because of poor therapeutic leadership, poor statement of problems, or similar procedural weaknesses. This points up the importance of superseding verbal, consulting-room therapy with techniques that minimize verbal stimulation and guidance, such as conditioning, restructuring of the environment, desensitization, and relaxation. Many patients develop an immunity to change through the discussion of their problems. Often discussion or analysis does not even lead to insight, much less to behavior change.

Second, failure may arise when the therapist is unable to enlist participation from the patient, through direct or indirect means. Consequently, although the first set of failure conditions may arise from a poor or unclear plan or an inaccurate knowledge of what to do, the second set of conditions arises from the inability to get the patient into action, even though the plan or change effort is understood. In this latter case, the therapist cannot get leverage on the patient, as he can through parents on children—although if he were bold, he might be able to, through such agents as courts, teachers, organization leaders, or employers. Programed instruction and good study habits lead the patient into activity that will result in his improvement, for he may be more amenable to a work situation that seems concrete and meaningful than to a verbal discussion devoid of overt activity.

As this book stresses, the therapist should be aware of the importance of making change plans and of change agents and change objects, and of how the three are related—whether the therapy takes place in a reconditioning sense or as verbal, face-to-face therapy. Equally important, of course, is the change plan that involved individuals other than the patient or variables other than those usually assigned to the patient and the therapist.

The therapy that comes closest to providing an effective change plan and procedure is the most active therapy, the most specific in the choice of variables, and the most operational in stating aims; it is centered in the present and treats the patient as the focal point in a matrix of variables. On the other hand, a therapy that focuses on internal variables, seeks an historical origin, and does not stress action or name specific problems seems inevitably to be more prone to fail.

The American Ethos of Efficiency

PRO

Preeminently the message of this book has been to set efficiency as the goal of psychotherapy, that is, increased efficiency of patients in achieving their goals. Since efficiency is equated with success (defined as the achievement of specified goals), inefficiency is the chief deterrent to success.

Yet the word "efficiency" in itself has acquired a connotation of superficiality that makes it suspect as a human value. To many, it is somehow alien to humanitarianism, as if it referred exclusively to shallow and inhumane traits. Obviously, this is not its meaning here, for an efficient therapy may help a person to become effectively humane. Here, it means the process of shedding irrelevant, self-defeating, and ineffective behavior that would otherwise seriously handicap one's effort to reach his goals and means also proceeding directly and effectively to such goals.

Specifying goals and working hard to reach them are particularly strong tendencies in the American culture. In a way, even the handling of drugs in the United States is a commentary on this characteristic. The use of narcotics is banned, tranquilizers require prescriptions, and persons who promote the advantages of drugs which enhance fantasying or passivity but which seem otherwise relatively harmless are generally ostracized. On the other hand, the use of stimulants is not banned; in fact, they are heavily used, together with aspirin and alcohol, in the apparent belief that they maintain or facilitate man's functioning as a hard-driving worker.

Although some control of narcotics is almost universal throughout the world, the rigid regulation of drugs that do not produce or perpetuate energy, such as tranquilizers, is fairly unique to the United States. Other countries may, of course, be accepting our way of living in trying to raise their standard of living, so that American views may eventually prevail internationally. Meanwhile, however, it can be questioned whether important values for which the American society is groping, including a sense of humanitarianism toward the whole world, do not call for some lessened efficiency in reaching for personal goals. Some deferral may be needed in the use of energy, some greater serenity in confronting daily problems, with some deliberately created passivity and leisure, to consider problems of living more broadly. In this sense, one should guard against setting himself prematurely to achieve efficiency in reaching immediate goals at the sacrifice of the leisure and pauses necessary to develop broader goals.

Much depends on the therapist's sense of values and on the extent to which he may focus upon these values in the therapeutic situation. If he discusses them with his patient, trying to distinguish between the trivial and the important and helping the patient to assign priorities among his problems and efforts, he is not likely to pursue efficiency for trivial purposes. But if he does not search intensively for the proper priorities, he may in the end be practicing and teaching only trivia.

Efficiency in reaching one's goals can never be harmful, it would seem, unless it becomes the goal instead of the means. It should be the therapist's job to see that this distortion does not happen.

CON

The above section stresses the concern that specificity, efficiency, and directness may sometimes be inimical to the preservation and growth of broader human values in therapy. This need not be the case at all. Although it is possible to overwork efficiency, it is also possible to overwork vague concepts of love, leisure, religion, and altruism when they are not given specific form or tested in real-life situations. The problem is not in the case but in the extreme example of the case.

If the patient wishes simply to ponder his own existence in therapy, and if the therapist and he agree that the sole outcome of therapy is to be the enlargement of his views, but not behavior change—fine. But such pondering should not be conducted in the name of therapy or with the implication of behavior change unless this is made explicit to the client and the therapist has no more pressing problems to attend to.

A lack of social priority about treatment has been one of the consuming ills of therapy—the treatment of the few who have somewhat vague philosophical interests, at the expense of the many who have acute and pressing problems of survival. The misallocation of therapeutic effort seems a far greater ill than the fact that one in therapy might not ponder richly and broadly enough on his own existence and that the therapy might thereby be more trivial than it could be.

Of course, therapy should not aim for efficiency solely to promote trivial or poorly considered personal gain. However, efficiency in behavior change is so sorely needed in the world today that to be concerned about the possibility of too much efficiency seems unnecessarily speculative and idealistic.

To place the term in its original perspective, efficiency is designed to reduce waste, and it is highly wasteful to the individual and to society to spend time in therapy that is not maximally productive and efficient. The therapist today can no longer proceed on the comfortable old assumptions of a previous era that deep or intensive therapy produces better results or that therapy is effective only with bright, talkative, or interested persons who function moderately well in their daily lives. There are simply no scientific data to support the first assumption, nor social priority to support the second. If a philosophy-oriented therapy were more productive of behavior change or had a longer-lasting effect, one might agree to its emphasis, at least in some special cases, but there is no evidence that this is true.

In one typical clinic, for example, the inefficiency was staggering. Patients were put on a waiting list sometimes for months. When they finally began in therapy, they dropped out quickly in great numbers, and those who stayed on usually came out with few firm gains. Many continued for years for no proved purpose. The inefficiency of this aimless approach is compelling. A single therapist in the same community working on a half-time private practice has been able to work with a larger case load than the entire staff of one such clinic and, according to the only research data available, to maintain a higher success rate than the clinic.

When do long-term cases only reflect slovenly habits of the therapist, and when are continued interviews needed? Why not try to enhance the efficiency of the clinic or the therapist by limiting the number or frequency of interviews or the length of time over which patients are seen and set goals are achieved? Is the matter of such efficiency not of primary importance to the public welfare—and to the individual as well?

Conclusions

We would end this simulated dialogue on a note of hope. If some aspects of it appear to be incompatible with the rest of the book, this is our burden of uncertainty. We have discussed these doubts with each other and with many other therapists, and will continue to weigh their significance in relation to the more decisive views and practices described in other chapters.

There is naturally much room for disagreement, for one therapist may agree more strongly with the views expressed here than another, just as one may be more confident in his practice of them than another. One may be more certain than another that he will not be likely to modify his approach in the future. Some may be impatient with these questions about traditional therapeutic practices that have partial merit but fall short of hopes for the more successful therapy that seems possible today.

These differences need not seriously affect the distinctiveness of therapy and its study, nor efforts to facilitate new scientific work on human behavior change. Raising such questions, regardless of whether they are wholly resolved, is like sifting grains in a sieve; hopefully, the larger grains of greatest significance to the behavior-change approach, will remain for concern.

Perhaps there can eventually be an addendum to resolve some of the misgivings expressed in this chapter. Perhaps even now, with more time and effort, one could find better resolutions, or perhaps the reader's own reactions and insight may suggest to him how therapists can differ in tone and detail while believing in and practicing the same basic method.

Bibliography

Adams, J. K. Laboratory studies of behavior without awareness. *Psychol. Bull.*, 1957, **54**, 383–405.

Adler, A. *Thinking machines.* New York: John Day, 1961.

Alexander, F. Principles and techniques of briefer psychotherapeutic procedures. In *Psychiatric treatment: Proc. Amer. Psychol. Ass., New York, 1951.* Baltimore: Williams & Wilkins, 1953.

Alexander, F., & French, T. M. *Psychoanalytic therapy.* New York: Ronald, 1946.

Allen, F. H. *Psychotherapy with children.* New York: Norton, 1942.

Allport, G. W. *The nature of prejudice.* Cambridge, Mass.: Addison-Wesley, 1954.

Alston, E. F. Psycho-analytic psychotherapy conducted by correspondence. *Int. J. Psychiat.*, 1957, **38**, 32–50.

Anderson, R. C. *Shaping logical behavior in six- and seven-year olds.* July, 1962. (Mimeographed)

Appel, K. E., Lhamon, W. T., Meyers, J. M., & Harvey, W. A. Long-term psychotherapy. In *Psychiatric treatment: Proc. Amer. Psychol. Ass., New York, 1951.* Baltimore: Williams & Wilkins, 1953.

Ashby, W. R. *An introduction to cybernetics.* New York: Wiley, 1958.

Ashem, B. The treatment of a disaster phobia by systematic desensitization. *Behav. Res. Ther.*, 1963, **1**, 81–84.

Ayllon, T. Some behavioral problems associated with hearing in chronic schizophrenic patients. Paper read at Amer. Psychol. Ass., Chicago, 1960.

Ayllon, T. Intensive treatment of psychotic behavior by stimulus satiation and food reinforcement. *Behav. Res. Ther.*, 1963, **1**, 53–62.

Ayllon, T., & Haughton, E. Control of the behavior of schizophrenic patients by food. *J. Exp. Anal. Behav.*, 1962, **5**, 343–352.

Ayllon, T., & Michael, J. The psychiatric nurse as a behavioral engineer, *J. Exp. Anal. Behav.*, 1959, **2**, 323–334.

Azrin, N. H., Holz, W., Ulrich, R., & Goldiamond, I. The control of the content of conversations through reinforcement. *J. Exp. Anal. Behav.*, 1961, **4**, 25–30.

Baker, E. Brief psychotherapy. *J. Med. Soc., N.J.*, 1947, **44**, 260–261.

Baller, W., & Shalock, H. D. Conditioned response treatment to enuresis. *J. Except. Child*, 1956, **22**, 233–236.

Bandura, A. Psychotherapy as a learning process. *Psychol. Bull.*, 1961, **58**, 143–159.

Bandura, A., & Walters, R. H. Aggression. In child psychology. *62nd Yearb. Nat. Soc. Stud. Educ.*, Part I. Chicago: Univer. of Chicago Press, 1963.

Barber, T. X. Hypnotizability, suggestibility, and personality, V. A. critical review of research findings. *Psychol. Rep.*, 1964, **14**, 299–320.

Barber, T. X. Physiological effects of hypnotic suggestions: a critical review of recent research. *Psychol. Bull.*, 1965, **63**, 201–222.

Batrawi, S. A. The differential effects of two therapeutic techniques on selected aspects of client behavior. Unpublished doctoral dissertation, George Washington Univer., 1964.

Beech, H. R., & Adler, F. Some aspects of verbal conditioning in psychiatric patients. *Behav. Res. Ther.*, 1963, **1**, 273–282.

Beer, S. The impact of cybernetics on the concept of industrial organization. *Proc. 1st Congr. Int. Ass. Cybernet.*, 1956.

Beer, S. The irrelevance of automation. *Proc. 2nd Congr. Int. Ass. Cybernet.*, 1958.

Beer, S. *Cybernetics and management.* London: English Univer. Press, 1960.

Bennett, D. H., & Robertson, J. P. S. The effects of habit training on chronic schizophrenic patients. *J. Ment. Sci.*, 1955, **101**, 664–672.

Bergin, A. E. The empirical emphasis in psychotherapy: a symposium. The effects of psychotherapy: negative results revisited. *J. Counsel. Psychol.*, 1963, **10**, 244–250.

Bieber, I. Homosexuality: a psychoanalytic study of male homosexuals. New York: Basic Books, 1962.

Binder, A., McConnell, D., & Sjohlern, N. A. Verbal conditioning as a function of experimenter characteristics. *J. Abnorm. Soc. Psychol.*, 1957, **55**, 309–314.

Blakemore, C. B., Thorpe, J. G., Barker, J. C., Conway, C. G., & Lewin, N. I. The application of faradic aversion conditioning in a case of transversion, *Behav. Res. Ther.*, 1963, **1**, 29–34.

Blau, P. M. *Exchange and power in social life.* New York: Wiley, 1964.

Boileau, V. K. New techniques in brief psychotherapy. *Psychol. Rep.*, 1958, **4**, 627–645.

Bonime, W. Some principles of brief psychotherapy. *Psychiat. Quart.*, 1953, **27**, 1–18.

Bordin, E. S. The implications of client expectations for the counseling process. *J. Counsel. Psychol.*, 1955, **2**, 17–21.

Brady, J. P., & Lind, D. L. Experimental analysis of hysterical blindness. *Arch. Gen. Psychiat.*, 1961, **4**, 331–339.

Broadbent, D. C. *Behavior: a survey of twentieth-century theory in behavioristic psychology.* New York: Basic Books, 1961.

Bullock, D. H. Some aspects of human operant behavior. *Psychol. Rec.*, 1960, **10**, 241–258.

Bullock, D. H., & Brunt, M. Y., Jr. The testability of psychiatric patients in an operant conditioning situation, *Psychol. Rec.*, 1959, 9, 165–170.

Burnham, W. H. *The normal mind*. New York: Appleton, 1924.

Cameron, D. E. Behavior concepts and psychotherapy. *Psychiat. Quart.*, 1950, 24, 227–242.

Cameron, N. *The psychology of behavior disorders*. Boston: Houghton Mifflin, 1947.

Carr, A. C. Specific modification of psychotherapy for specific symptoms. *E.P.A. Symp.* New York: 1963.

Cartwright, D. S., & Rath, I. Success and satisfaction in psychotherapy. *J. Clin. Psychol.*, 1957, 13, 20–26.

Chicago Institute for Psychoanalysis. Third psychotherapy council, Oct. 16–18, 1946. Chicago: Author, 1946.

Church, R. M. The varied effects of punishment on behavior. *Psychol. Rev.*, 1963, 70, 369–402.

Clark, D. F. The treatment of hysterical spasm and agoraphobia by behavior therapy. *Behav. Res. Ther.*, 1963, 1, 245–250. (a)

Clark, D. F. The treatment of monosymptomatic phobia by systematic desensitization. *Behav. Res. Ther.*, 1963, 1, 63–69. (b)

Clark, L. Sex education by mail. *Int. J. Sexol.*, 1953, 7, 31–33.

Colby, K. M. *A primer for psychotherapists*. New York: Ronald, 1951.

Cooper, A. J. A case of bronchial asthma treated by behavior therapy. *Behav. Res. Ther.*, 1963, 1, 351–356.

Cowden, R., & Ford, L. Systematic desensitization with phobic schizophrenics. *Amer. J. Psychiat.*, 1962, 119, 241–245.

Daniels, G. E. Brief psychotherapy in diabetes mellitus. *Psychiatry*, 1944, 7, 121–128.

Danielson, P. J., & Rothney, J. W. M. The student autobiography: structured or unstructured? *Personnel Guid. J.*, 1954, 33, 30–33.

DeLatil, P. *Thinking by machine*. Boston: Houghton Mifflin, 1957.

Deutsch, F. *Applied psychoanalysis: selected lectures on psychotherapy*. New York: Grune & Stratton, 1949.

Dinoff, M., Richard, H. C., Selzberg, H., & Sipprelle, C. N. An experimental analogue of three psychotherapeutic approaches. *J. Clin. Psychol.*, 1960, 16, 70–73.

Dollard, J., Doob, L., Miller, N. E., Mowrer, O. H., & Sears, R. R. *Frustration and aggression*. New Haven, Conn.: Yale Univer. Press, 1939.

Dollard, J., & Miller, N. *Personality and psychotherapy*. New York: McGraw-Hill, 1950.

Dubos, R. *Mirage of health*. New York: Harper & Row, 1959.

Eaton, J. W., & Weil, R. J. *Culture and mental disorders*. New York: Free Press, 1955.

Ellis, A. New approaches to psychotherapy techniques. *J. Clin. Psychol.*, 1955, 208–260. (a)

Ellis, A. Psychotherapy techniques of use with psychotics. *Amer. J. Psychother.*, 1955, 9, 452–476. (b)

Ellis, A. Outcome of employing three techniques of psychotherapy. *J. Clin. Psychol.*, 1957, 13, 344–350.

Ellis, A. Rational psychotherapy. *J. Gen. Psychol.*, 1958, 59, 35–49.

Ellis, A. *Reason and emotion in psychotherapy.* New York: Lyle Stuart, 1962.

Ellul, J. *The technological society.* New York: Knopf, 1964.

Ends, E. J., & Page, C. W. A study of three types of group psychotherapy with hospitalized male inebriates. *Quart. J. Studi. Alcohol.*, 1957, 18, 263–277.

English, H. B., & English, A. C. *A comprehensive dictionary of psychological and psychoanalytic terms.* New York: Longmans, 1958.

English, O. S., & Pearson, G. H. J. *Emotional problems of living.* (3d ed.) New York: Norton, 1963.

Eysenck, H. J. *The scientific study of personality.* London: Routledge, 1952.

Eysenck, H. J. *Dynamics of anxiety and hysteria.* London: Routledge, 1957.

Eysenck, H. J. Learning theory and behavior therapy. In H. J. Eysenck (Ed.), *Behavior therapy and the neuroses.* New York: Pergamon Press, 1960.

Eysenck, H. J. *Handbook of abnormal psychology.* New York: Basic Books, 1961.

Fairbairn, W. R. D. Theoretical and experimental aspects of psychoanalysis. *Brit. J. Med. Psychol.*, 1952, 25, 122–127.

Farber, D. J. Written communication in psychotherapy. *Psychiatry*, 1953, 16, 365–374.

Faries, M. Short-term counseling at the college level. *J. Counsel. Psychol.*, 1955, 2, 182–184.

Ferguson, D. C., & Buss, A. H. Operant conditioning of hostile verbs in relation to experimenter and subject characteristics. *J. Consult. Psychol.*, 1960, 24, 324–327.

Ferster, C. B., & DeMyer, M. K. The development of performances in autistic children in an automatically controlled environment. *J. Chron. Dis.*, 1961, 13, 312–345.

Feshback, S. The catharsis hypotheses and some consequences of interaction with aggressive and neutral play objects. *J. Pers.*, 1956, 24, 449–462.

Fine, S. Personal communication. Based on paper read at Sympos. Behav. Change, Psychol. Clin., George Washington Univer., November, 1963.

Finney, B. C. Personal communication. 1964.

Ford, D. H., & Urban, H. B. *Systems of psychotherapy: a comparative study.* New York: Wiley, 1963.

Ford, J. J. The Soviet exploitation of cybernetics. In R. E. Weber (Ed.), *A proposal for a new capability for individual and societal growth and development.* Washington, D.C.: Department of Health, Education, and Welfare, June, 1964.

Frank, J. D. Emotional reactions of American soldiers to an unfamiliar disease. *Amer. J. Psychiat.*, 1946, 102, 631–640.

Frank, P. Metaphysical interpretations of science. *Brit. J. Phil. Sci.*, 1950, 1, 60–74, Part I. (a)

Frank, P. Metaphysical interpretations of science. *Brit. J. Phil. Sci.*, 1950, 1, 77–91, Part II. (b)

Frankl, V. E. Paradoxical intention: a logotherapeutic technique. *Amer. J. Psychother.*, 1960, **14**, 520–535.

Franks, C. M. Alcohol, alcoholism and conditioning: a review of the literature and some theoretical considerations. *J. Ment. Sci.*, 1958, **104**, 14–33.

Franks, C. M. *Conditioning techniques in clinical practice and research.* New York: Springer, 1964.

Friedman, J. H. Short-term psychotherapy: "phobia of travel." *Amer. J. Psychother.*, 1950, **4**, 259–278.

Fromm-Reichmann, Frieda. *Principles of intensive psychotherapy.* Chicago: Univer. of Chicago Press, 1950.

Gagne, R. M. Military training and principles of learning. *Amer. Psychologist,* 1962, **17**, 83–91.

Garetz, F. K., Kogl, R. C., & Wiener, D. N. A comparison of random and judgmental methods of determining mode of outpatient mental hygiene treatment. *J. Clin. Psychol.*, 1959, **15**, 401–402.

Garner, H. H. A confrontation technique used in psychotherapy. *Comprehens. Psychiat.*, 1960, **1**, 201–211.

Gliedman, L. H., Nash, E. H., Imber, S. D., Stone, A. R., & Frank, J. D. Reduction of symptoms by pharmacological inert substances and by short-term psychotherapy. *Amer. Med. Ass. Arch. Neurol., Psychiat.*, 1958, **79**, 345–351.

Goldhamer, H., & Marshall, A. W. *Psychosis and civilization.* New York: Free Press, 1953.

Goldiamond, I. Justified and unjustified alarm over behavioral control. 1964. (a)

Goldiamond, I. Operant behavior in relation to clinical psychology. Series of ten lectures given at George Washington Univer. Psychol. Clin., October–December, 1964. (b)

Goldiamond, I. Personal communication. Based on lecture given at George Washington Univer., May 7, 1964. (c)

Grandall, W. L. A method of treating nocturnal enuresis. *J. Clin. Psychol.*, 1946, **2**, 175–178.

Greenspoon, J. The effect of two nonverbal stimuli on the frequency of numbers of two verbal response classes. *Amer. Psychologist,* 1954, **9**, 384. (Abstract)

Greenspoon, J. The reinforcing effect of two spoken sounds on the frequency of two responses. *Amer. J. Psychol.*, 1955, **68**, 409–416.

Greniewski, H. *Cybernetics without mathematics.* New York: Pergamon Press, 1960.

Grinker, R. R. Brief psychotherapy in psychosomatic problems. *Psychosom. Med.*, 1947, **9**, 78–103.

Group for the Advancement of Psychiatry. G.A.P. Collaborative research in psychopathology, Report No. 24. Topeka, Kans.: Author, 1954.

Gutheil, E. A. Psychoanalysis and psychotherapy. *J. Clin. Psychopathol. Psychother.*, 1944, **6**, 207–230.

Haddock, J. N., & Mensh, I. N. Psychotherapeutic expectations in various clinic settings. *Psychol. Rep.*, 1957, **3**, 109–112.

Haring, N. G., & Phillips, E. L. *Educating emotionally disturbed children.* New York: McGraw-Hill, 1962.

Harper, R. A. *Psychoanalysis and psychotherapy: 36 systems.* Englewood Cliffs, N.J.: Prentice-Hall, 1959.

Harris, D. H., Firestone, R. W., & Wagner, G. M. Brief psychotherapy and enuresis. *J. Consult. Psychol.,* 1955, 19, 246.

Harris, R. E., & Christiansen, C. Prediction of response to brief psychotherapy. *J. Psychol.,* 1946, 21, 269–284.

Heckel, R. V., Wiggins, S. L., & Salzberg, H. C. Conditioning against silence in group therapy. *J. Clin. Psychol.* 1962, 18, 216–217.

Herzberg, A. Short treatment of neurosis by graduated tasks. *Brit. J. Med. Psychol.,* 1941, 19, 36–51.

Herzberg, A. *Active psychotherapy.* New York: Grune & Stratton, 1945.

Hoffer, E. *The true believer.* New York: New American Library, 1951.

Hollingshead, A. B., & Redlich, F. C. *Social class and mental illness.* New York: Wiley, 1958.

Holt, E. B. *Animal drive and the learning process.* New York: Holt, 1931.

Hood-Williams, J. The results of psychotherapy with children: a reevaluation. *J. Consult. Psychol.,* 1960, 24, 84–88.

Isaacs, A. F. Survey of research on the gifted. In E. P. Trapp & P. Himelstein (Eds.), *Readings on the exceptional child.* New York: Appleton-Century-Crofts, 1962.

Jahoda, M. *Current concepts of positive mental health.* New York: Basic Books, 1958.

Jensen, M. B., & Yanagi, O. H. Directive treatment of long-term closed ward schizophrenics. *J. Clin. Psychol.,* 1961, 139–141.

Jones, M. C. Conditioned fear in children, *J. Exp. Psychol.,* 1924, 7, 383. (a)

Jones, M. C. The elimination of children's fears. *Pedag. Sem.,* 1924, 31, 308–315. (b)

Katz, M. M., Lorr, M., & Rubinstein, E. A. Remainer patient attributes and their relation to subsequent improvement in psychotherapy. *J. Consult. Psychol.,* 1958, 22, 411–413.

Kelly, G. A. *The psychology of personal constructs.* Vols. I and II. New York: Norton, 1955.

King, G. F., Armitage, S., & Tilton, J. A therapeutic approach to schizophrenics of extreme pathology. *J. Abnorm. Soc. Psychol.,* 1960, 61, 276–286.

King, J. A. Parameters relevant to determining the effect of early experience upon the adult behavior of animals. *Psychol. Bull.,* 1958, 55, 46–58.

Kirtner, W. L., & Cartwright, D. S. Success and failure in client-centered therapy as a function of initial in-therapy behavior. *J. Consult. Psychol.,* 1958, 22, 259–264. (a)

Kirtner, W. L., & Cartwright, D. S. Success and failure in client-centered therapy as a function of initial in-therapy behavior. *J. Consult. Psychol.,* 1958, 22, 329–333. (b)

Klein, M. *The psychoanalysis of children.* New York: Norton, 1935.

Knight, R. P. Evaluation of the results of psychoanalytic therapy. *Amer. J. Psychiat.,* 1941, 98, 434–446.

Komoski, P. K. Use of programed instruction with the academically talented. Address at Conf. Programed Instruction, Roanoke, Va., December, 1963.

Koye, I. A community agency experiment in short-term methods. *Nerv. Child.*, 1949, **8**, 360–374.

Krasner, L. The use of generalized reinforcers in psychotherapy research. *Psychol. Rep.*, 1955, **1**, 19–25.

Krasner, L. Studies of the conditioning of verbal behavior. *Psychol. Bull.*, 1958, **55**, 148–170.

Krasner, L. The therapist as a social reinforcement machine. In H. H. Strupp & L. Luborsky (Eds.), *Research in psychotherapy.* Washington, D.C.: Amer. Psychol. Ass., 1962.

Krasner, L., & Ullmann, L. P. *Research in behavior modification.* New York: Holt, 1965.

Lagey, Joseph. Personal communication. 1964.

Lagey, Joseph. Community treatment programs for multi-problem families. Research Dept., Community Chest, Vancouver, B.C., Canada, 1962.

Lagey, Joseph. Priority determination plans. Community Chest, Vancouver, B.C., Canada, 1960.

Landis, C., & Page, J. D. *Modern society and mental disease.* New York: Farrar & Rinehart, 1939.

Landsman, T. The therapeutic use of written materials. *Amer. Psychologist*, 1951, **6**, 347.

Lang, G. *Mental health: the reference shelf.* Vol. 1. New York: H. W. Wilson, 1958.

Lang, P. J., & Lazovik, A. D. Experimental desensitization of a phobia. *J. Abnorm. Soc. Psychol.*, 1963, **66**, 519–525.

Lawrence, D. H., & Festinger, L. *Deterrents and reinforcement.* Stanford, Calif.: Stanford Univer. Press, 1962.

Lazarus, A. A. The elimination of children's phobias by deconditioning. In H. J. Eysenck (Ed.), *Behavior therapy and the neuroses.* New York: Pergamon Press, 1960.

Lazarus, A. The results of behavior therapy in 126 cases of severe neuroses. *Behav. Res. Ther.*, 1963, **1**, 69–79.

Lazovik, D., & Lang, P. J. A laboratory demonstration of systematic desensitization psychotherapy. *J. Psychol., Stud.*, 1960, **11**, 238–247.

Lehner, G. F. J. Negative practice as a psychotherapeutic technique. *J. Gen. Psychol.*, 1954, **51**, 69–82.

Leighton, A. H. *My name is legion.* New York: Basic Books, 1959.

Levitt, E. E. The results of psychotherapy with children. *J. Consult. Psychol.*, 1957, **21**, 189–196.

Levitt, E. E. Psychotherapy with children: a further evaluation. *Behav. Res. Ther.*, 1963, **1**, 45–51.

Lorr, M., Katz, M. M., & Rubinstein, E. A. The prediction of length of stay in psychotherapy. *J. Consult. Psychol.*, 1958, **22**, 321–327.

Lovibond, S. H. The mechanism of conditioning treatment of enuresis. *Behav. Res. Ther.*, 1963, **1**, 17–22.

Lowinger, P., & Huston, P. E. Transference and the physical presence of the physician. *J. Nerv. Dis.*, 1955, **121**, 250–256.

McClelland, D. C. *Personality.* New York: Sloane, 1951.

McKee, J. Programed instruction as a therapeutic tool. *Amer. Psychologist,* 1963, **18**, 385.

Maier, N. R. F. *Frustration: the study of behavior without a goal.* New York: McGraw-Hill, 1949.

Malamud, W. Brief psychotherapy in medical practice. *Med. Clin. N. Amer.,* 1948, 1195–1206.

Maruyama, M. The second cybernetics: deviation amplifying mutual causal processes. *Amer. Scientist,* 1963, **51**, 164–179.

Mead, Margaret. *Continuities in cultural evolution.* New Haven, Conn.: Yale Univer. Press, 1964.

Meehl, P. E. Schizotaxia, schizotypy, and schizophrenia. *Amer. Psychologist,* 1962, **17**, 827–838.

Meiers, J. I. Therapy at a distance. *Int. J. Sociomet.,* 1957, **1**, 109–111.

Mendelson, W. (Ed.). *Felix Frankfurter: a tribute.* New York: Reynald, 1964.

Messinger, E. Auto-elaboration: an adjuvant technique in the practice of psychotherapy. *Dis. Nerv. Syst.,* 1952, **13**, 339–344.

Meyer, A. *The commonsense psychiatry of Dr. Adolph Meyer.* New York: McGraw-Hill, 1948.

Meyer, A. *Psychobiology: a science of man.* Springfield, Ill.: Charles C Thomas, 1958. (Trans. and comp. by E. E. Winters & A. M. Bowers.)

Miller, J. G. The implications of psychoanalytic theory for the evaluation of psychotherapy. *Psychol. Serv. Center J.,* 1950, **2**, 123–129.

Morton, R. B. A controlled experiment in psychotherapy based on Rotter's social learning theory of personality. Unpublished doctoral dissertation, Ohio State Univer., 1949.

Morton, R. B. An experiment in brief psychotherapy. *Psychol. Monogr.,* 1955, **1**, No. 9.

Mowrer, O. H. A stimulus-response analysis of anxiety and its role as a reinforcing agent. *Psychol. Rev.,* 1939, **46**, 553–565.

Mowrer, O. H. Learning theory and the neurotic paradox. *Amer. J. Orthopsychiat.,* 1948, **18**, 571–610.

Mowrer, O. H. Neurosis, psychotherapy, and two-factor learning theory. In O. H. Mowrer (Ed.), *Psychotherapy: theory and research.* New York: Ronald, 1953.

Mowrer, O. H. Payment or repayment? The problem of private practice. *Amer. Psychologist,* 1963, **18**, 577–580.

Mowrer, O. H., & Mowrer, W. M. Enuresis: a method for its study and treatment. *J. Orthopsychiat.,* 1938, **8**, 436–457.

Muench, G. A. An investigation of time-limited psychotherapy. *Amer. Psychologist,* 1964, 19. (Abstract)

Munroe, R. *Schools of psychoanalytic thought.* New York: Dryden Press, 1955.

Murray, E. J. The empirical emphasis in psychotherapy: a symposium. Learning theory and psychotherapy: biotropic versus sociotropic approaches. *J. Counsel. Psychol.,* 1963, **10**, 250–255.

Murray, H. A. *Explorations in personality.* Fairlawn, N.J.: Oxford Univer-
Press, 1938.

Murray, H. A. Studies of stressful interpersonal disputations. *Amer. Psychologist,* 1963, 18, 28–36.

Myrdal, G. *Economic theory and underdeveloped regions.* London: Duck-
worth, 1957.

Myrdal, G. *An American dilemma: the Negro problem and modern democracy.* (20th anniversary ed.) New York: Harper & Row, 1964.

National Association for Mental Health. *Fact sheet.* New York: Author, 1963.

Neale, D. H. Behavior therapy and encopresis in children. *Behav. Res. Ther.,*
1963, 1, 139–150.

New York Times. Magazine section. Sept. 27, 1965.

Oppenheimer, J. R. Filler, in *Contemp. Psychol.,* 1960, 5, 219.

Orlando, R. *References on behavior modification with operant conditioning
techniques.* 1964. (Mimeographed)

Orlansky, H. Infant care and personality. *Psychol. Bull.,* 1949, 46, 1–48.

Pascal, G. R. *Behavior change in the clinic: a systematic approach.* New York:
Grune & Stratton, 1959.

Pascal, G. R., & Zax, M. Psychotherapeutics: success or failure? *J. Consult.
Psychol.,* 1956, 20, 325–331.

Pask, G. *An approach to cybernetics.* New York: Harper & Row, 1961.

Peffer, P. A. Money: a rehabilitative incentive for mental patients. *Amer. J.
Psychiat.,* 1953, 110, 84–92.

Phillips, E. L. Attitudes toward self and others: a brief questionnaire report.
J. Consult. Psychol., 1951, 15, 79–81.

Phillips, E. L. *Psychotherapy: a modern theory and practice.* Englewood
Cliffs, N.J.: Prentice-Hall, 1956.

Phillips, E. L. Metaphysical interpretations in psychotherapy and personality
theory. *Amer. Psychologist,* 1959, 14, 336. (Abstract)

Phillips, E. L. Parent child psychotherapy: a follow-up study comparing two
techniques. *J. Psychol.,* 1960, 49, 195–202.

Phillips, E. L. Logical analysis of childhood behavior problems and their treatment. *Psychol. Rep.,* 1961, 9, 705–712.

Phillips, E. L., & Batrawi, S. A. Learning theory and psychotherapy re-visited:
with notes on illustrative cases. *Psychother.: Theory, Res. Pract.,* 1964,
1, 145–150.

Phillips, E. L., & Johnston, M. H. S. Theoretical and clinical aspects of short-
term, parent-child psychotherapy. *Psychiatry,* 1954, 7, 267–275.

Phillips, E. L., & Mattoon, C. U. Interference vs. extinction as learning models
for psychotherapy. *J. Psychol.,* 1961, 51, 399–403.

Phillips, E. L., Raiford, A. W., & Batrawi, S. A. The Q-sort re-evaluated.
1966. In press.

Phillips, E. L., Test, L. R., & Adams, N. M. Multiple approaches to short-term
psychotherapy. *Amer. Psychologist,* 1964, 19, 475. (Abstract)

Philpott, W. H., & Boyer, H. Personal communication. Discussion paper at
George Washington Univer., Psychol. Clin., April, 1964.

Pierce, W. H. Redundancy in computers. *Sci. Amer.,* 1964, 210, 103–112.

Plunkett, R. J., & Gordon, J. E. *Epidemiology and mental illness.* New York: Basic Books, 1960.

Prugh, D. G., & Brody, B. Brief relationship therapy in the military setting. *Amer. J. Orthopsychiat.*, 1946, **16**, 707–721.

Pumpian-Mindlin, E. Considerations in selection of patients for short-term therapy. *Amer. J. Psychother.*, 1953, **7**, 641–652.

Rachman, S. Treatment of anxiety and phobic reactions by desensitization. *J. Abnorm. Soc. Psychol.*, 1959, **102**, 421–427.

Rachman, S. Sexual disorders and behavior therapy. *Amer. J. Psychiat.*, 1961, **46**, 57–70.

Rachman, S. Child psychology and learning theory. *J. Child Psychol. Psychiat.*, 1962, **3**, 149–163.

Rachman, S. Introduction to behavior therapy. *Behav. Res. Ther.*, 1963, **1**, 3–15.

Rank, O. *Will therapy and truth and reality.* New York: Knopf, 1947.

Raymond, J. J. Case of fetishism treated by aversion therapy. *Brit. Med. J.*, 1956, **2**, 845–856.

Ricco, A. C. The status of the autobiography. *Peabody J. Educ.*, 1958, **36**, 33–36.

Rickard, H. C., Dignam, P. J., & Horner, R. F. Verbal manipulation in a psychotherapeutic relationship. *J. Clin. Psychol.*, 1960, **16**, 364–367.

Rogers, C. R., & Dymond R. (eds.). *Psychotherapy and personality change.* Chicago: Univer. of Chicago Press, 1954.

Rogers-Skinner debate. Tape recording made in Duluth, Minn., 1962.

Rosen, J. N. The treatment of schizophrenia psychosis by direct analytic therapy. *Psychiat. Quart.*, 1947, **21**, 3–37, 117–119.

Rosen, J. N. *Direct analysis.* New York: Grune & Stratton, 1953.

Rosenthal, D., & Frank, J. D. The fate of the psychiatric clinical outpatient assigned to psychotherapy. *J. New Ment. Dis.*, 1958, **127**, 330–343.

Rothenberg, S. Brief psycho-dynamically oriented therapy. *Psychosom. Med.*, 1955, **17**, 455–457.

Rotter, J. B. *Social learning and clinical psychology.* Englewood Cliffs, N.J.: Prentice-Hall, 1954.

Rotter, J. B. Psychotherapy. In *Annual Review of Psychology. 1960.* Vol. 11. Palo Alto, Calif.: Annual Review, 1960. Pp. 381–414.

Ruesch, J., & Bateson, G. *Communication: the social matrix of society.* New York: Norton, 1951.

Rusk, H. A. *New hope for the handicapped.* New York: Harper & Row, 1949.

Rusk, H. A. *Rehabilitation medicine.* St. Louis: Mosby, 1958.

Rusk, H. A., & Taylor, E. J. *Living with a disability.* New York: McGraw-Hill, 1953.

Salter, A. *Conditioned reflex therapy.* New York: Creative Age, 1949.

Salter, A. *Conditioned reflex therapy.* (Reissued.) New York: Capricorn Books, 1961.

Salzberg, H. C., Clark, J. B., Drennen, W. T., Hamilton, J. W., Heckel, R. B., Long, T. E., & Marr, M. J., The effects of multiple therapists in relinquishing a delusional system. *J. Clin. Psychol.*, 1962, **18**, 218–220.

Saul, L. J. A note on the telephone as a technical aid. *Psychoanal. Quart.*, 1951, 287–290. (a)

Saul, L. J. On the value of one or two interviews. *Psychoanal. Quart.*, 1951, **20**, 613–615. (b)

Schoenberg, B., & Carr, A. C. An investigatioon of brief psychotherapy of neurodermatitis. *Psychosom. Med.*, 1963, **25**, 253–263.

Schwitzgebel, R., & Kolb, D. A. Inducing behavior changes in adolescent delinquents. *Behav. Res. Ther.*, 1964, **1**, 297–304.

Sears, R. R. Experimental studies of projection. I. Attribution of traits. *J. Soc. Psychol.*, 1936, **7**, 151–163.

Sears, R. R. Survey of objective studies of psychoanalytic concepts. *Soc. Sci. Res. Council Bull.* **51**, 1943.

Seitz, P. F. D. Dynamically oriented brief psychotherapy: psychocutaneous excoriation syndrome. *Psychosom. Med.*, 1953, **15**, 200–242.

Shaffer, E. E., Jr. The autobiography in secondary school counseling. *Personnel Guidance J.*, 1954, **32**, 395–398.

Shah, S. Behavior therapy and psychotherapy with delinquents. Paper read at Amer. Psychol. Ass., Philadelphia, 1963. (a)

Shah, S. A program for the rehabilitation of offenders. Paper read at Amer. Psychol. Ass., Philadelphia, 1963. (b)

Shaw, F. J. A stimulus-response analysis of repression and insight in psychotherapy. *Psychol. Rev.*, 1946, **53**, 36–42.

Shaw, F. J. The problem of acting and the problem of becoming. *J. Humanist. Psychol.*, 1961, **1**, 64–69.

Sheerer, E. T. An analysis of the relationship between acceptance of and respect for self and acceptance of and respect for others in ten counseling cases. *J. Consult. Psychol.*, 1949, **13**. 169–175.

Shlien, J. M. An experimental investigation of time-limited client centered therapy. *Univer. of Chicago Counsel. Cent. Paper*, 1958, **2**, No. 23.

Shlien, J. M., Mosak, H. H., & Dreikurs, R. Effects of time limits: a comparison of client-centered and Adlerian psychotherapy. *Amer. Psychologist*, 1960, **15**, 415. (Abstract)

Shlien, J. M., Mosak, H. H., & Dreikurs, R. Effects of time limits: a comparison of two psychotherapies. *J. Counsel. Psychol.*, 1962, **9**, 31–34.

Shoben, E. J., Jr. A learning theory interpretation of psychotherapy. *Harvard Educ. Rev.*, 1948, **18**, 129–145.

Shoben, E. J., Jr. Some observations on psychotherapy and the learning process. In O. H. Mowrer (Ed.), *Psychotherapy: theory and research.* New York: Ronald, 1953.

Shoben, E. J., Jr. Psychotherapy as a problem in learning theory. In H. J. Eysenck (Ed.), *Behavior therapy and the neuroses.* New York: Pergamon Press, 1960.

Shoben, E. J., Jr. The empirical emphasis in psychotherapy: a symposium. The therapeutic object: men or machines? *J. Counsel. Psychol.*, 1963, **10**, 264–268.

Shor, R. E. Recorder self-therapy: a technique. *J. Counsel. Psychol.*, 1955, **2**, 150–151.

Siegel, S. *Nonparametric statistics*. New York: McGraw-Hill, 1956.

Skinner, B. F. *Science and human behavior*. New York: Macmillan, 1953.

Snyder, W. U. Clinical methods: psychotherapy. In *Annual Review of Psychology, 1950*. Vol. 1, Palo Alto, Calif.: Annual Review, 1950.

Snyder, W. U. Psychotherapy. In *Annual Review of Psychology, 1958*. Vol. 9. Palo Alto, Calif.: Annual Review, 1958.

Solomon, R. I. Punishment. *Amer. Psychologist*, 1964, **19**, 239–253.

Stein, M. I. *Contemporary psychotherapies*. New York: Free Press, 1961.

Stendal, S. W., & van der Veen, F. Length of therapy in relation to counselor estimates of personal integration and other case variables. *J. Consult. Psychol.*, 1957, **21**, 1–9.

Stevenson, I. Is the human personality more plastic in infancy and childhood? *Amer. J. Psychiat.*, 1957, **114**, 152–161.

Stevenson, I. Processes of spontaneous recovery from the psychoneuroses. *Amer. J. Psychiat.*, 1961, **117**, 1057–1064.

Stieper, D. R., & Wiener, D. N. The problem of interminability in outpatient psychotherapy. *J. Consult. Psychol.*, 1959, **23**, 237–242.

Stieper, D. R., & Wiener, D. N. *Dimensions of psychotherapy: an experimental and clinical approach*. Chicago: Aldine, 1965.

Stine, L. A., & Ivy, A. C. The effect of psychoanalysis on the cause of peptic ulcer: a preliminary report. *Gastroenterology*, 1952, **21**, 185–211.

Stone, H. C., & Simos, I. A follow-up study of personal counseling versus counseling by letter. *J. Appl. Psychol.*, 1948, **32**, 408–414.

Strupp, H. H. Nature of therapist's contribution to treatment process. *Arch. Gen. Psychiat.*, 1960, **3**, 219–231. (a)

Strupp, H. H. *Psychotherapists in action*, New York: Grune & Stratton, 1960. (b)

Sundberg, N. D., & Tyler, L. E. *Clinical psychology*. New York: Appleton-Century-Crofts, 1962.

Szasz, T. S. The myth of mental illness. *Amer. Psychologist*, 1960, **15**, 113–118.

Szasz, T. S. The uses of naming and the origin of the myth of mental illness. *Amer. Psychologist*, 1961, **16**, 59–65.

Szasz, T. S. *The myth of mental illness*. New York: Harper & Row, 1964.

Taft, Jessie *The dynamics of therapy in a controlled relationship*. New York: Macmillan, 1933.

Taylor, J. W. Relationship of success and length in psychotherapy. *J. Consult. Psychol.*, 1956, **20**, 332.

Test, Laurence R. A comparative study of four approaches to short-term psychotherapy. M.A. thesis, George Washington University, Washington, D.C., 1964.

Thibault, J. H., & Coules, J. The role of communication in the reduction of interpersonal hostility. *J. Abnorm. Soc. Psychol.*, 1952, **47**, 770–778.

Thorpe, J. G., Schmidt, E., & Castell, D. A comparison of positive and negative (aversive) conditioning in the treatment of homosexuality. *Behav. Res. Ther.*, 1963, **1**, 357–362.

Todd, A. L. *Justice on trial: the case of Louis D. Brandeis.* New York: Mc-Graw-Hill, 1964.

Tompkins, S. S., & Messick, S. *Computer simulation of personality.* New York: Wiley, 1963.

Truax, C. B. The empirical emphasis in psychotherapy: a symposium. Effective ingredients in psychotherapy: an approach to unraveling the patient-therapist interaction. *J. Counsel. Psychol.,* 1963, 10, 256–263.

Ullmann, L. P., & Krasner, L. *Case studies in behavior modification.* New York: Holt, 1965.

Von Bertalanffy, L., & Rapoport, A. *General systems.* Vol. I. Ann Arbor, Mich.: General Systems Research , 1956. (Vol. II, 1957; Vol. IV, 1959.)

Walton, D., & Black, D. A. The application of learning theory to the treatment of stammering. *J. Psychosom. Res.,* 1958, 3, 170–179.

Walton, D., & Black, D. A. The application of modern learning theory to the treatment of chronic hysterical aphonia. *J. Psychosom. Res.,* 1959, 3, 303–311.

Walton, D., & Mather, M. D. The application of learning principles to the treatment of obsessive-compulsive states in the acute and chronic phases of illness. *Behav. Res. Ther.,* 1963, 1, 163–174. (a)

Walton, D., & Mather, M. D. The relevance of generalization techniques to the treatment of stammering and phobic symptoms. *Behav. Res. Ther.,* 1963, 1, 95–120. (b)

Watson, J. B., & Morgan, J. J. B. Emotional reactions and psychological experimentation. *Amer. J. Psychol.,* 1917, 28, 163–174.

Watson, J. B., & Rayner, R. Conditioned emotional reactions. *J. Exp. Psychol.,* 1920, 3, 1–14.

Weiss, R. L., Krasner, L., & Ullmann, L. P. Responsivity to verbal conditioning as a function of emotional atmosphere and pattern of reinforcement. *Psychol. Rep.,* 1960, 6, 415–426.

Whitehorn, J. C. Therapeutic goals and their significance for therapeutic strategy. In *Psychiatric treatment: Proc. Amer. Psychol. Ass., New York, 1951.* Baltimore: Williams & Wilkins, 1953.

Whitehorn, J. C., & Betz, B. J. A comparison of psychotherapy relationships between physicians and schizophrenic patients. *Amer. J. Psychiat.,* 1954, 111, 321–331.

Whitehorn, J. C., & Betz, B. J. A comparison of psychotherapy relationships between physicians and schizophrenic patients when insulin is combined with psychotherapy, and when psychotherapy is used alone. *Amer. J. Psychiat.,* 1957, 113, 901–910.

Whitehorn, J. C., & Betz, B. J. Further studies of the doctor as a crucial variable in the outcome of treatment of schizophrenic patients. *Amer. J. Psychiat.,* 1960, 117, 215–223.

Widroe, J., & Davidson, J. The use of directed writing in psychotherapy. *Bull. Menninger Clin.,* 1961, 25, 110–119.

Wiener, D. N. The effect of arbitrary termination on return to psychotherapy. *J. Clin. Psychol.,* 1959, 15, 335–338.

Wiener, D. N., Feinberg, P., Nagobads, I. J., Westendorf, F., & Warren, P. W. Effects of withdrawal of tranquilizers. *Arch. Gen. Psychiat.*, 1963, **9**, 513–519.

Wiener, N. *Cybernetics.* New York: Wiley, 1948.

Wiener, N. *Cybernetics: human use of human beings.* (2d rev. ed.) Garden City, N.Y.: Doubleday, 1954.

Wiener, N. *God and Golem, Inc.* Cambridge, Mass.: M.I.T., 1964.

Willoughby, R. R. An operational approach to the problem of emotional re-adjustment. *J. Abnorm. Soc. Psychol.*, 1938, **33**, 261–264.

Winder, C. L. Psychotherapy. In *Annual Review of Psychology*, 1957. Vol. 8. Palo Alto, Calif.: Annual Review, 1957.

Wolberg, L. R. *The technique of psychotherapy.* New York: Grune & Stratton, 1954.

Wolfle, D. *America's resources of specialized talent.* New York: Harper & Row, 1954.

Wolpe, J. Objective psychotherapy of the neurosis. *So. African Med. J.*, 1952, **26**, 825–829.

Wolpe, J. Reciprocal inhibition as the main basis of psychotherapeutic effort. *Amer. Med. Ass. Arch. Neurol. Psychiat.*, 1954, **72**, 205–229.

Wolpe, J. Learning versus lesions as the basis of neurotic behavior. *Amer. J. Psychiat.*, 1956, **112**, 923.

Wolpe, J. *Psychotheraapy by reciprocal inhibition.* Stanford, Calif.: Stanford Univer. Press, 1958.

Wolpe, J. Explaining the durability of "control of fear." *Amer. J. Clin. Hypnosis*, 1961, **4**, 24–25. (a)

Wolpe, J. The prognosis in unpsychoanalyzed recovery from neurosis. *Amer. J. Psychiat.*, 1961, **117**, 35–39. (b)

Wolpe, J. The systematic desensitization treatment of neurosis. *J. Nerv. Ment. Dise.*, 1961, **132**, 189–203. (c)

Wolpe, J., Salter, A., & Reyna, L. J. *The conditioning therapies: the challenge in psychotherapy.* New York: Holt, 1965.

Yates, A. J. Symptoms and symptom substitution. In H. J. Eysenck (Ed.), *Behavior therapy and the neuroses.* New York: Pergamon Press, 1960.

Zax, M., & Klein, A. Measurement of personality and behavior change following psychotherapy. *Psychol. Bull.*, 1960, **57**, 435–448.

Zolick, E. S., & Hollon, T. N. Further characteristics of patients' responsiveness to brief psychotherapy. *Amer. Psychologist*, 1960, **15**, 387. (Abstract)

Index